02

India's
Communication
Revolution

India's Communication Revolution

from bullock carts to cyber marts

Arvind Singhal
Everett M. Rogers

Sage Publications
New Delhi/Thousand Oaks/London

First published in 2001 by

Sage Publications India Pvt Ltd
M 32 Market, Greater Kailash I
New Delhi 110 048

Sage Publications Inc
2455 Teller Road
Thousand Oaks, California 91320

Sage Publications Ltd
6 Bonhill Street
London EC2A 4PU

Published by Tejeshwar Singh for Sage Publications India Pvt Ltd, type-set in 10pt Baskerville by Line Arts, Pondicherry, and printed at Chaman Enterprises, Delhi.

Library of Congress Cataloging-in-Publication Data

Singhal, Arvind, 1962–
    India's communication revolution: from bullock carts to cyber marts/
    Arvind Singhal, Everett M. Rogers.
        p. cm.   (cloth)   (pbk.)
    Includes bibliographical references and index.
        1. Telecommunication—India. 2. Telecommunication—Social
    aspects—India. 3. India—Economic conditions—1947– I. Rogers,
    Everett M. II. Title.
    HE8374.S56   303.48'33'0954—dc21   2000   00–055385

ISBN: 0–7619–9471–8 (US-Hb)   81–7036–946–0 (India-Hb)
        0–7619–9472–6 (US-Pb)   81–7036–947- 9 (India-Pb)

Sage Production Team: Aruna Ramachandran, M.S.V. Namboodiri and
Santosh Rawat

This book is dedicated to Dr N. Bhaskara Rao, our longtime friend, founder of the Center for Media Studies, New Delhi, and a selfless leader of India's communication revolution, and also to the pioneering spirit of Vikram Sarabhai, Sam Pitroda, and Chandrababu Naidu, visionary leaders of India's informatization.

Contents

Tables

Figures

Plates

Preface

In recent decades, the United States, Japan, and most European nations have become *information societies*, defined as countries in which information workers are more numerous than such occupational categories as farmers, industrial workers, or service workers. *Information workers* are individuals whose main job responsibilities are to gather, process, or distribute information, or to produce information technologies like computers or telecommunications equipment that are used by other information workers. Typical information workers are computer programmers, teachers, journalists, and managers. In the United States today, more than two-thirds of the workforce are information workers.

India as a nation is still far from becoming an information society. About 25 percent of workers in India are engaged in service occupations, while 60 percent are farmers and 15 percent work in factories. Of those engaged in service occupations, however, tens of millions are information workers. India has more information workers than Japan, and about the same number as the United States. So India has an information society within this nation of approximately one billion people. These millions of information workers are mostly urban and educated, living lifestyles similar to information workers in Silicon Valley, Tokyo, or London. The present book is especially about this Indian information society, and the communication technologies that have led to its creation over recent decades, particularly in the 1990s.

What causes the important social changes leading to the creation of an information society? The communication technologies of the computer, including its various applications (in telecommunications, radio, television, cable, satellites, Internet, etc.) are driving this social shift toward an information society. These technologies, once considered as distinctive components, are converging today so that the point at which one technology stops and the next one begins is no longer clear. Consider a long-distance telephone call made from a cell-phone in Bangalore, India, to San Jose, California. The caller dials the number on a handset, the call is then transmitted through a cellular microwave system to a switching computer, beamed up to a communication satellite, then down to another computer-controlled switch and several miles of fiber optic cable, causing the destination's telephone set to ring. The message then transmitted may be computer data, video, or pictures, rather than spoken words. A similar communication exchange could be established through the Internet between Bangalore and San Jose using computer keyboards, rather than telephone handsets, at a fraction of the cost of the long-distance telephone call. Here we see an example of the multiple ways in which communication technologies converge. The traditional differences between telephone, fax, and computer communication are lessening.

Notice also the importance of information, the basic element in an information society. The voice or words transmitted in our example comprise "information." So do pictures, data-sets, and email. *Information* is patterned matter-energy that affects the choices available to an individual making a decision. Information can take the form of ink on paper, of electrical impulses traveling through a wire, or of light waves falling on a darkened screen. In an Information Society, information is the crucial ingredient, as energy was in the Industrial Society and manual labor in the Agricultural Society. The computer is to the Information Society what the steam engine was to the Industrial Society.

India is a developing nation that is making remarkable progress toward development through the *informatization* strategy, the process through which communication technologies are used as a means of furthering socio-economic development. Gradually, over recent decades, we have realized that telephones, the Internet, and other communication technologies can greatly increase business activity by connecting individuals and organizations into the global economy. Such informatization can benefit all levels of society, including highly profitable high-tech companies like Wipro or Infosys in Bangalore, a peasant village in Andhra Pradesh, or a *paanwallah* in Uttar Pradesh. Informatization fits with free-market capitalism, the dominant economic ideology of the West, adopted by the Indian government in 1991. Informatization also presents opportunities to use communication technology to improve delivery of education, health, and nutrition, especially in rural India. It also fits with the notion of creating an efficient, responsive, and transparent government, as exemplified by the infotech policies of Andhra Pradesh's Chief Minister Chandrababu Naidu. India represents a unique path to development characterized by informatization and globalization.

India is an unusual setting in which to analyze the communication revolution. While the new communication technologies of cable television, computers, the Internet, satellites, and telecommunications are impacting Indian society in dramatic ways, the subcontinent is still mainly a developing nation in which many citizens depend on the bullock cart[1] for transportation and on human labor for making a daily living. In the 53 years since independence from Britain in 1947, India has made remarkable progress in certain sectors: the life expectancy of its citizens has doubled from 32 years to 63 years; the literacy rate has increased from 18 percent to 62 percent; and infant mortality has been cut down by half from 134 to 69 deaths per thousand. However, during this time, India's population has risen from 350 million to over one billion people, of which 350 million live in abject poverty in villages and urban slums. India has more university students than any other nation in the world today, but also the most illiterates. While India has world-class Indian Institutes of Technology (IITs) and Indian Institutes of Management (IIMs), few Indian universities are research universities, conducting R&D and teaching graduate students how to conduct research. So most brainy young Indians migrate to America to pursue scientific training for Master's and Ph.D. degrees. Many thus join the Indian diaspora of 20 million people. Although Indian society has strong historical roots in socialism,[2] the young Indian businessmen and women who are pioneering high-technology companies, private television networks, and the advertising industry, are super-capitalists. The Indian government in 1991 made a radical policy shift toward free-market forces, which strongly impacted the informatization of Indian society, opening the nation's boundaries to Coca Cola, McDonalds, *Baywatch* and Nike, and to the highly profitable exports of its computer software companies. The New Economic Policy of 1991 allowed India to become a major player in the global village. However, globalization and material progress have done little to improve the quality of life of India's poor. Their preoccupation is with raising two square meals a day, not with McDonalds and Coca Cola.

The purpose of this book is to describe and analyze India's journey on the informatization path, including the recent changes in Indian society resulting from the applications of new communications technologies. Hence the main title of our book, *India's Communication Revolution*. Dramatic changes occur as a nation of bullock carts becomes a nation of cyber marts,[3] presenting a fascinating picture of paradox, contradiction, and uncertainty. That is why we subtitle our book *From Bullock Carts to Cyber Marts*, implying a society in transition.

Metaphorically, to us, the bullock cart symbolizes the "past," the "traditional," the "rural," the "disadvantaged," the "agricultural," the "slow," the "disconnected," and the "local;" the cyber mart, on the other hand, symbolizes the "future," the "modern," the "urban," the "elite," the "informational," the "fast," the "connected," and the "global." Indian society, at the turn of the century, is caught between these dialectical forces. We are enthusiasts for this communication revolution, as well as critics of the greater socioeconomic inequality and other social problems that accompany the obvious benefits. We seek to present in this book a balanced picture of the Indian information society. Informatization is powerful, but everything about it may not be beneficial, especially for the disadvantaged sections of Indian society.

The intended audience for this book includes (*a*) scholars and students in India who seek to understand the rapid social changes that are under way in their nation, and (*b*) their counterparts in the United States and other nations who seek to understand the development process in developing nations as it is facilitated by informatization. India has played a dominant role in theory and research on development, perhaps because its development problems are so huge. For instance, no other nation has such a grave population problem, has tried longer through government family planning programs to control it, and has become more frustrated in its attempts to achieve its demographic goals. India's population has tripled in the half-century since independence. Each year, the government has to educate millions of new citizens and help them find jobs. India also has many development successes, such as the Green Revolution of the 1970s and the White Revolution (in milk production and marketing) of the 1980s and 1990s, both on equally grand scales. Will the informatization revolution, which began in the 1990s, boost India to becoming a major world power? Will the benefits of information technology be harnessed to enhance the quality of life of India's poor?

We use American English throughout this book, using "defense" instead of "defence," and "color" instead of "colour," for example. We state all money values in U.S. dollars rather than Indian rupees, with one dollar equivalent to 43 rupees at the time of writing, although this exchange rate fluctuates.[4]

We owe gratitude to many individuals and organizations who helped us in writing this book: Dr N. Bhaskara Rao, founder and Chairman of the Center for Media Studies (CMS), New Delhi, who has collaborated with us on several research projects, and who provided detailed feedback on the manuscript; his daughter Vasanti, a social psychologist at CMS, who provided many information sources for the present book; Mrs Usha Bhasin, Controller of Programs at the Prasar Bharati Corporation; Dr S.N. Singh, Tom Carter, Dr N.V. Belavadi, Dr Arun Wayangankar, and Dattatray Ghanekar of the National Dairy Development Board (NDDB), with whom we have worked in India for the past decade; Mr Kiran Karnik, Managing Director of Discovery Channel (India); and Tejeshwar Singh, Managing Director of Sage Publications India Pvt. Ltd. We especially acknowledge Dr Sheena Malhotra, Assistant Professor of Communication at Cal State University; Dr David V. Gibson of the IC^2 Institute at the University of Texas at Austin;

Dr Sandhya Rao, Associate Professor of Mass Communication, Southwest Texas State University, San Marcos, Texas; and an external reader for providing detailed suggestions to improve the present book.

Our special thanks to Arjun Malhotra, co-founder of Hindustan Computers Ltd (HCL) in India and presently CEO of Techspan; Vinod Khosla, co-founder of Sun Microsystems and a partner in the Silicon Valley venture capital firm of Kleiner, Perkins, Caufield & Byers; Sabeer Bhatia, co-founder of Hotmail and CEO of Arzoo.com; Sam Pitroda, Chairman of WorldTel in London; Azim Premji, Chairman of Wipro in Mumbai; N.R. Narayana Murthy, President of Infosys Technologies in Bangalore; Gururaj "Desh" Deshpande, founder of Sycamore Networks; Love Goel, Chief Operating Officer of the E-Commerce Business Unit of Federated Department Stores in Minneapolis; Atin Malaviya of Unisphere Solutions in Boston; and our Silicon Valley–based Indian friends Nitin Parekh, Manish Mehta, Anurag Agrawal, Amitabh Arora, Sanjay Gangal, and Raj Baronia, for providing various important inputs to this book. Jianying Zhang and Krishna P. Kandath, graduate students at the School of Interpersonal Communication, Ohio University, provided invaluable research assistance on this project, and Peggy Sattler and Saumya Pant of Ohio University helped us with the artwork and the photographs.

Finally, we acknowledge the Internet for serving as an invaluable resource in researching, writing, and illustrating the present book. We accessed a number of Indian newspapers, magazines (such as *India Today*, *Computers Today*, and others), and hundreds of other relevant Web-sites (for instances, the WorldTel Web-site to catch up with Sam Pitroda's present mission) while sitting in our offices in Athens, Ohio, and Albuquerque, New Mexico. We used the Internet to request photographs from the Vinod Khoslas and Sabeer Bhatias in Silicon Valley, and from the Azim Premjis and Narayana Murthys in India. Most of the photographs in this book, including permissions to use them, were provided to us as email attachments. In several cases, we found a picture on a Web-site that we liked, for instance, the picture of Chief Minister of Andhra Pradesh Chandrababu Naidu with Chairman of Microsoft Bill Gates, and then went about tracking down the source (once again through the Internet) to seek permission to use it here. We also shared drafts of the book's various chapters, as we wrote them, through the Internet, bridging in an instant the physical distance of about 2,000 miles between our two locations.

About the Authors

The co-authors of this book represent a combination of different nationalities and backgrounds who share a fascination with the communication revolution in India, and who have collaborated over many years in studying the informatization process. Everett Rogers, presently Regents' Professor at the Department of Communication and Journalism at the University of New Mexico, has taught, researched, and lived in India off and on over the past 36 years. His early studies dealt with the diffusion of agricultural innovations that led to the Green Revolution. In the early 1970s he studied the communication of family planning methods in India, and served as a Ford Foundation consultant to the Indian government's family planning program. During the 1980s and 1990s, Rogers collaborated with Arvind Singhal in several studies of the effects of an entertainment–education television soap opera (*Hum Log*) and a radio soap opera (*Tinka Tinka Sukh*). With Singhal, Rogers served as an FAO consultant to the NDDB in the 1990s in efforts to empower women dairy farmers.

Arvind Singhal, son of an Indian Railways engineer, earned his Bachelor's degree in engineering from the University of Delhi, an M.A. in broadcasting at Bowling Green State University, and his Ph.D. degree in communication theory and research from the University of Southern California. Singhal is presently Professor at the School of Interpersonal Communication at Ohio University, where he teaches and from where he conducts research on organizing for social change projects in Bangladesh and India and on the effects of entertainment–education programs in India, the People's Republic of China, and South Africa. He has taught in Thailand and Malaysia, and has offered development communication workshops in various countries for the World Bank, the Food and Agriculture Organization of the United Nations, UNAIDS, and the U.S. Agency for International Development.

We have previously collaborated in writing two books, *India's Information Revolution* (1989) and *Entertainment–Education: A Communication Strategy for Social Change* (1999). When we wrote *India's Information Revolution*, several of our colleagues thought the title of our book should have ended with a question mark. We disagreed, as an information society was already beginning to emerge in India in the late 1980s. Since our 1989 book, television audiences in India have multiplied four-fold, the number of telephones has increased six-fold, cable television—which was then almost non-existent in India—has reached 35 million homes, and Indian computer software exports have increased fifty-fold! In the process of writing the present book, we realized gradually that it bears little resemblance to its predecessor. India has changed so much in the past decade that our present book represents a focus on the informatization path to development. This book is not just about Indians in India, it is also about Indians in Silicon Valley or wherever they are today in the Indian diaspora. We write here about the Subhash Chandras, Sam Pitrodas, Vinod Khoslas, Sabeer Bhatias, Azim Premjis, Arjun Malhotras, Narayana Murthys, and other pioneers and visionaries. Their personal narratives characterize, and personalize, India's informatization.

We hope that the present volume will increase your understanding of the communication revolution under way in India.

Arvind Singhal
Athens, Ohio

Everett M. Rogers
Albuquerque, New Mexico

Notes

1. A wooden cart pulled by bullocks, commonly found in Indian cities, towns, and villages. In remote, rural Indian villages, the bullock cart still serves as the main carrier of people and goods. In 2000, India had 77 million buffaloes and 20 million bullock carts; bullocks plowed 100 million acres in India, about two-thirds of the cultivated farmland.
2. When India gained independence from Britain in 1947, it inherited an economy that had grown at an average annual rate of seven-tenths

of 1 percent since 1897. Post-independence, during the Nehru era, India's economy grew at about 3 percent annually. In the 1990s, India's economy grew at about 6.5 percent annually, in large measure as a consequence of the New Economic Policy (NEP) of 1991.

3. Called variously cyber cafes, cyber *dhabas*, cyber kiosks, and tele-centers, which provide public access to Internet, telephony, and computer services.

4. For instance, in 1975, one U.S. dollar equaled only eight Indian rupees.

I India's communication revolution

"We all know that distance is dead. What used to be far is near, what is local is global."

> SAM PITRODA (2000, p. 92), Chairman of WorldTel and the visionary technologist who spearheaded India's telecommunications revolution.

"Our government has decided to create conditions that will enable more and more successful information technology enterprises to grow on Indian soil—and to grow world class. This is not only for wealth creation, but also for employment generation."

> ATAL BEHARI VAJPAYEE, Prime Minister of India (quoted in *The Hindu Business Line*, 1999, p. 7).

"We just skipped over the Industrial Revolution."

> NARAYANA MURTHY, Chairman of Infosys Technologies (quoted in Niejahr, 1997, p. 31).

T he theme of the present book is the communication revolution that new communication technologies are bringing
about in India. No other nation provides a better example of the
role of the new communication media in the development process
through which a country moves from being an agriculture-based
economy toward becoming an information society. India's rising
information society is not just a function of Indians in India; it is
fueled by Indians in Silicon Valley from half a world away, or from
wherever some 20 million Indians reside in their global diaspora
(Khadria, 1999). Such forces as globalization, free-wheeling capitalism, entrepreneurship, and opportunity represent the key
ingredients in the making of an information society.

❑ Migrant Indian Cyberworkers[1]

Silicon Valley in Northern California is the mecca of high-technology.
Here entrepreneurs combine technological innovation, venture capital, and vision to produce products that drive the worldwide revolution
in microelectronics, computers, telecommunications, and the Internet.
At the turn of the century, over 130,000 skilled Indian professionals
lived in the San Francisco Bay area, of which an estimated 80,000
worked for Silicon Valley high-tech companies (*Computers Today*,
1999a).[2] Nearly 40 percent of all new start-ups in Silicon Valley had
Indian co-founders![3] These tens of thousands of Indians in Silicon Valley
have established a reputation for their technical competence, and, in
recent years, for their entrepreneurial excellence (Saxenian, 1999).
Indians like Vinod Khosla, co-founder of Sun Microsystems, and Sabeer
Bhatia, co-founder of Hotmail, are much-admired icons. These entrepreneurs, and others like them, have generated enormous amounts of
wealth for themselves and their companies. In short, they are living in a
high-tech paradise.

But is Silicon Valley a paradise for all Indians? Consider the case of
migrant cyberworker Satish Appalakutty, who earned a Master's degree in computer science from the University of Poona, and now
works for a Silicon Valley high-tech firm. Hired in India by a contracting
company that supplies engineers to Silicon Valley firms, Appalakutty is
one of the thousands of foreign workers who enter the U.S. every year
under a temporary work visa (H-1B) program (Richter, 2000). In 1998,

some 30,000 Indian engineers were granted H-1B visas (Lewis, 1999).[4] Appalakutty is paid about $ 50,000 a year by his contracting company, a fortune by Indian standards, but about 50 percent less than what other Americans or Indian permanent residents (green-card holders) are paid for comparable work. In addition to relatively lower salaries, H-1B workers earn fewer and smaller raises, are ineligible for stock options, and as salaried employees often work long hours without overtime pay. Further, temporary workers like Appalakutty "are beholden to the employers who sponsor their visas" in what some critics call "a form of indentured servitude" (Branigin, 1998, p. 2). It is very difficult for them to change jobs: they need new work visas, and are often fined $10,000 to $20,000 by their employers for breach of contract.

What keeps migrant cyberworkers like Appalakutty from complaining? First, they earn much larger salaries in the U.S. than they could earn in India (up to 10 to 15 times more). Second, they are reluctant to offend their employers, who often dangle before them the promise of changing their status to that of U.S. permanent residents. Given that H-1B temporary work visas are issued for six years, the change to permanent resident status may not occur soon, if at all.

Appalakutty shares a small, sparsely furnished apartment with three other Indian computer programmers in Sunnyvale, sleeping two to a bedroom. His apartment is a curious mix of Indian culture and bachelor cyberworker lifestyle. The living room furniture consists of a television set and a stereo with an Indian calendar on the wall. His company laptop, mobile phone, and pager compete for space in his messy bedroom, littered with soiled clothes and Indian newspapers. "Most of the Indians I know here are living this way," he says (cited in Branigin, 1998, p. 1). Chinese and Indians account for about 65 percent of the residents in the large apartment complex where Appalakutty lives.

What is Appalakutty's future? Like his roommates, he is saving for the day when he will return to India. Each dollar he saves will fetch 43 rupees back home, making him wealthy by Indian standards. If good fortune allows, he can become a permanent U.S. resident, and perhaps someday start his own software company. Appalakutty's roommate, Srinivasan, speaks in awestruck tones: "I drive past companies like Intel and IBM every day. It is thrilling. All the technology in the world originates here. It inspires you and you can really think big" (quoted in Branigin, 1998, p. 4).

Many hundreds of H-1B cyberworkers from India do obtain their permanent resident cards in the U.S. each year. Several have gone on to launch their own companies in Silicon Valley. A notable example is K.B. Chandrasekhar (Chandra), a former Wipro employee in India who came to the U.S. to work for Rolta, an Indian company, in their Silicon Valley office. In 1992, he quit Rolta to found a software design company called Fouress, Inc. Two years later, he founded Exodus Communications, an Internet services company that went public in 1998, doubling its stock value the first day. By spring 2000, the stock price of Exodus had exploded by 3,000 percent, raising its market capitalization to $25 billion, and making Chandra superrich (*Siliconindia*, 2000a, p. 104). Chandra notes: "The entrepreneurial spirit and the dynamic environment [in Silicon Valley] helped me start my company" (cited in K. Bhatt, 1998, p. 1). Chandra believes his company's success resulted from the powerful Indian network in the Valley: "Kanwal Rekhi [a successful Indian entrepreneur in Silicon Valley] validated my dreams. Once he did that, others started getting involved in my project" (ibid.). Rekhi, who provided venture capital for Chandra's company and mentored him during the initial crunch,[5] describes Exodus Communications as being in the business of providing the "picks and shovels" for the Internet gold rush of today. Entrepreneurs like Chandra are the heroes of migrant cyberworkers like Appalakutty and his roommates. However, for every Chandra who makes it big in the United States, many hundreds of Appalakuttys spend years trying, but never quite achieving, the American dream.

Migrant Indian cyberworkers like Appalakutty and Chandra signify the tremendous competitive advantage that Indians hold in the cutthroat global information economy, where brainpower, computer competence, and English-language skills are the keys to wealth creation and material success. Their story also reflects some of the problems that can accompany free-wheeling capitalism, such as exploitative employer–employee relationships and wide socio-economic inequalities.

The New Communication Technologies

New communication technologies such as satellites, cable television, wireless telephony, the Internet, and computers are bringing about noticeable changes in Indian society. *Communication technology* includes the hardware equipment, organizational structures, and social values by which individuals collect, process, and exchange information. The new media have certain characteristics that are similar in some respects to those of both interpersonal and mass media communication, but that are different in many other respects. *Interpersonal communication* consists of a face-to-face exchange between two or more individuals. The message flow is from one to a few individuals, feedback is immediate and usually plentiful, and the messages are often relatively high in socio-emotional content. In contrast, *mass media communication* includes all those means of transmitting messages such as radio, television, newspapers, and film, that enable a source of one or a few individuals to reach a large audience. Some type of hardware equipment is always involved in mass communication, feedback is limited and delayed, and the messages are often relatively low in socio-emotional content. An evening news broadcast on Doordarshan, the Indian national network television, is an example of mass communication.

The new media integrate the characteristics of both interpersonal and mass communication. Communication that occurs through these media often links two individuals or a small number of people. In this sense, the new media are like interpersonal communication, in that the messages are targeted to specific individuals (this is often called de-massification). But interactive communication via the new media, like email on the Internet, is somewhat like mass media communication in that hardware equipment (computers, satellites, and telephone lines in this case) is necessarily involved. Information exchange via the new media is *interactive*, meaning that the participants in a communication process have control over, and can exchange roles in, their mutual discourse. Such interactivity is also particularly characteristic of face-to-face interpersonal communication.

The interactive technologies of communication are at the heart of the communication revolution that is occurring in India. The computer and its various applications in satellite and cable television, telecommunications, and the Internet are driving the social changes in India. These technologies, once distinctive, are converging today to deliver data, voice, and video in ways not possible before. Here we imply a causative relationship: the new communication technologies are leading to changes in society. *Technological determinism* is an approach that considers technology as the main cause of social change. We generally take the perspective of communication-technological determinism in this book, but we also acknowledge that certain changes in society occur because of non-technological forces, such as government policies (like the New Economic Policy of the Indian government in the 1990s), international politics, and public opinion. These are social forces, and their use in explaining social change is called social determinism. For example, several decades ago, in the late 1970s, the Indian government pursued a policy that drove IBM (and Coca Cola) out of India by requiring dominant ownership of these companies by Indian citizens. In the 1980s, after a government policy change, IBM and other foreign computer companies returned to India, as microcomputers replaced many of the computing functions once performed by mainframes. By the 1990s, computers were being used for communication purposes (such as email) rather than as number-crunchers, their original use. Therefore, social forces like government policies combined with technological innovations (in the form of semiconductor advances, which made the miniaturization of computers possible) fostered the communication revolution in India.

Social values, policies, and religion may help shape the nature of technologies. This *social construction of technology* is the process through which people give meaning to a new technology by discussing it among themselves. For instance, later in this book, we show how the Cold War era in which the Internet was developed served to determine its decentralized nature, which makes it difficult for governments to censor it today. In the 1960s, U.S. computer scientists, fearing a nuclear attack from the Soviet Union, worked with funds provided by the Pentagon to design ARPANET. The predecessor of the Internet, ARPANET did not have a central headquarters. Each computer passed along a message to another computer in the direction of the message's ultimate destination (indicated by its address) by means of an open telephone line, with no predetermined or prescribed route. Thus an email message from Delhi to Chicago may travel through any one of many millions of possible routes.

The decentralized nature of the Internet today makes it extremely difficult for governments or other agencies to censor

pornographic or other objectionable material, as there is no cen-
tralized point through which all electronic messages pass. Gate-
keeping is impossible on the Internet. The decentralized nature of
the Internet also makes it a potentially powerful tool for connecting citizens with local, regional, and national government departments and officials. For instance, several Indian states (led by
Andhra Pradesh) are establishing Internet community centers
(ICCs), where citizens can access government forms, file griev-
ances, and monitor land records on the Internet.

For several decades, computer networks were perceived as a
useful tool for exchanging personal messages, like sending letters
to colleagues or family members or business contacts. During the
1990s, the Internet also began to be perceived as a means of buying products (with a credit card), which were then delivered by an
overnight delivery service to the consumer. The social meaning of
the Internet changed, creating a host of business opportunities in
the United States and in other countries. A cadre of entrepreneurs
rushed in to found Internet-related companies, and several dozen
became billionaires overnight. Several of these new Internet billionaires were from India.

Development Communication

Development is a widely participatory process of directed social
change in a society, intended to bring about both social and material advancement (including greater equality, freedom, and other
valued qualities) for the majority of people through their gaining
greater control over their environment (Rogers, 1976). When the
nations of Latin America, Africa, and Asia gained their independence from European colonial powers in the years following the
end of World War II, the first priority of the new governments in
many of these countries (including India) was development. These
developing countries were poor, and so raising per capita income
was of the highest importance. To do so meant increasing agricultural production, industrialization, urbanization, improved housing, better health, and higher education. These are major social
changes in a society.

Such widespread behavior change could only be attained if the mass media were harnessed for that purpose. *Development communication* is the use of communication to further development. Government policy-makers have utilized the mass media to decrease the number of infant deaths in their countries, to produce more food so as to decrease hunger, and to overcome certain limitations of illiteracy (Melkote, 1991). These development goals are of unquestionable benefit for society; no one has opposed them. However, the most appropriate strategies for utilizing communication for development have been contentious. Europeans and North Americans were often involved as designers, funders, advisors, or evaluators of these development communication programs.

In Europe and North America the mass media are used mainly for entertainment. Government policies generally encourage this entertainment function of the media, or at least do not discourage it. The media are privately owned and are managed to make a profit, leading to certain social problems. For example, the American public is attracted to sex and violence on television and in films. Media companies provide this anti-social content because it leads to larger audiences, which can be sold to advertisers for higher profits. But in India and many other developing nations, the mass media were expected to encourage development by serving an educational function. This educational content is often perceived as relatively dull by mass audiences. For instance, many urban teenagers in India in the 1990s preferred to watch Madonna in a spiked bra on MTV, rather than to watch a show about improving potato production. So Indian television, increasingly driven by audience preferences and advertising revenues, provides more and more television shows like MTV, and fewer and fewer educational programs.

Thus, one policy conflict is between the educational and the entertainment functions of the mass media in a nation like India. One solution, in which India has played a pioneering role,[6] is the strategy of *entertainment–education*, the process of purposely designing and implementing media messages to both entertain and educate, in order to increase audiences' knowledge about educational issues, create favorable attitudes, and change overt behavior (Singhal and Rogers, 1999). Recent experiences with the entertainment–education strategy in over 100 countries suggest that such programs can be commercially viable *and* socially responsible (Singhal and Brown, 1996; Piotrow et al., 1997). However, the rapid spread of private television systems in India in the 1990s, especially in urban areas, represents a move toward emphasizing the entertainment function of the media.

India's development problems are not just in its villages. For example, *mega-cities* are metropolitan areas that have grown to such large size that they are virtually unmanageable. India has at least four mega-cities: Calcutta with a population of over 17 million, Mumbai with 14 million, Delhi with 13 million, and Chennai with 10 million. As agricultural production in many countries like India reaches increased efficiency, millions of villagers previously employed in agriculture migrate to urban centers. The mass media, particularly in advertising messages, generally depict urban life as attractive, thus encouraging rural–urban migration. Unfortunately, the reality of urban living, at least in a mega-city, is quite different. Unemployment rates are high, adequate housing is unavailable or unaffordable, the civic infrastructure is poor, and the city environment is very badly polluted from over-population.

In recent years, developing countries such as India have become increasingly interested in the possible uses of new communication technologies such as computers, telecommunications, and the Internet to enhance connectivity, boost businesses, streamline governance, and improve the quality of life of their citizens. There is also a recognition of the importance of, and enthusiasm for, promoting high-technology industries (including telecommunications, computer software, and the Internet), given their potential to create jobs, wealth, and taxable income. This information-technology-led movement toward socio-economic growth, which we generally call "informatization" in this book, complements the previous mass-media-led approach to bringing about social change, called development communication.

The Informatization Route to Development[7]

The world today is aptly described as a "Global village", in which a web of information networks interconnects individuals as well as organizations in nearly instantaneous global communication. The global village is a world that is increasingly interconnected by communication technologies and that is tending toward a global culture. The Internet and the World Wide Web are dramatic examples of these interconnections. At a superficial level, large cities across the world today resemble Western cities in the consumer products sold, air conditioning, traffic, and fast food. Coke, burgers, and fries are sold in every city, although in nations like India the burger may be a muttonburger or a veggieburger.

The global village has many benefits for humankind, although the increasing degree of interconnectivity also causes certain problems. Much of the strength of the U.S. economy in the 1990s was based on the ability of U.S. firms to expand into global markets and to develop new market segments in Asia, Africa, and Latin America. The vulnerability of the global village was illustrated by the 1997 Asian financial crisis, when the financial market in Thailand collapsed, quickly followed by market crises in Malaysia, the Republic of Korea, Indonesia, and other Asian nations. Eventually, the Asian financial crisis of 1997 had a depressing effect on the U.S. stock market, as the Asian demand for consumer electronics, food, and other American exports dropped. This was compounded by the Brazilian and Russian economies also nosediving. However, a strong world economy withstood the threat from Asia, and in 1999 the Asian markets began to recover. The global village is like an electronic spider web connecting all nations; an event in any one place may have repercussions throughout the world.

The basic raw material driving the information society is silicon, the most plentiful element on the earth's surface (silicon is found in beach sand and in most rocks) (Table 1.1). The minute amount of physical material in a semiconductor chip is worth about as much as an ordinary staple pin. So why does a semiconductor, made of silicon, cost up to $300? What makes the semiconductor valuable is the information that is etched on this thin slice of silicon in the form of tiny electronic circuits. Semiconductor chips are the core technology in computers, mobile telephones, and in most other communication devices.

The Internet and other communication technologies are highly concentrated in Western industrialized countries (Mody, 2000).

Table 1.1

Comparison of the Agricultural Society, Industrial Society, and the Information Society

Key Characteristics	Agricultural Society	Industrial Society	Information Society
1. Time period	10,000 years (and continues today in most developing countries)	200 years (began in about 1750 in England)	Began in about 1955 in the U.S.
2. Key element/ basic resource	Food	Energy	Information
3. Main type of employment	Farmers	Factory workers	Information workers
4. Key social institutions	Farms	Steel factories	Research universities
5. Basic technology	Manual labor	Steam engines	Microelectronics, computers, and the Internet
6. Nature of mass communication	One-way print media (newspapers)	One-way electronic media (radio, television, film)	Interactive media that are de-massified in nature

Source: Based upon Rogers (1986, p. 13).

High-income countries, such as the 23 nations (mainly in Europe and North America) comprising the Organization for Economic Cooperation and Development (OECD), represent 15 percent of the world's population, but account for 97 percent of Internet host computers, 91 percent of all Internet users, and 68 percent of the world's telephones (Mansell and When, 1998). The other 168 nations of the world, including India, have 85 percent of the world's people and only 3 percent of Internet hosts. About 75 percent of the world's population has never made a telephone call. And the entire African continent has fewer telephone lines than the city of Tokyo.[8]

It will be many decades, if ever, before the average citizen of India has a private telephone and owns a personal computer. Meanwhile, telephone and Internet access is increasingly provided by telephones and computers situated in public places, as in India's 650,000 public call offices (PCOs), the many thousands of

Internet community centers (ICCs), cyber cafes, and telecenters. Here, for a small fee of a few cents, an individual can surf the Net, send a fax, or make a long-distance call. Thus, increasing numbers of people are gaining access to information technologies without having to own them. Nevertheless, a wide "digital divide" presently separates the urban, information-rich elite in India from their rural counterparts who are information-poor.

■ Informatization

Informatization is the process through which new communication technologies are used as strategies for furthering socio-economic development. The informatization strategy has been particularly important in Northern California's Silicon Valley, and, in India, in the Bangalore technopolis and in the emerging technopolis of Hyderabad. A *technopolis* is a geographically concentrated high-technology complex characterized by a large number of entrepreneurial spin-off firms. Another route to informatization is via telecommunications, such as improved telephone service and access to the Internet, which speeds up the rate of business activity in a society like India. Scholarly research does not demonstrate convincingly that improving telecommunications causes economic development, but a high correlation certainly exists.

Along with the informatization of a nation usually comes commercialization, consumerism, and capitalism. The United States is the leading economy in the world, accounting for more than 12 percent of all exports and more than 17 percent of all imports. The U.S. strongly promotes globalization, and the competitive, free-market forces that accompany capitalism, throughout the world (McMichael, 2000). India ranks as the 31st largest exporter in the world and the 29th largest importer. China, with an approximately equal-sized population of around a billion people, ranks as the world's 10th largest exporter and 12th largest importer.

To simplify somewhat, the world is politically and economically dominated by the United States, Japan, and Germany. Experts predict that five other nations are emerging as world economic powers: Brazil, China, India, Indonesia, and Russia. What common factors characterize these five? Large population, an expansive territory, and vast natural resources. Starting from a relatively low economic base, these nations can demonstrate rapid economic growth (Mansell and When, 1998). For example, China more than doubled its per capita income from 1980 to 1996. China's per capita income rose from just 4 percent of the United States' per capita income in 1980, to 12 percent in 1996, an amazing advance.

In addition to Japan's economic "miracle"[9] in the decades following World War II, three other Asian economies, Hong Kong, Singapore, and Taiwan, have achieved spectacular success.[10] All three have relatively small populations and limited territories, and literate, motivated workforces. Their population consists of people with a predominantly Chinese ancestry. Importantly, the economic development of these regions was driven by new communication technologies: semiconductors, computers, mobile telephones, other electronic equipment, and, most of all, the Internet. For instance, Singapore is called the "intelligent island" because it is so thoroughly informatized; by the year 2000 every household was linked by cable into a nationwide computer network. Some 25 percent of Singapore's population used the Internet in 2000, compared to 30 percent in the United States. This small island nation has a population of only three million, all of whom live in one city. Can India, with a huge population of almost one billion and a vast territory, and with relatively high illiteracy, follow a similar route to development? Certainly not, although certain pockets within India (the Bangalore and Hyderabad technopolises,[11] for example) are clearly pursuing an informatization path to development.

Other nations in the world may offer useful strategies that could be adapted by India, or at least by technopolises within India, to spur economic development. For example, in the late 1990s, Costa Rica, a small Spanish-speaking Central American nation, emphasized English-language training in all schools so as to encourage its citizens' participation in the world marketplace. Computer training was also stressed, and all government services were provided through the Internet. The State of Andhra Pradesh in India, led by its chief minister Chandrababu Naidu, during the late 1990s pioneered the search for an informatization pathway to development and governance. Naidu has a vision of creating a technopolis in Hyderabad, spurring new jobs and investments in the information technology (IT) sector, and showcasing how electronic governance can benefit the implementation of development programs targeted to the poor. Naidu views information technology as the means by which the 80 million citizens of Andhra Pradesh may be empowered through ready access to knowledge, resources, and government officials, hitherto the privilege of a few. Naidu's societally conscious informatization vision has not gone unnoticed in India, and the rest of the world. Inspired by Naidu, the Indian national government established a Ministry of Information Technology in 1999.

❑ Electronic Governance: Information Technology for Public Service[12]

In November 1999, in a three-day national conference on e-governance (electronic governance) held in Bangalore, IT secretaries from 32 Indian states and union territories issued the following joint declaration: "We are committed to providing a one-stop, non-stop, efficient, effective, responsive, and transparent citizen governance through the use of information technology" (quoted in Katakam, 1999, p. 78). While implementing such a declaration in India may require several years (Plate 1.1), some states, notably Andhra Pradesh (AP), Karnataka, Tamil Nadu, and Kerala, are taking rapid strides toward e-governance.

Chief Minister Chandrababu Naidu is leading AP state speedily along the informatization path, vigorously promoting the establishment of high-tech industries (as we discuss in detail later in Chapter 4), and applying information technology to create a SMART (simple, moral, accountable, responsive, and transparent) government. Naidu, a believer in the efficient delivery of government services to people, business, and industry, is spearheading a massive e-governance program that involves the computerization *and* networking of all government departments, linking villages to blocks, blocks to districts, and districts to the state headquarters (Katakam, 1999). This is informatization, squared.

Andhra Pradesh has already implemented four e-governance initiatives: (a) Computer-Aided Administration of Registration Department (CARD); (b) Andhra Pradesh State-Wide Area Network (APSWAN),

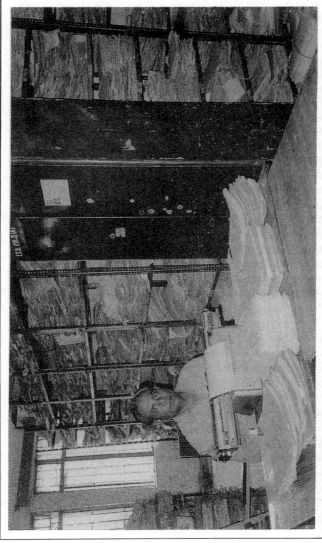

Plate 1.1: A revenue clerk in India's Uttar Pradesh state surrounded by tens of thousands of income-tax files

A great potential exists to use telecommunications, computers, and the Internet to streamline government bureaucracy in India. The State of Andhra Pradesh leads the way in using information technology to create an efficient, responsive, and transparent government.

Source: Saumya Pant (used with permission).

(c) Andhra Pradesh State Secretariat Campus Network (APSCAN), and (d) Twin Cities Network Services (TWINS) Project.

Under CARD, consumer registration processes are being computerized in 29,000 villages of AP's 23 districts. Prior to CARD's implementation, several weeks were required to register a newly purchased piece of land, to ascertain its market value, transfer duty, and file registration fee; a dozen different forms needed to be filled and filed at half a dozen locations. With CARD in place, this whole process takes 15 to 20 minutes at a one-stop location.

Andhra Pradesh State-Wide Area Network represents the statewide backbone of a high-speed digital network for voice, data, and video communication. In its first phase, the state capital of Hyderabad was linked to Vijayawada and Tirupati (two major cities in AP state) and to 23 district headquarters, using fiber optic links. Naidu conducts his weekly videoconferences with district officials using APSWAN. In the second phase, APSWAN is being extended to all block headquarters, followed by all villages in the state. The local area networks (LAN) that are operational in the state's various government offices are also being linked to APSWAN. Through APSCAN, all offices in the state's Secretariat have been connected to each other and to the various administrative units at the district headquarters. Eventually, all government offices at the state, district, block, and village levels will be connected through APSCAN and APSWAN.

The TWINS Project operates a chain of integrated citizen service centers. The eventual purpose of TWINS is to integrate several administrative services and offer them to citizens at one location. So whether one needs to renew a driver's license, or pay one's electricity bill, it can be done at a single window. Initially, the TWINS project offered 20 citizen services, provided by six departments, on a pilot basis in the twin cities of Hyderabad and Secunderabad. There are plans to scale up both the number of services and the number of citizen service centers statewide.

The State of Andhra Pradesh is leading India's march to informatization. Naidu views informatization as a means of job and wealth creation, and, more importantly, of improving the quality of life of ordinary citizens.

India's Road to Informatization

Government policies are highly influential in shaping the development agenda of any country. In the 1940s, Mohandas K. Gandhi and his protégé Jawaharlal·Nehru disagreed about the role of industrialization in India's development. Gandhi knew that cloth manufacture had once been the premier industry in India, until the British colonizers systematically destroyed the spinning and dyeing of cotton cloth by Indian businessmen, moving cloth manufacturing to their Manchester mills. The result was massive unemployment and poverty in India, and a ruralization of India as former clothing workers were forced to move back to villages.

Thus, Gandhi made hand-spun, hand-woven cloth (*khadi*) the centerpiece of his program for Indian independence (Bean, 1989, p. 355). He spun his own yarn on a spinning wheel each day, and urged his followers to do the same (Shridharani, 1946; Mehta, 1977). Further, he dressed only in a *khadi* loincloth and a *khadi* cap (inspired by the prison cap that he had worn in South African jails). This costume was a communication message, distinctively all-Indian (cutting across caste, religious, regional, and social class differences) and strongly anti-British. Gandhi's clothes were a statement of *swadeshi*, the promotion of indigenous products. The Indian National Congress in 1921, at Gandhi's urging, voted to require its officers and workers to spin and wear *khadi* and to boycott foreign cloth. *Khadi* also became the uniform of Indian government officials. The spinning wheel was adopted as the symbol of the National Congress, and placed at the center of the party's flag. *Khadi* cloth emporia are still found today throughout India, a lasting vestige of India's Gandhian heritage. Gandhi's clothing policy had opponents, who considered it ridiculous. For example, the Bengali poet Nobel Laureate Rabindranath Tagore argued that trying to liberate 350 million people by making them all spinners was like urging them to drown the English by all spitting together (Bean, 1989, p. 371).

Nehru believed that industrialization was crucial for the economic development of India, and when he became prime minister at India's independence in 1947, he instituted industrialization policies. Foreseeing the need for vastly increased numbers of

Indian engineers, he created the Indian Institutes of Technology (IITs) to prepare technologists, and the Indian Institutes of Management (IIMs) to train the future managers of plants and factories. These Institutes later played a key role in providing the skilled human resources that are leading India toward becoming an information society. Given the long intellectual tradition of numeracy in India,[13] many young Indians took easily to engineering and to computer science.

The Indian government in the 1950s and 1960s launched a massive industrialization program of building steel mills, hydroelectric dams, and other heavy industry. Only decades later, beginning with the policies instituted by Prime Minister Rajiv Gandhi in the late 1980s, did the government begin to adopt the informatization of Indian society as a more effective route to development. In the 1990s, Indian entrepreneurs in India and abroad utilized their business acumen to amass considerable wealth by combining technical expertise with risk-taking skills. In the contemporary meritocracy of the global village, Indian brainpower is transformed into wealth creation.

■ The New Economic Policy

The trend toward the informatization strategy of development in India during the 1990s was accompanied by a fundamental shift from the Nehruvian socialist-style policy to a free-market policy in which India opened its borders to foreign investment and foreign consumer products: Reebok, T.G.I. Friday, Pierre Cardin, Drakkar Noir, KFC, Pepsi, Coke, and McDonalds pervaded the Indian landscape. Many urban middle-class individuals thronged to buy these foreign products, and to accept the Western values that often accompanied them.

How did this revolution in economic policy occur? The architect of India's New Economic Policy (NEP) was Finance Minister Manmohan Singh in Prime Minister P.V. Narasimha Rao's government.[14] Singh, with his trademark sky-blue turban, is an economist educated at Oxford and Cambridge. He served as a career civil servant in India's bureaucracy and as India's representative to the World Bank, and then rose to be Minister of Finance.

In 1991, with India facing a severe balance-of-payments crisis, Singh proposed to throw out India's economic policy that had stood since independence. Gone were licenses and controls, government-owned key industries, and protection against the invasion of foreign businesses. The NEP opened India to foreign money flows, provided a much greater role for private enterprises, streamlined government clearance procedures, and stimulated economic growth. As Nandan Nilekani, Managing Director of Infosys Technologies in Bangalore, notes: "Prior to 1991, it took six to eight months of delays and 10 to 15 visits to New Delhi to get an import license for something worth $1,500. Today, it takes less than half-a-day and a single visit to the Software Technology Park office, half a mile away from our office, to import a machine worth several million dollars" (quoted in *Upside*, 2000, p. 3). The NEP was an economic revolution.

The intellectual origins of the NEP trace back to Charles Darwin's theory of evolution published in his famous book, *On the Origins of Species*, in 1859, and to Adam Smith's "invisible hand" theory, the notion that the best economic decisions are made by the market rather than by government interventions (Rogers, 1994). The best price for a product or service should be set by the competitive forces in the marketplace, according to the theory of free-market forces. So, under the NEP, the role of the government in India's economy shrank, and laissez-faire policies prevailed instead. However, India's brand of free-wheeling capitalism in the 1990s has probably done little, at least to date, to help the underprivileged in Indian society, like the landless in Indian villages and the urban poor. Greater socio-economic inequality usually accompanies a free-market policy, although that need not always be the case. A great potential exists in India to practice "compassionate capitalism" whereby information technology and business prowess are consciously channeled to improve the productivity of poor people (Murthy, 2000; Yunus, 2000).

■ Information Technology Policy

When, in 1998, India's prime minister Atal Behari Vajpayee inaugurated the Hyderabad Information Technology and Engineering

Consultancy (HITEC) City, a modernistic 10-story building with the amenities needed by global and local information technology (IT) firms, he said: "IT is India's tomorrow." To put the weight of official government policy squarely behind the informatization strategy, Vajpayee, in 1999, established a Ministry of Information Technology. The mission of the new ministry is to boost India's IT industry, create new wealth and jobs, harness opportunities provided by converging communication technologies (such as cable television and the Internet), enact and implement cyber laws, and facilitate the use of IT in electronic governance, public service, and distance education.[15] Almost all state governments in India have established IT departments and instituted IT policies, mostly a phenomenon of the late 1990s.[16] However, doubts exist about whether increased governmental control will eventually enhance or stymie India's informatization progress.

The Indian government became enthusiastic about pursuing an informatization route to development in the 1990s, carrying forward policies inaugurated by Prime Minister Rajiv Gandhi in the 1980s. The remarkable success of Indian computer software exports, which rose from $100 million in 1990 to $2.6 billion in 1998, and to $5 billion in 2000 (almost 2 percent of India's gross national product) contributed to this enthusiasm.[17] The National Task Force on IT, established by Prime Minister Vajpayee in 1998, set a target of $60 billion in software exports for India by 2008. McKinsey, the global consulting company, pegs software exports even higher, at $100 billion by the year 2010. If these goals are met, Indian software exports alone will contribute 10 to 15 percent of India's gross national product (GNP) by 2010, and over 2.5 million professionals will be employed in this sector. India will become a computer software powerhouse of the world.

India's enthusiasm for communication technology is reflected in several other policies and programs (Venkataram, 1999). For instance, subsequent to the formation of the World Trade Organization (WTO) in 1995, the Indian government became a signatory to the Global Telecom Agreement and the Information Technology Agreement (Vittal, 1999). These international commitments provided external pressure on India to revamp its tariff regime and to establish a legal framework for rapid adoption of communication technology. The establishment of a National IT Task Force in 1998,[18] under the co-chairmanship of Andhra Pradesh's chief minister Chandrababu Naidu, was a watershed event in India's road to informatization. The Task Force made 108 specific recommendations on how the country could become an IT powerhouse, which were accepted by the Indian government. Furthermore, in 1999, the central government created a $25 million venture capital fund to fuel computer software start-ups, and introduced the momentous Information Technology Bill in Parliament. The purpose of the IT Bill is to facilitate e-business and e-commerce, provide a framework for cyber regulation and laws, and empower government departments to create, file, and store official documents in digital format. Despite the slow pace of implementation, these and other policy initiatives symbolize India's resolve to move toward greater informatization.

Indian government leaders, goaded by champions like Chief Minister Chandrababu Naidu in Andhra Pradesh, realize that investments in information technology create jobs and wealth for Indians, given the country's competitive advantage of cheap skilled labor costs, technical excellence, and English-language ability. Unlike other areas of the economy, information technology has the potential to transform society in important new ways, through such means as electronic governance, distance education, and electronic commerce. India's challenge is to use information technology to boost the productivity of poor people, alleviating poverty, hunger, malnutrition, and illiteracy (Yunus, 2000). These results are unlikely to be achieved if left to market forces.

India is showing early signs of becoming a world power (Nayar, 1999). This nation has the numeracy, the English-language ability, the huge population, the technological proficiency, and the drive to reach this vision.[19] The democratic government of India guarantees individual freedom to Indian citizens to create new businesses, criticize government policies, or migrate to the Gulf or to America if they wish. China and India are the two mega-nations of the world, each with over one billion people. Together, these two Asian nations have over one-third of the world's population of six billion people. The importance of the democratic system for India's future is demonstrated by comparison with China, where individual freedoms are very limited. China is also pursuing a high-tech route to informatization, but cannot do so effectively until the government in Beijing someday allows individual freedoms.[20]

The growing importance of the informatization route to development is reflected in the rapid rise of high-tech companies such as Wipro and Infosys Technologies in India and Microsoft and Oracle in the U.S. These software giants act like monster money machines, making their leaders multibillionaires. Bill Gates of Microsoft and Larry Ellison of Oracle are two of the richest men in the world. Their net worth of over $50 billion each in 2000 was higher than the gross domestic product (GDP) of 175 countries, including Indonesia, Kuwait, New Zealand, and the Philippines. And Azim Premji of Wipro is the richest man in India.

❑ Azim Premji: India's Cyber Czar[21]

Fifty-four year-old Azim Premji (Plate 1.2), Chairman of Wipro, has an estimated wealth of U.S. $26 billion (*India Abroad*, 2000, p. 38). Most of Premji's wealth was created in the past few years in the information technology business, especially computer software exports.

Back in 1966, Azim Premji was within a few months of completing his B.S. degree in engineering at Stanford University when he received the sad news of his father's death. Premji dropped his studies in Palo Alto and returned to Mumbai to manage his father's business, the Western Indian Vegetable Products Limited (Wipro). Premji had observed the rise of high-technology semiconductor companies in Northern California's Silicon Valley, where Stanford University is located, and vowed to start a computer company in India.

But the immediate problem facing Premji on his return to Mumbai was to manage the family business in cooking oil, one of the most traditional of products. Premji worked tirelessly to professionalize Wipro's business. At that time, a customer would go to a retail shop to buy 50 or 100 grams of *vanaspati* (solidified fat). The shopkeeper would scoop it out of an open bulk container, often along with flies and other insects. Premji's innovative solution to this sanitation problem was to package the cooking oil in consumer containers.

Plate 1.2: Indian cyber czar Azim Premji, Chairman of Wipro

Premji is the richest Indian in the world. He works 90 hours a week, and leads Wipro's employees by personal example. Most of his wealth was generated in the late 1990s in the computer software business.

Source: Wipro (used with permission).

When IBM exited from India in the late 1970s, Premji quickly moved to fill the vacuum in the information technology business. A subsidiary, Wipro Infotech, was launched to manufacture computers, at first with many of the key components purchased by Wipro from American computer companies like Hewlett-Packard and Sun Microsystems. Wipro later formed a joint venture with Acer, the Taiwanese personal computer manufacturer, so as to capitalize on the higher price that consumers were willing to pay for foreign-name computers in India.

Wipro-Acer achieved 8 percent of market share for computer sales in India in 1999.

In 1990, foreseeing an enormous business opportunity, Premji steered Wipro into the computer software and services business. By 1999, software formed the bedrock of Wipro's earnings, making up 80 percent of the company's profits. The value of Wipro's stock on the Indian stock exchange began to rocket in the late 1990s, as investors scrambled to own a piece of this highly profitable company. Wipro's sales in the financial year 1998–99 amounted to U.S. $500 million; its market capitalization in spring 2000 was about $35 billion (*Siliconindia*, 2000b, p. 104). Wipro introduced stock options for its employees in 1983, long before other Indian IT companies. In 2000, some 30 percent of Wipro's employees owned company stock.

Premji is known for his hard work (he averages 90 hours a week), and for his unfailing dedication to excellence and quality. A corporate vision for Wipro was charted in 1972, which is regularly reviewed and updated. Wipro's core corporate values include unfailing integrity, providing innovative solutions, and offering customers value for their money. Organizational processes are aligned to meet customer needs. Top IIT and IIM graduates are recruited to build Wipro's intellectual firepower. Like General Electric's celebrated chief executive officer (CEO), Jack Welch, Premji personally teaches and coaches future leaders of Wipro, often by personal example. Wipro holds the distinction of being the first company in the world to receive the highest global quality ranking of SEI-CMM Level 5 from the Software Engineering Institute of the USA for the quality of its software services. Wipro is also the first Indian company to adopt the Six Sigma quality program, pioneered by Motorola and made famous by General Electric. Implementation of Six Sigma has boosted productivity at Wipro through significant reductions in defects and cycle time.

Now, 34 years after his return from Stanford University, Premji is India's undisputed cyber czar. Wipro still sells cooking oil, but the rapid growth of the company is due to its computer software operations. The computer software industry in India has created many Indian millionaires in recent years, including N.R. Narayana Murthy of Infosys Technologies, the first Indian company to be listed on the U.S. NASDAQ stock market (see Chapter 6). When we met with Premji several years ago at his Mumbai headquarters office, he pointed out the advantages of growing a computer company out of a cooking oil enterprise. The venture capital to start up the computer division was provided by the existing enterprise. Many of the original managers of the computer division had prior experience in the corporation's cooking oil division. Thus, Wipro was able to get off to a fast start in the computer industry.

So one way to establish a computer company in India is to start with a cooking oil company. Another essential in the case of Wipro was the young, entrepreneurial Premji, who identified business opportunities early, and seized them with a vengeance.

■ India's Informatization Score

Various scholars have created indices to measure the relative positions of nations on a scale of informatization. One such index includes three variables: (a) the availability of direct-dial international telephone service, (b) the number of fax machines per capita; and (c) computing power per capita (measured in millions of computer instructions per second). On this scale, the top 15 nations (in descending order) are: the United States, Sweden, Denmark, Finland, Australia, Hong Kong, Canada, the Netherlands, Japan, the United Kingdom, New Zealand, Switzerland, Ireland, France, and Singapore. Of the 45 nations that were ranked on this index, India was 43rd, followed only by Poland and China.

Notice that this informatization index does not include an indicator of Internet activity (probably because this index was developed before the Internet became such a dominant means of communication all over the world), nor does it fully account for high-volume usage of telephones, faxes, or computers at public access facilities, as occurs every day in public call offices (PCOs) and Internet community centers (ICCs) across India. Nevertheless, a nation like India has a long way to go before catching up in informatization with leading nations like the United States and Sweden (Ebiri, 1999). However, certain sectors within India, as noted previously, are approaching the world leaders in informatization (*India Abroad*, 1999a). "Fertile spots" of informatization in a large country, like the Bangalore and Hyderabad technopolises in India, can multiply development effects throughout the rest of the country. The Bangalore and Hyderabad technopolises are strongholds of the computer software industry. Furthermore, if the informatization index were calculated for India's 250 million urban educated elites, rather than for the whole population of one billion people, this information sector would rank near the top of the scale.

☐ **Astounding Achievements by Indian High-Tech Entrepreneurs[22]**

- Indians in Silicon Valley represent about 5 percent of the total workforce but 40 percent of the start-ups in 1999.
- Several of the 24 new billionaires in Silicon Valley, who reached this economic status during 1999 by founding Internet-related companies, are Indians. Many of the others are immigrants from Taiwan and Hong Kong.
- India rose rapidly during the 1990s to become a world power in computer software, with exports of $5 billion in 2000. Software exports are expected to rise to $100 billion by 2010. Bangalore and Hyderabad, two emerging technopolises, house several of the new Indian software companies.
- The market capitalization of the 150 IT companies listed on the Bombay Stock Exchange was a whopping U.S. $82 billion, accounting for one-third of the total stock market capitalization in early 2000.
- The richest people in India—Azim Premji, Shiv Nadar, N.R. Narayana Murthy, Rajendra Pawar, Aditya Birla, Vijay Thadani, and others—are all billionaire owners of IT companies.

Is there something about Indian cultural values that makes Indians particularly successful in high-technology businesses? Can the same technologies that are creating enormous amounts of wealth for some entrepreneurs help raise the quality of life of India's poor?

The Rate of Adoption of Communication Media in India

India's forward movement on the informatization road is reflected in the recent expansion of information technology. Figure 1.1

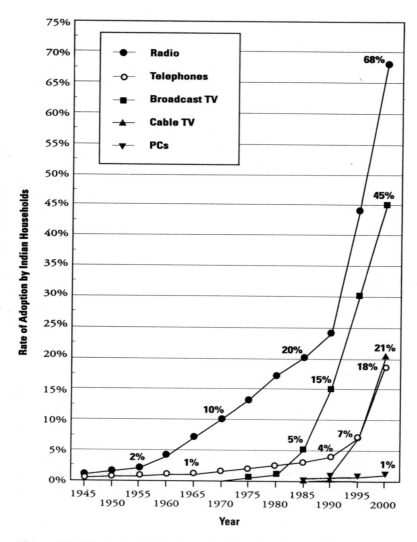

Figure 1.1: The rate of adoption of radios, broadcast television, cable television, telephones, and personal computers by Indian households

A tremendous increase has occurred in the rate of adoption of each of the communication media shown here, as India begins to move toward becoming an information society. Because of this rapid growth in the use of communication technologies, we speak of the television revolution, the telecommunications revolution, and the computer revolution in this book.

shows the rate of adoption of selected communication media over recent decades in India: radio, broadcast television, cable television, telephones, and computers. A similar pattern of growth can be observed for each new communication medium, with a relatively slow early rate of adoption, followed by a rapid spurt in the number of adopters per year, and eventually a leveling-off in the rate of adoption. This S-shaped diffusion curve characterizes the rate of adoption of most innovations (Rogers, 1995). In the case of India, the adoption of communication media is still rising at an increasing rate. Between 1950 and 2000, the combined reach of all mass media (including print, radio, television, and film) increased from 15 percent of the Indian population to an impressive 65 percent. However, 35 percent of India's present population of one billion, some 350 million people, is still untouched by India's communication revolution.

■ The Press

India publishes more daily newspapers than any other country in Asia, covering a range of languages and cultural diversity that is unparalleled in the world. In 2000, there were over 27,000 newspapers and periodicals in India published in 93 languages. Some 5,000 dailies are read by over 100 million readers in 14 languages (Kripalani, 1997). But in a nation with a high rate of illiteracy (40 percent), the effects of these newspapers and periodicals are limited to an elite audience.

Indian newspapers are owned mainly by individuals or by private firms and, in this sense, are relatively free from government control. A magazine boom occurred in India in the late 1970s, as newly founded newsmagazines like *India Today* capitalized on Indian readers' unfulfilled needs for news and other information during the Emergency years of 1975 to 1977, when press freedom was revoked. This boom occurred because of improvements in printing technology and the sale of commercial advertising, especially color advertisements, which greatly enhanced the attractiveness of magazines. Detailed, investigative news coverage by magazines provided an attractive alternative to most newspaper coverage.

In the late 1980s and the 1990s, Indian newspapers also underwent a facelift in order to keep up with magazines and with the rise of television, which represents a major competitor for advertising revenues. Stolid political coverage has been scaled down and colorful features on lifestyles, business, and entertainment have been added. During the 1990s, many publishing groups, such as Living Media Private Limited (publishers of *India Today*, something like *Time* and *Newsweek* in the U.S.) and Bennett Coleman (publishers of another leading news medium, *The Times of India*) moved into the production of television programs and launched Internet portals, gaining a wider audience as compared to the print media.

■ Radio

Radio broadcasting began in India during the British colonial era in 1923. When India gained independence, there were only six radio stations in India, located in metropolitan cities. By 2000, broadcasts of All India Radio (now part of India's Prasar Bharati Corporation) programs were heard in 110 million households (two-thirds of all Indian households) in 24 languages and 146 dialects (see Figure 1.1). After a slow start in the late 1990s, FM radio is coming of age in the new millennium.

Radio has unique advantages under Indian conditions. Unlike the press, radio gets through to the illiterate population. Compared to television or film, radio is relatively cheaper per person reached. Also, radio broadcasts can be localized to each community, so as to cover local news events and thus appeal to local audiences. However, radio only involves a sense of hearing and cannot convey visual messages. In India, at the turn of the century, radio was the most effective channel for reaching the vast audience of villagers and urban poor. However, the rise of television in India has relegated radio to the back burner.

■ Broadcast Television

Film has a long history in India, one of the most movie-crazy nations of the world. "Bollywood"[23] produces more films annually than any other country. However, Bollywood films have not played an important role in the development process. One might expect that India, with such a rich film tradition, would have moved quickly into television.[24] This was not the case.

Television began in India in 1959 as an educational project supported by the United Nations Educational, Scientific and Cultural Organization (UNESCO), and grew very slowly during the 1960s. Like radio broadcasting, television in India was based on the BBC model of a public broadcasting system, rather than American-style private, commercial networks. The big leap toward expansion of the television audience occurred in the mid-1970s with the Satellite Instructional Television Experiment (SITE), which broadcast to 2,400 villages in six Indian states. The American satellite ATS-6 transmitted educational programs for the development of rural India, and helped Indian technologists gain television broadcasting expertise prior to launching their national satellite, INSAT, eight years later.

Prime Minister Indira Gandhi, who had previously been Minister of Information and Broadcasting, supported the expansion of satellite-based television in India. Under her patronage, color television was introduced for the 1982 Asian Games. The communication satellite INSAT was launched in 1983 in order to expand the public's access to television signals. Mrs Gandhi viewed television as an important tool for development in rural India, although her critics contended that her real aim was to create a propaganda tool for her political objectives.

By 2000, Indian television had become mainly an entertainment medium driven by ratings and revenues, with its development potential largely unfulfilled and forgotten. About 50 percent of India's population regularly watches television (see Figure 1.1). The growth of the television audience is due to (a) the investments made in creating an infrastructure of about 1,000 ground-based transmitters, which repeat the satellite signal to their surrounding area, and (b) appealing television programs, beginning with *Hum Log* (*We People*) in 1984–85.

■ Cable and Private Television Networks

The mid-1980s saw the rising popularity of television serials (*Hum Log*, for example) which triggered an increase in the number of television sets purchased, and created a need for changes in the nature of television programming (as most of Doordarshan's programs were perceived as boring and educational). Thus, a niche market for alternative entertainment fare was created, and small-time cable television entrepreneurs fulfilled this need for the urban public in India.

Cable television began in Maharashtra and Gujarat in the mid-1980s through the efforts of private entrepreneurs, who wired apartment buildings and charged a monthly subscription fee to transmit films and serials via a central video-playing unit. Cable services took off in popularity throughout India in 1991–92 with the availability of foreign satellite channels. Only the government-controlled television system Doordarshan, however, was allowed to broadcast from Indian soil. A private, Hong Kong–based television network, STAR-TV, began beaming BBC and other news programs into India via satellite in 1991, at the time of the Gulf War. A vast cadre of cable television operators purchased satellite dishes and wired apartment buildings or urban neighborhoods. Because the private networks were uplinking their satellite signals from Hong Kong, Singapore, or other foreign sites, they were not violating the government regulations that gave Doordarshan a monopoly over broadcasting from Indian soil.

By 2000, more than 40 private television networks were broadcasting in India, including private networks like Zee-TV, STAR-TV, SONY, CNN, BBC, and many others. The programming consisted of either Western entertainment imports or Indian-produced serials, game shows, talk shows, and news and current affairs. These private television programs have greatly multiplied the choices available to Indian audiences. Coupled with the New Economic Policy in the 1990s, and the accompanying invasion of the Indian market by American and other foreign companies, private television has brought about many important social changes.

■ Telecommunications

Until a few decades ago, the telephone service in India was one of the worst in the world. There was only about one telephone for every 200 persons. Telephone service was considered a luxury, and accorded a low priority by government policy-makers. This perspective was replaced, beginning in the mid-1980s, with a view that telecom services are essential for business, industry, and economic development. The revolution in telecommunications services began under the leadership of India's "high-tech" prime minister, Rajiv Gandhi, and Satyen (Sam) Pitroda, a U.S.–returned expatriate Indian.

The telecommunications revolution gathered further momentum during the 1990s, spurred by the sweeping economic reforms of the Narasimha Rao government. While the pace of telecommunications reform has been slow, and the government-run Department of Telecommunications is reluctant to part with its monopoly status, private sector investment in telecommunications is increasing. Telephone density in 2000 had risen steeply to one telephone for 34 people, still low for a nation pursuing an informatization path to development. Telephone services reach out to India's villages and market towns, aided by the establishment of digital automatic exchanges and some 650,000 public call offices, which are to be found everywhere.

In the absence of reliable telecommunications links, the Bangalore technopolis would not have seen the establishment of a Texas Instruments R&D center for semiconductor design in the 1980s. The TI center represented a turning point in the rise of Bangalore as a technopolis, and for India's software exports (see Chapter 4).

■ The Internet

We previously traced the origins of computer communication to the ARPANET, which was established in 1969. This computer network had evolved into the Internet by 1989, when the total number of users worldwide began to explode. Compared to other communication channels like postal mail or long-distance telephone calls, email via the Internet is quicker, cheaper, and better in other ways. The early 1990s saw a very rapid rate of adoption of the Internet, including the World Wide Web, especially after the development of MOSAIC, a software technology that made the Internet much more user-friendly. One reason that the Internet was adopted so rapidly was the widespread prior adoption of personal computers. This spread of the Internet in the 1990s meant that computers were increasingly used for communication, rather than as number-crunchers, a radical change from the early functions of mainframe computers.

Most communication on the Internet is in the English language, and here India has a huge advantage over many other nations. India has a larger number of English-speakers than does England. The combination of English-language ability and the huge number of computer software professionals in India has boosted India into a leading position worldwide in computer software development and in remote-processing services.

❑ **NavinMail: Bridging the Distance between the U.S. and India**

Compared to other expatriate communities, U.S.–based Indians spend heavily on calling their families and friends back home. However, many people in India do not have telephone service, so many U.S.–based Indians rely on "snail mail" to keep in touch. NavinMail (literally "new mail") is an Internet-based alternative to overseas telephone calling and to postal mail. Expatriate Indians in America can now exchange voice messages (although not carried out in a real-time conversation) with their families and friends in India simply by making a local U.S. telephone call (Springer, 1999a). The voice data are compressed and transmitted through NavinMail's Internet servers in the U.S. and in India. The voice message is then locally accessed in India, usually at an Internet cafe, or by a local Internet vendor. NavinMail service costs only $10 a month for up to 200 minutes of talk time; users in India pay nothing because they are sponsored by the subscribers in the U.S. NavinMail is already on-line in Hyderabad, Chennai, Pune, Mumbai, Delhi, Ahmedabad, and Bangalore. The on-line menu in each city is in English, Hindi, and the regional language of the area.

NavinMail is the brainchild of Vishwas Godbole, an Indian engineer in Silicon Valley with expertise in high-speed Internet access. Godbole did not have a formal business plan for NavinMail, but explained the project informally to Jayashree Patil, a co-volunteer for a local event.

> Jayashree shared the idea with her husband Suhas Patil, co-founder of Cirrus Logic, who provided venture capital and advice to take the project to the market (Springer, 1999a).

The Role of Research Universities in High-Technology

As explained previously, information is the crucial ingredient in the information society. Institutions that create new information through R&D, and that convey technological innovations to receptor organizations, are the growth engines of the information society. Research universities are crucial institutions in the United States and in many other information societies. For example, California's famous Silicon Valley centers around Stanford University. Boston's Route 128 technopolis was stimulated by MIT, and Austin's Silicon Hills could not have happened without the University of Texas. Similarly, Cambridge University in England was key to the formation of the Cambridge technopolis, and the University of Tsukuba was important to Tsukuba Science City, located north of Tokyo. During the 1990s, the main factor explaining the degree of economic growth of metropolitan areas in the United States was high-tech industry, which in turn was driven by the presence of research universities (DeVol, 1999).

■ IITs and IIMs

The Indian Institutes of Technology (IITs) and the Indian Institutes of Management (IIMs) played a role similar to that of research universities in other nations. The IITs were envisioned by Prime Minister Jawaharlal Nehru in the 1950s as a means of applying scientific and technological knowledge for India's industrial development. Engineers were needed to design and operate steel plants, hydroelectric dams, and manufacturing facilities. A foreign university was invited to assist in establishing each IIT. For example, IIT Madras (Chennai) was founded with technical assistance from Germany.

The late Vikram Sarabhai, an influential technocrat, believed that science and engineering education in India should be complemented by business management training. What benefit would society receive from a well-designed steel plant that was managed in an ineffective manner? So several Indian Institutes of Management were established, the first in 1962 in Calcutta with the collaboration of MIT. A second IIM followed in Ahmedabad, Sarabhai's home city, assisted by the Harvard Business School. Today several other IIMs—in Bangalore, Cochin, Jaipur, and Lucknow—dot the Indian landscape.

Many of the entrepreneurs leading India's communication revolution are graduates of the IITs and IIMs, although high-quality expertise is also provided by several regional engineering colleges[25] and private management institutes. Many engineers from the IITs and other Indian institutions then travel overseas, often to the United States, for graduate work. In 1998, 33,000 Indian students arrived in the U.S. to earn degrees, mostly in engineering and business administration. Enrollments of Indian students in computer science at American universities were up by 20 percent in 1998 compared to the previous year (Pais, 1998). Many of these brainy, young Indians stay on to work in high-tech companies in Silicon Valley or in other technopolises. Previously, this migration was perceived negatively as a "brain drain" from India. Today, the migrants are looked upon as a brain bank.

■ IT Training in India

For India to progress on the informatization road, a tremendous need exists to train human resources in IT occupations.[26] In the late 1990s, two Indian Institutes of Information Technology (IIITs) were established in Bangalore and Hyderabad (India's leading technopolises) to provide cutting-edge teaching and research in the area of high-tech microelectronics, telecommunications, and computer and Internet technologies. Most of the IITs have also established new teaching and research programs in information technology, in order to reach world-class competence in this high-technology arena.

The Indian computer software sector employs an estimated 325,000 people, and needs at least an additional 55,000 every year to keep pace with its goals of expansion.[27] Flexible, need-based, market-driven training and education in computer hardware and software are also offered by private sector companies outside the purview of universities and colleges. Organizations such as the National Institute of Information Technology (NIIT), Aptech, ZED, STG, and ISTE offer a variety of computer certification courses in about 2,000 training centers spread across India. For instance, in 2000, NIIT had over 800 training centers in India, and sales of $100 million just from its computer education business. Training in computer hardware and software is becoming a big business in India. For instance, Advanced Technology Labs Pvt. Ltd (ATL) offers a Certified Middleware Engineer (CME) course for U.S. $7,500, which can be completed in six months, a year, or two years. The courseware and training materials, developed by Catapult Inc. in the U.S., are highly focussed on Microsoft technologies. Individuals with this training are in big demand in the U.S. and in the global market. Increasingly, IT training companies in India, such as NIIT, Aptech, and ZED, offer Web-based computer training[28] and certification courses, a business which is rapidly growing.

Conclusions

A new pathway to development identified in recent decades, *informatization* is the process through which new communication technologies are used as a means of furthering socio-economic development. The economic prowess of this strategy has been demonstrated in several small Asian nations like Hong Kong and Singapore, and in several larger Asian nations like Japan, Taiwan, and Korea. India lags far behind, dragged down in its economic performance by its huge population of rural and urban poor. But within certain high-technology enclaves in India, such as Bangalore and Hyderabad, informatization is well under way, led by visionary leaders who seek to create technopolises and use information technology to improve the quality of life of ordinary citizens. The challenge facing India is to create mechanisms so that communication technology is consciously used to boost literacy, health, and nutrition among its rural poor.

The communication revolution in India was brought about by new communication technologies like satellites, cable television, telecommunications, computers, and the Internet, accompanied by a radical change in government policies represented by the New Economic Policy of 1991. The NEP stimulated the economy by removing many government regulations, and by opening India's large population to the global market. As a consequence, the state-owned mass media apparatus in India faced increased competition from both domestic and foreign corporations, and was forced to improve the production quality of its programs.

Notes

1. This case draws upon Branigin (1998).
2. These numbers are at best estimates, given the high mobility of Indians in and out of Silicon Valley, especially that of H-1B workers.
3. In 1998, Dun & Bradstreet estimated that there were 788 Silicon Valley high-tech companies led by Indians, of which 385 were founded between 1995 and 1998 (constituting about 10 percent of all start-ups) (Frauenheim, 1999). Indian involvement in dot-com start-ups shot up dramatically in 1999. By mid-2000, several of these dot-coms had become "dot-bombs", i.e., companies that failed to survive.
4. In the late 1990s, the U.S. government allocated increasing numbers of H-1B visas to high-tech information workers, due to the industry need for such employees in America.
5. Apart from providing invaluable business advice, Rekhi asked Chandra to hire a speech therapist to dull his South Indian accent, learn how to make effective presentations, and how to effectively interact with Americans he wanted to hire.
6. Over two thousand years ago, Indian religious epics like the *Mahabharata* and *Ramayana*, as well as children's fables like the *Panchatantra*, combined the art of storytelling with a moral and educational commentary.
7. This section draws upon Mansell and When (1998).
8. See the brochure of WorldTel Ltd, a London-based company founded by Sam Pitroda to develop telecommunications capabilities in developing countries.
9. Fueled by Western aid to rebuild Japan.
10. Per capita incomes in Singapore and Hong Kong exceed those in Britain, their erstwhile colonial ruler (Aiyar, 2000).

11. We prefer, for simplicity, to use "technopolises" as the plural form of technopolis, although some scholars prefer "technopoleis," which would be the appropriate spelling in light of the word's Greek origin (see Gibson et al., 1992).

12. For more information on Andhra Pradesh's e-governance initiatives, visit http://www.andhrapradesh.com/.

13. So-called "Arabic" numbers (including zero) were created in India, and then introduced to Europeans by Arabic people. Arabic numerals replaced the clumsy Roman numerals.

14. The Rao government's sweeping economic reforms were in part influenced by the bold reforms of Mikhail Gorbachev in the former Soviet Union.

15. Some analysts fear that the new Ministry of Information Technology may lead to further bureaucratization of the Indian IT sector, spurring turf battles with the existing Ministries of Information and Broadcasting, Communications, and Science and Technology, and the Departments of Telecommunications, Electronics, and Space.

16. In fact, there is now a healthy competition among various state governments in India (spurred by Andhra Pradesh's vigorous push toward informatization) to attract foreign capital and to implement IT-friendly policies and e-governance systems. The state government of Karnataka, for instance, has created an IT-led Vision 2004 initiative, and directed that 5 percent of each administrative department's budget be used for promoting or implementing IT initiatives.

17. The Indian software industry is growing at twice the rate of the software sector in the U.S.

18. For more information on the IT Task Force's activities, visit http://it-taskforce.nic.in/it-taskforce/index.html.

19. However, India faces monumental challenges in its efforts to raise the quality of life of its 350 million people who live below the poverty line, who are uneducated, and whose lifestyles are relatively untouched by the advances made by India's unfolding communication revolution.

20. However, in the past 50 years, China has fared better than India in terms of providing literacy, health care, and adequate nutrition to its citizens (A. Sen, 1999).

21. The present case illustration is based mainly on Karp (1999) and S. Mitra (1999). We also thank Renee Jhala of Wipro's Corporate Communication Division for her inputs.

22. This case draws upon *India Abroad* (2000).

23. A term combining Bombay and Hollywood that was coined by the popular press.

24. However, Hindi films and *Chitrahaar* (a compilation of popular songs and dances from Hindi films) were highly popular on Indian television.

25. Some 150,000 engineers graduate from about 700 Indian engineering schools every year.

26. The need for trained personnel in information technology occupations is a worldwide phenomenon. Canada has an immediate shortage of over 15,000 IT personnel. Canada introduced the Software Development Worker Pilot Project (SDWPP) in 1997 in order to ease its shortage of IT workers. The project enabled Canadian firms to hire foreign workers expeditiously. Some 46 percent of the foreign workers hired to date under SDWPP are from the Indian subcontinent (Krishna, 1999a).

27. Various state governments are also gearing up to inculcate a computer culture in schools. Kerala has officially set a goal to become an "intelligent" state. Other states, like Karnataka, Gujarat, Tamil Nadu, and Andhra Pradesh, are introducing computer education at the primary school level. For instance, the Tamil Nadu government contracted the National Institute of Information Technology (NIIT) to provide computer training to 371 schools across the state. Some 742 teachers were recruited, trained, and certified for this task by NIIT.

28. The Indira Gandhi National Open University (IGNOU) is also incorporating Web-based distance learning methodologies. In collaboration with Satyam Infoway Ltd, a private Internet service provider, IGNOU in 1999 launched a unique distance learning project called the Virtual Campus Initiative (VCI). All registered students of IGNOU's School of Computer Information Sciences (SOCIS) are provided courseware on a compact disc (CD), which includes the software for Internet access. Students then conduct on-line interaction with faculty members, peer groups, and external experts.

2 The public broadcasting revolution[1]

"Since television was considered only an extension of radio broadcasting, it was natural that the baby be born in the mother's own house, almost in her lap, and grow up under her care, only to overshadow and dwarf the procreator when it grew up."

S.C. BHATT (1994, p. 18)

"Indian television has come to reflect the ambivalence, the genteel hypocrisy of our system, which is supportive of inertia. It also reflects the political, moral, and intellectual confusion into which we have landed, choosing the easy path of a loosely-structured evolution as against either a principle-based revolution or a carefully conceived and sustained evolution along pre-determined lines."

The late HARISH KHANNA, former Director General of Doordarshan (1987, p. 1).

"There is something supremely reassuring about television; the worst is always yet to come."

JACK GOULD (cited in *Forbes*, 1999, p. 160).

I n 2000, India had one of the largest radio, television, and satellite/cable systems in the world.[2] For instance, America's 260 million television viewers are dwarfed by India's 500 million viewers. The present chapter explores the growth of public broadcasting services in India. The rise of All India Radio, the Indian national radio network, and of Doordarshan, the Indian national television network, is analyzed here. Challenges to public broadcasting from private competition, commercialization, and foreign broadcasters are investigated. The scorecard of India's public broadcasting service fares well with respect to the expansion of hardware, but is very uneven in terms of establishing a public service policy, and even poorer in terms of implementing this policy. Vast changes have occurred in public broadcasting in India in recent decades, including increased competition from private cable and satellite television channels, the rise of media entrepreneurship, and the growth of regional broadcasting.

Radio Broadcasting in India

Radio broadcasting began in India as a private enterprise when, in 1927, Indian businessmen, enthused by the entertainment and profit potential of radio, cobbled together existing amateur radio clubs in Calcutta, Madras, Bombay, and Lahore to form the Indian Broadcasting Company (IBC). This event was perceived as so momentous that Lord Irwin, Viceroy of India, personally inaugurated IBC's services (AIR, 1996). However, IBC lost money and was closed down three years later. In 1930, the British government took over radio broadcasting, establishing the Indian State Broadcasting Service, which was renamed All India Radio (AIR) a few years later. The British felt that "broadcasting" was a difficult word for Indians to pronounce, so it was not used in the name of the network (Kumar, 1998).

During World War II, AIR launched an External Services Division and a Monitoring Service as part of the British Military Intelligence Wing. Like its model, the BBC, AIR broadcast anti-Nazi and anti-Japanese propaganda (often in local languages) into neighboring Asian countries. Meanwhile, on Indian soil, the British denied radio access to Indian nationalist leaders, who were waging a struggle for independence. In several Indian cities, clandestine underground radio helped fuel nationalist sentiments (Kumar, 1998). The British also used AIR to counter the pro-nationalist propaganda of Indian leaders through the press.

When India gained independence in 1947, All India Radio had an infrastructure of six radio stations, located in metropolitan cities.[3] The country had 280,000 radio receiver sets for a population of 350 million people (Figure 2.1). Post-independence, the Nehru government gave priority to the expansion of the radio broadcasting infrastructure, especially in state capitals and in border areas. Programming on AIR in the late 1940s and 1950s in India consisted mostly of news, current affairs, drama, and music (to cater to "highbrow" or "high-culture" tastes). Indian film songs and commercials were considered "low-culture," and were banned. So Indian listeners tuned their shortwave radio sets to Radio Ceylon (broadcasting from neighboring Sri Lanka) and to Radio Goa (broadcasting from Goa, then under Portuguese rule) in order to enjoy Indian film music, commercials, and other entertainment fare. The popularity of these "foreign" broadcasts in India spurred radio listening and the sale of radio sets. When purchasing a radio set, the buyer would invariably confirm with the vendor that the set could be tuned to Radio Ceylon and Radio Goa (S.C. Bhatt, 1994).

The Indian government was slow in responding to the challenge of this foreign competition for radio audiences (a scenario repeated in the case of television in the 1990s, as we detail later in this chapter). Only in 1957, 10 years after independence, did AIR launch a Vividh Bharati entertainment channel, broadcasting Indian film music and other entertainment fare. Commercials on Vividh Bharati were allowed 10 years later, beginning in 1967.

Over the years, All India Radio has developed a formidable infrastructure for radio broadcasting in India. It operates a three-tiered—national, regional, and local—service to cater to India's geographic, linguistic, and cultural diversity. Over 97 percent of India's population lives in areas that have access to radio broadcasts, served by 195 AIR radio stations scattered across the country. In 2000, AIR's programs could be heard in two-thirds of all Indian households in 24 languages and 146 dialects, over some

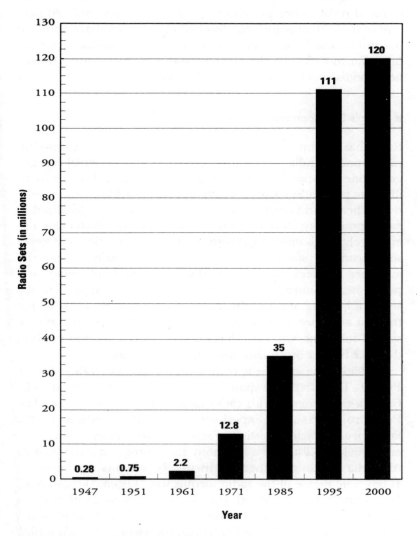

Figure 2.1: Growth in the number of radio sets in India

Source: All India Radio (1996); http://air.kode.net/; Kumar (1998).

120 million radio sets (AIR, 1996). While radio's potential reach in India, at least in aggregate terms, far exceeds that of any other mass medium (see Figure 1.1), the emergence of television has reduced radio's once prominent position. In 2000, only 20 percent of the Indian population listened to radio regularly; some 50 percent watched television.[4] However, radio still holds enormous potential to carry development messages to poor, rural Indian households which cannot afford television sets.

■ Radio's Development Potential

Radio has certain unique advantages for development communication under Indian conditions. However, this potential has largely gone untapped. Unlike the press, radio gets through to an illiterate population. Compared to television or film, radio is relatively cheap and portable, so radio broadcasts can be localized to each community, thus appealing to local people. Radio can also effectively reach individuals with less formal education and lower socio-economic status; these individuals are usually the priority audience segment for rural development, family planning, and public health initiatives. Even though radio only appeals to the sense of hearing, it is still the most effective channel for reaching the vast audience of rural and urban poor. However, the expansion of television and cable has unfortunately relegated radio to the back burner on Indian policy-makers' agenda.

In 1956, India was the site of the famous Pune Radio Farm Forum Project. The UNESCO-sponsored Pune Project was inspired by Canada's experience with radio farm forums in the 1940s. The Pune Project was a field experiment to evaluate the effects of radio farm forums, each consisting of several dozen villagers who gathered weekly to listen to a half-hour radio program (broadcast by All India Radio) and then to discuss its contents (Kivlin et al., 1968). The theme of the radio forums was "Listen, Discuss, Act!" For example, one of the radio broadcasts might deal with rodents as a problem. Following discussion of this topic in a radio forum, villagers would mount a rat-control campaign in their community.

The research evaluation showed that the Pune radio farm forums helped to "unify villages around common decisions and common actions," widening "the influence of the *gram panchayat* [village government] and broadening the scope of its action" (Mathur and Neurath, 1959, p. 101). The farm forums spurred discussions among villagers, leading to decisions about digging wells, adopting purebred bulls and Leghorn chickens, and establishing *balwadis* (children's enrichment centers). At the village level, the radio forums acted like voluntary organizations "whose members were neither appointed by authority nor elected to represent specific group interests," signifying an important experiment in village democracy (ibid.). Members voluntarily engaged in village clean-up drives, planting papaya trees, and building pit latrines. The radio farm forums, for several years, became a permanent feature (as opposed to just an experiment), and included more music, folklore, and *bhajans* (devotional songs) (ibid., p. 106).

The evaluation results were spread with UNESCO's help from India to other developing countries, many of which subsequently launched radio forums (Neurath, 1962). However, AIR over time failed to capitalize on the lessons of the Pune Project, notably the role of radio in sparking community discussions and activities (later in this chapter we discuss how Doordarshan, the Indian national television network, also failed to capitalize on the lessons of SITE and the Kheda Communication Project). And as more and more Indian households acquired radio sets, group listening declined. Eventually, in the 1970s, the radio farm forums disappeared from the Indian scene.

■ Entertainment–Education

A more recent and promising idea in AIR's development programming repertoire is the use of entertainment–education serials. As defined previously, *entertainment–education* is the process of purposely designing and implementing a media message to both entertain and educate, in order to increase audience members' knowledge about an educational issue, create favorable attitudes, and change overt behavior (Singhal and Rogers, 1999). Entertainment–education seeks to capitalize on the popular appeal of entertainment media in order to show individuals how they can live safer, healthier, and happier lives (Singhal and Brown, 1996;

Piotrow et al., 1997). Since 1987, the Central Educational Broadcasting Unit (CEBU) of All India Radio has produced several entertainment–education serials dealing with such topics as social forestry, sex education, substance abuse, gender equality, literacy, and family size (Table 2.1).

All India Radio's serials have adopted various entertainment formats, such as soap operas, variety programs, interactive talk shows, and features to engage audiences while educating them at the same time. For instance, *Jeevan Saurabh* (Fragrance of Life), a 13-episode radio series broadcast in 1988, addressed various adolescent problems—teenage sexuality, intergenerational conflicts, and career choices. *Jeevan Saurabh* broke new ground at AIR by addressing a hitherto sensitive and taboo issue: teenage sexuality. This radio program also employed a highly participatory message design strategy, using the actual "voices" of the target audience (Indian youth), their parents, and experts to identify adolescent problems and to explore solutions (Bhasin and Singhal, 1998).

All India Radio's more recent entertainment–education serials—such as *Dehleez* (Threshold), *Tinka Tinka Sukh* (*Happiness Lies in Small Pleasures*), and *Yeh Kahan Aa Gaye Hum* (*Where Have We Arrived?*)—have employed a soap opera format to both entertain and educate audience members. Research evaluations of these radio programs showed that they reached large audiences: *Tinka Tinka Sukh*, for instance, had an estimated audience of 35 to 40 million people in the seven Hindi-speaking states of North India (Singhal and Rogers, 1999).

Usha Bhasin, a career Indian Broadcasting Service official, was instrumental in launching these entertainment–education serials on AIR. She produced *Jeevan Saurabh* and *Jeevan Saurabh II* in the late 1980s, and pioneered the concept of long-running entertainment–education radio serials such as *Dehleez*, *Tinka Tinka Sukh*, and *Yeh Kahan Aa Gaye Hum*. These programs were designed on the basis of a prior audience needs assessment, and employed a team of writers and subject matter specialists. Pre-program publicity was orchestrated in the broadcast areas, employing a variety of mass media (including the vernacular press). Various techniques were used to enhance the "interactivity" of the radio programs with their target audience members. Thousands of listeners were

Table 2.1

Educational radio serials broadcast by All India Radio

Program (Year of First Broadcast)*	Number of Episodes	Educational Theme	Number of Broadcast Languages (Area)	Number of Registered Listeners**
1. *Nisarg Sampada* (1987–88)	13	Social forestry	18 (countrywide)	88,000
2. *Jeevan Saurabh* (1988)	13	Adolescent sex education	1 (Hindi Belt)	6,000
3. *Vigyan Vidhi* (1989)	13	Methods of science	17 (countrywide)	140,000
4. *Jeevan Saurabh II* (1989)	13	Marital harmony	18 (countrywide)	10,000
5. *Radio Date* (1990)	30	Substance abuse	16 (countrywide)	100,000
6. *Cheer* (1992–93)	156	Child enrichment	3 (4 states)	18,200 centers
7. Project on Radio Education for Adult Literacy (PREAL) (1990–91)	26	Adult literacy	1 (Hindi Belt)	108,000
8. *Manav ka Vikaas* (1991–94)	144	Human evolution	18 (countrywide)	100,000

Table 2.1 continued

Table 2.1 continued

Program (Year of First Broadcast)*	Number of Episodes	Educational Theme	Number of Broadcast Languages (Area)	Number of Registered Listeners**
9. Dehleez (1994–95)	52	Sexuality and population issues	7 (13 states)	66,000
10. Tinka Tinka Sukh (1996–97)	104	Gender equality, family size, and community empowerment	7 (13 states)	6,000
11. Yeh Kahan Aa Gaye Hum (1998)	52	Environmental conservation	1 (Hindi Belt)	6,000

Note: Only the educational serials broadcast by the Central Educational Broadcasting Unit (CEBU) of All India Radio are listed here.

* Several programs were later rebroadcast or transcreated into regional languages.

** A registered listener enrolls with All India Radio to listen to all episodes of a program and to provide feedback on the program's content.

Source: Bhasin (1997) and Bhasin and Singhal (1998).

encouraged to register to listen to these radio programs in advance of the programs' broadcasts (see Table 2.1), assuring an audience for the programs when the broadcasts began. These registered listeners were encouraged to write letters in response to the various social issues raised in the radio programs. These letters about the serials were then discussed in specific listener interaction programs, and prizes were awarded for viewer responses.

The impact of these entertainment–education radio serials, originally produced in the Hindi language, was multiplied by Bhasin through the process of *transcreation*, which involves adapting an existing serial's plot, characters, and context to suit the needs of another audience. For instance, the Hindi version of *Tinka Tinka Sukh* was transcreated in four additional languages in four South Indian states.[5] The plot of the radio program was modified to create realistic *local* characters and to address the subtleties of *local* norms with respect to the depicted educational issues. For instance, gender issues depicted in *Kochu Kochu Mohangal* (*Little Little Hopes*), the Malayalam version of *Tinka Tinka Sukh*, which was set in Kerala, a predominantly matriarchal society, differed in important ways from the gender issues portrayed in the Hindi version of the program, targeted to audience members in the patriarchal system of North India. This transcreation process institutionalized the methodology of producing entertainment–education serials in several AIR regional centers. The four transcreations were broadcast in the four South Indian states in 1999–2000.

◻ Community Effects of Radio in Lutsaan[6]

The present authors conducted a case study of the effects of entertainment–education radio in village Lutsaan, Uttar Pradesh state, starting in 1997. Our study showed that radio programs can create a climate for social change by stimulating interpersonal discussions and encouraging collective action at the village level.

How did we become interested in Lutsaan? In December 1996, a colorful 21-inch by 27-inch poster-letter-manifesto, initiated by a village tailor in Lutsaan, with the signatures and thumbprints of 184 villagers, was mailed to All India Radio in New Delhi (Plate 2.1). At that time,

Plate 2.1: The poster-letter from village Lutsaan, including the signatures and thumbprints of 184 community members pledging not to give or take dowry

Saumya Pant, a member of our research team, holds the letter-manifesto in the headquarters of All India Radio (AIR), New Delhi, in the company of Usha Bhasin (center), Executive Producer of *Tinka Tinka Sukh*, and Lalni Bharadwaj (right), a member of the radio serial's production team.

Source: Personal files of the authors.

All India Radio was broadcasting the entertainment–education soap opera *Tinka Tinka Sukh*. We were in charge of evaluating its impacts. The poster-letter stated: "Listening to *Tinka Tinka Sukh* has benefitted all listeners of our village, especially the women.… Listeners of our village now actively oppose the practice of dowry—they neither give nor receive dowry." This unusual letter was forwarded to the present authors by Usha Bhasin, the program's executive producer at AIR. Just prior to the writing of this letter, a tragic dowry death (the suicide of a newly married young woman that was instigated by her greedy in-laws) had occurred in an episode of *Tinka Tinka Sukh*.

We were immediately intrigued by the poster-letter. We visited village Lutsaan in August 1997. The poster-letter suggested that *Tinka Tinka Sukh* had had a strong impact on this village. We wondered whether or not the villagers had been able to actually change their dowry behavior, a practice deeply ingrained in Indian culture. Upon our arrival, we learned that the village had a Shyam Club (named after the Hindu god Krishna) with about 50 active members. The Club carried out various self-development activities, including village clean-up, fixing broken waterpumps, and reducing religious and caste tensions in the village. The village postmaster, Om Prakash Sharma (called "Bapu" or respected father by the villagers), is chair of the Club. In 1996–97, stimulated by *Tinka Tinka Sukh*, the Shyam Club devoted its main attention to such gender equality actions as encouraging girl children to attend school and opposing child marriage and dowry.

The plot of *Tinka Tinka Sukh's* 104 episodes centered around the daily lives of a dozen main characters in Navgaon (New Village), who provided positive and negative role models to audience individuals for the educational issues of family planning, female equality, and HIV prevention. Shyam Club members told us that they perceived Navgaon village in *Tinka Tinka Sukh* as much like their own village, progressive yet traditional in many ways, and with a cast of local characters much like those in their village.

Listeners to the radio soap opera in Lutsaan said they were "emotionally stirred" by Poonam's character in *Tinka Tinka Sukh*. Poonam, a young bride, is beaten and verbally abused by her husband and in-laws for not providing an adequate dowry, the payment made by a bride's parents to the groom's parents. She lives after marriage in her in-law's home, so they are in a good position to torment her if her family does not make the dowry payments they have agreed to. In recent decades, dowry payments in India have become exorbitant, usually including cash or gold, a television set, or a refrigerator. If the dowry payment is inadequate, the bride may be mistreated by the husband's family. In extreme cases, the bride is burned to death in a kitchen "accident," called a "dowry death." In the radio soap opera, Poonam was humiliated and sent back to her parents after being incorrectly accused by her in-laws of infidelity to her husband. In desperation, she commits suicide. Lutsaan's poster-letter noted: "It is a curse that for the sake of dowry, innocent women are compelled to commit suicide. Worse still... women are murdered for not bringing dowry. The education we got from *Tinka Tinka Sukh*, particularly on dowry is significant.... People who think differently about dowry will be reformed; those who practice dowry will see the right way and why they must change."

Tinka Tinka Sukh also opposed child marriage. In the soap opera, Kusum is married before the legal age of 18, becomes pregnant, and dies in childbirth. While child marriage is illegal, it is common in Indian villages. Equal opportunity for girls was also stressed in the radio soap opera. The poster-letter stated: "In comparison with boys, education of girls is given less importance. Even if some girls wish to develop themselves through their own efforts and assert their individuality, their family is not supportive.... Whenever girls were given equal opportunities for educating themselves, they have done as well as the boys." Family planning/population size issues were stressed in *Tinka Tinka Sukh*. The poster-letter stated: "Our society has to take a new turn in their thinking concerning family size. As the cost of living rises, having more children than one can afford is inviting trouble.... This message of *Tinka Tinka Sukh* comes across very clearly."

Efficacy is the degree to which an individual feels he/she can control his/her future. Individual efficacy and collective efficacy were emphasized in the radio soap opera. A young bride, Sushma, takes charge of her life after her husband leaves her by starting a sewing school. She is rewarded in the storyline for this efficacious behavior. Efficacy is also demonstrated by Sunder, a drug abuser, who gets clean and then obtains a job. Ramlal, a pampered son and male chauvinist, represented a negative role model in the early episodes of *Tinka Tinka Sukh*. Later he reforms and becomes a development officer, leading Navgaon village in a variety of progressive activities. The tailor in Lutsaan identified with this transitional role model, Ramlal, as he stated in the poster-letter: "I saw myself, in fact many of my anti-social ways, reflected in Ramlal who is also reformed." Such parasocial involvement with a transitional role model in the mass media is one way in which entertainment–education effects behavior change.

Collective efficacy was also stressed in *Tinka Tinka Sukh*, as Navgaon village displays collaborative spirit in solving its problems. For example, the village constructs a new hospital, rejecting government assistance and raising the needed funding themselves. As the poster-letter stated: "The problems of the village are tackled collectively, and in the event of any major problem, the matter is put before the *panchayat* [village council] for resolution."

The relatively strong effects of *Tinka Tinka Sukh* in village Lutsaan may be traced to two villagers, the tailor Birendra Singh Khushwaha and the postmaster Bapu. While they are a generation apart in age, and differ socio-economically, they have much in common. Both are in occupations that bring them in contact with many villagers on a daily basis. Both the tailor and the postmaster are sparkplugs for social change in Lutsaan. The tailor is a hyperactive fan of All India Radio, listening eight to 10 hours a day, and writing an average of four to five letters to AIR per day! His shop is located centrally in the village, and its door is always open, with the radio on. Several people are usually sitting in the tailor's shop, gossiping, listening to All India Radio, and discussing the program.

Om Prakash Sharma (Bapu), the 55-year-old postmaster of Lutsaan, is known for his altruism in helping his fellow villagers. He has a small buffalo corral in the courtyard of his home. Villagers bring their sick buffalo to him for treatment. Bapu barters the drugs for milk. Like the tailor, he was a devoted fan of *Tinka Tinka Sukh*, often delaying his evening meal in order to listen. Bapu often discussed each episode with his friends after they had listened to the radio program. These discussions helped spark collective action, such as the pledge by community members to not give or accept dowry.

Our subsequent visits to Lutsaan in 1998 and 1999 showed that the effects of the radio soap opera continued (perhaps they were magnified somewhat by the impacts of our previous visits).[7] For instance, enrollment in Lutsaan's primary school in 1999 comprised about 40 percent girls and 60 percent boys; in 1996, before the broadcasts of *Tinka Tinka Sukh*, the ratio had been 10 percent girls and 90 percent boys. Villagers in Lutsaan attributed this notable change in the gender ratio of the student body to the interpersonal discussions about gender equality that were stimulated by the radio soap opera. Further, male and female radio listening clubs were organized for AIR's follow-up entertainment–education program, *Yeh Kahan Aa Gaye Hum*, about preserving the environment. Several large hand-painted signs appeared in the village, stating: "After *Tinka Tinka Sukh* listen now to *Yeh Kahan Aa Gaye Hum*, broadcast from All India Radio." Members of the listening clubs donated a dollar per month toward the cost of radio batteries, paint and poster supplies, and tree seedlings (the radio program promoted reforestation).

However, in our visits to Lutsaan, we encountered cases which show the complexities of radio-sparked social change. For instance, in our first visit to Lutsaan we encountered a just-married 14-year-old girl, suggesting that *Tinka Tinka Sukh* was not completely effective in changing village norms. Marriage meant that this child had to drop out of school. Her father, a low-caste community member, told us that he knew that child marriage and paying dowry were illegal in India, but he did not expect the police to interfere (they did not). Bapu, the postmaster, while visibly angered by the child marriage, shrugged it off as being a problem of the lower caste. This suggests that radio can only do so much to change strongly held norms of behavior.

Why was radio so effective in stimulating social changes in Lutsaan? Exposure to radio, and to *Tinka Tinka Sukh*, was higher in Lutsaan than elsewhere in North India. Prior conditions in the village helped magnify the effects of radio: a hyperactive radio listener (the tailor), a highly respected village leader (the postmaster), group listening to the radio episodes, and the activities of a village self-help group.

Our research in Lutsaan demonstrates the potential of radio in spurring rural development. For radio to be effective, villagers need to listen to the programs, discuss them, and then act upon them.

Private FM Radio

In 1993, frequency-modulated (FM) radio broadcasts were launched in India on an AIR channel to serve a half-dozen metro cities. FM radio has a shorter range than AM broadcasts, usually 30 to 40 kilometers, and has higher-quality sound (and is less affected by weather conditions) than AM radio. Several private companies like Times FM and Radio 1 began broadcasting FM radio programs, mostly geared to urban youth. FM programs include music, talk shows, and telephone call-ins. In Delhi alone, top-rated FM broadcasts garner audiences of three to four million listeners.

One popular program produced by Times FM in 1994–95 was *Balance Barabar* (*Balance Always*), which used popular music and a "Hinglish" (Hindi–English) talk show format to engage the youth audience. It was sponsored by Population Services International (PSI) and provided information on AIDS and STDs, encouraging listeners to ask questions through letters and telephone calls.

In 1998, in an ad hoc move, the Indian government canceled all private programs on FM radio, and the programs immediately went off the air. In 1999, the government approved the establishment of 150 private FM radio stations in 40 Indian cities, and in principle allowed non-governmental organizations, educational institutions, and citizens' groups to establish community radio stations. In 2000, AIR's FM network covered just 17 percent of India's geographical area and 21 percent of India's population. So a tremendous potential exists for the expansion of FM radio services in India. As with television (discussed later), AIR's monopoly in radio services is gradually being broken.

❑ Internet Broadcasting: Anyplace, Anytime

Indians now also have access to Internet broadcasting, although the number of Indians who access Internet broadcasting is very low. However, this situation may change as Internet access rises steeply and the cost of Internet services comes down. Internet broadcasting offers certain advantages over traditional broadcasting services. In traditional over-the-air broadcasting, audience members cannot access their favorite stations outside of the broadcast area. Also, the broadcast stations, not the individual audience members, determine what programs are broadcast. However, through Internet broadcasting audience members can receive their favorite broadcast programs anytime, anywhere.

Prior to 1996, few broadcast stations existed on the Internet. By 1999, the Internet had over 500 TV stations and 1,900 radio stations, and several were being added each day (Kaur, 1999a). Technological innovations like "streaming" video and audio helped this boom; audience members can now watch/listen to a program while it is being downloaded to their computer.

The year 1999 witnessed a boom in Internet radio (a boom in Internet television will likely follow), especially in America. An Internet hub, Lycos, launched Lycos Radio. Its rival Yahoo! paid $5 billion (U.S.) for Internet-media distributor Broadcast.com, which offers a comprehensive selection of programs including sports coverage, talk and music radio, news, commentary, and several hundred audio books. Each day, some 1.1 million users access its broadcast offerings over 410 radio stations. America On-Line (AOL) followed with its $400 million acquisition of a radio firm, Spinner Networks Inc., and a music technology company, Nullsoft Inc. It is no surprise that Microsoft's latest browser has a "radio bar" to access Net radio.

It is unlikely that Internet broadcasting will ever completely replace AM and FM radio or over-the-air television broadcasting. Radio and television penetration is far, far higher than computer penetration worldwide. Also, most personal computer users do not have the bandwidth to receive video or audio files as is possible with conventional broadcasting.

The Internet is also blurring the traditional broadcasting dichotomy between source and receiver. Today, almost anyone with a PC and a modem can become a publisher or a broadcaster.

The Television Revolution in India

Television was introduced in India as an experimental educational service in Delhi in 1959, with regular daily broadcasts beginning six years later (Table 2.2). In the mid-1960s, Dr Vikram Sarabhai, a visionary technocrat and founder of India's space program, began arguing in policy-making circles that a nationwide satellite television system could play a major role in promoting economic and social development. At Sarabhai's initiative, a national satellite communication group (NASCOM) was established in 1968. Based on its recommendations, the Indian government approved a "hybrid" television broadcasting system consisting of communication satellites as well as ground-based microwave relay transmitters. Sarabhai envisaged that the satellite component would allow India to leapfrog into state-of-the-art communication technology, speed up the development process, and take advantage of the lack of infrastructure (until 1972, there was only one television transmitter in India, located in Delhi).

Table 2.2

Main events in the development of television in India

Year	Event
1959	Television is introduced in Delhi as an experimental educational service under a grant from UNESCO.
1965	Television service is regularized in Delhi with daily broadcasts of entertainment and educational programs.
1969	The Government of India signs an agreement with the United States' National Aeronautics and Space Administration (NASA) to launch the Satellite Instructional Television Experiment (SITE) in India.
1972–75	Regular television service begins in Bombay, Srinagar, Amritsar, Pune, Calcutta, Madras, and Lucknow.
1975–76	SITE broadcasts television programs to 2,400 Indian villages from NASA's ATS-6 satellite for one year.
1980	The first television commercial is aired on Indian television.
1982	Indian television switches from black-and-white to color in order to broadcast the Asian Games in New Delhi.
1983	INSAT-1B is launched by the U.S. space shuttle, Challenger, and begins television broadcasting in India.
1984–85	Over 120 television transmitters are installed in India to rapidly increase television coverage. Indigenous soap operas become popular, starting with *Hum Log* (1984–85), *Buniyaad* (1986–87), *Ramayana* (1987–88), *Mahabharat* (1988–90), and others.
1986	The first regional television network is launched in Maharashtra.
1990	The Prasar Bharati Bill granting autonomy to Doordarshan and All India Radio is passed by Parliament but is not implemented until 1997–98 because of political wrangling.
1991–92	Private cable and satellite television channels begin to diffuse rapidly in India after the Gulf War, competing for audiences and advertising revenues with the state-run Doordarshan. The private television channels broadcast from satellite transponders to the dish receivers of thousands of cable operators.
1993–94	Doordarshan reorganizes to cope with the cable onslaught, launching the metro entertainment channel in metropolitan cities and several regional-language channels from state capitals.
1995	Doordarshan launches an international channel (DD-International).
1997–98	Doordarshan and AIR are delinked from the Ministry of Information and Broadcasting and an autonomous Prasar Bharati Corporation is established. Meanwhile, competition from private cable and satellite channels intensifies, gradually eating into Doordarshan's advertising revenues.

Table 2.2 continued

Table 2.2 continued

Year	Event
2000	Almost 500 million Indians (50 percent of the population) watch television regularly. Doordarshan broadcasts some 20 channels by satellite and its 1,000 ground transmitters to provide potential access to about 90 percent of India's population. Some 40 private television networks are currently broadcasting.

Source: Singhal and Rogers (1989); Doordarshan (1998); http://www.ddindia/net/.

Satellite broadcasting fits naturally with India's immense size, and with the ability of satellites to overcome natural barriers to television signals like mountains. Who first thought of broadcasting from satellites? Arthur C. Clarke, author of the science fiction book and movie, *2001: A Space Odyssey*, originally proposed the idea of communication satellites in 1945. He argued that a satellite positioned 22,300 miles above the Equator would be stationary with respect to a given point on the earth's surface. Thus, a satellite in this geo-stationary orbit would be a perfect platform for television broadcasting. The footprint of the television signal would cover about one-third of the earth's surface. Essentially, satellite communication removes the cost of distance in transmitting television (or telephone) messages.

Many years passed before Clarke's idea could be implemented. The launch of Sputnik by the Soviet Union in 1957 set off a space-race between the United States and the U.S.S.R., leading to more powerful rockets that could be utilized to put satellites in space. The first U.S. communication satellite, WESTAR 1, was launched in 1974. Today hundreds of communication satellites are boosted into space each year in order to transmit television broadcasts, long-distance telephone calls, and other voice–picture–data. Recently, the increasing demand for cellular telephones required that many more satellites be launched; in 1999, several hundred satellites went into space. In fact, satellites now face a parking problem in space!

■ SITE and INSAT

Sarabhai's NASSCOM planning group prepared the blueprint for INSAT, the Indian national satellite, but also realized that before embarking on INSAT, which involved tremendous expenditures on communication infrastructure, a pilot experiment was essential. The Satellite Instructional Television Experiment (SITE) was a one-year pilot project in 1975–76 utilizing NASA's ATS-6 satellite to broadcast directly to satellite-receiving dishes in 2,400 Indian villages in order to reach tens of millions of rural people (Plate 2.2), most of whom watched television for the first time. Its objectives were to improve rural primary school education, provide teacher training, improve agriculture, health and hygiene, and nutritional practices, and contribute to family planning and national integration (Agrawal, 1981). Useful lessons were learned during SITE about satellite hardware, television software, costs, and field-based operational management issues on a smaller scale prior to the launch of INSAT (Mody, 1979).

  · The first Indian national satellite, INSAT-1A, was constructed in the U.S. and launched in 1982 by NASA. However, it developed technical snags and was deactivated within months. A second satellite, INSAT-1B, was built by Ford Aerospace in California's Silicon Valley, and launched on the U.S. space shuttle Challenger on 15 October 1983. Over one hundred Indian engineers were in residence at Ford Aerospace while INSAT-1B was built to Indian technical specifications (Mody, 1987).

  INSAT-1B, followed by other generations of the INSAT satellite, led to a major expansion of television broadcasting in India. Prior to 1983, television access in India was limited to 28 percent of the nation's population. Only 30 million Indians (less than 5 percent of the population), mostly located in metropolitan cities, regularly watched television (Figure 2.2). Five years later, in 1988, 62 percent of the population could access television signals, and over 100 million Indians regularly watched television. In 2000, some 90 percent of India's population could access television signals, and over 500 million Indians (50 percent of the population) regularly watched television.

  This increase in viewership is due to the large-scale installation of ground-based television transmitters in India. Television programs are uplinked from production studios to the INSAT satellite, and then downlinked to these television transmitters, which then rebroadcast the television programming to the surrounding

Plate 2.2: Television viewing is making inroads into rural India

By 2000, approximately half of India's population had regular exposure to television broadcasts either from Doordarshan, the public broadcasting television network, or from over 40 private broadcasting networks that transmit their programs by satellite and cable distribution. During the 1990s, television in India turned away from its educational and development goals to become primarily focussed on earning advertising profits by maximizing audience ratings.

Source: Saumya Pant (used with permission).

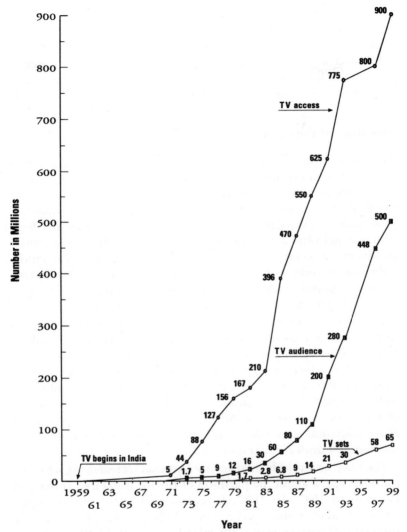

Figure 2.2: Growth in the number of people who have access* to television, the number of people who watch television, and the number of television sets in India

A television revolution has occurred in India in recent decades, as attractive programs have led to 50 percent of the population having regular exposure.
* Those who live in a geographical area where a television signal can be received.

Source: Singhal and Rogers (1999); http://www.ddindia/net/.

area. The number of television transmitters in India increased from one in 1959 to five in 1973, 19 in 1983, 175 in 1985, 220 in 1988, and about 1,000 in 2000. Despite this widespread access, rural households and those of lower socio-economic status are least likely to have television access.

The Rise of Entertainment

The rapid expansion of television hardware in India in the 1980s increased the need for developing more program software to fill the broadcast hours. Television broadcasting, by its very nature, is like feeding a hungry elephant. Program production, previously a monopoly of Doordarshan, the government-run national television system in India, was then opened to an outside pool of artists, producers, directors, and technicians. Many of these talented individuals were connected previously with the Mumbai film industry.

Highly popular television soap operas, beginning with *Hum Log* (*We People*) in 1984–85, sparked a programming revolution at Doordarshan. The main lesson learned from this experience was that an indigenous television program could attract and build a large loyal audience over the duration of the serial, generating big profits. The advertising carried by *Hum Log* promoted a new consumer product in India, Maggi 2-Minute Noodles. The public rapidly accepted this new consumer product, suggesting the power of television commercials. Advertisers began to line up to purchase television advertising, and the commercialization of Doordarshan got under way (Figure 2.3).

Hum Log was quickly followed by *Buniyaad* (*Foundation*), a historical soap opera about the partition of British India into India and Pakistan in 1947. In 1987, *Ramayana*, a Hindu religious epic, attracted smash ratings, to be then eclipsed by the phenomenally successful *Mahabharata* in 1988–89 (Bhargava, 1987; Bhatia, 1988; Ananda Mitra, 1993). In the 1990s, it was serials galore on Doordarshan: big hits included historical serials such as *The Sword of Tipu Sultan* and *The Great Maratha*, religious serials such as *Shri Krishna, Jai Hanuman*, and *Om Namah Shivay*, fantasy serials like *Shaktimaan*, and family serials like *Shanti, Hum Raahi*, and *Udaan*. These popular television programs attracted large audiences, and

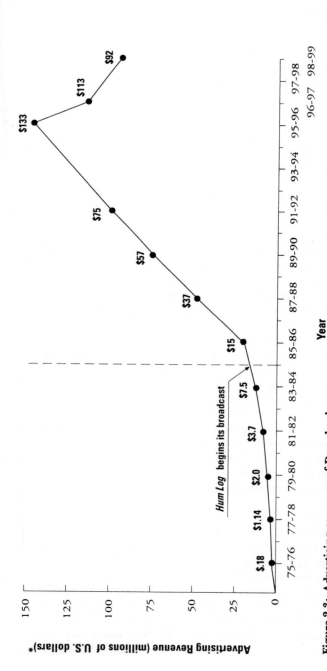

Figure 2.3: Advertising revenues of Doordarshan

Beginning with the broadcast of *Hum Log* in 1984–85, the commercialization of Doordarshan increased rapidly, as advertising sales shot up. Then, in the mid-1990s, competition from private television networks, who dominated in attracting the urban elite audience, led to a decline in Doordarshan's advertising revenues.

* One U.S. dollar equaled 43 Indian rupees.

Source: Singhal and Rogers (1999) and http://www.ddindia.net/.

generated vast advertising earnings for the Indian government through Doordarshan. Advertisers quickly understood the advantages of advertising their products on a medium that reached a huge national audience.

❑ *Hum Log*: A Turning Point

Because the broadcasting of *Hum Log* in 1984–85 was such an important turning point in the growth of television in India (see Figure 2.3), we describe here how this unusual program came to be.

Hum Log was India's first long-running soap opera. A *soap opera* is a dramatic serial that is broadcast mainly in order to entertain audience members. The term "soap opera" originated in the United States because the sponsors of these daytime broadcasts were mainly soap companies like Procter and Gamble. Soap operas are called *telenovelas* (literally "television novels") in Latin America, where they are the most popular genre of television programming.

Hum Log was a special kind of soap opera, however. This pioneering program utilized the entertainment–education strategy by intentionally placing educational content in this entertainment message (Singhal and Rogers, 1999). The idea of an entertainment–education soap opera came to India from Mexico, where Miguel Sabido, a brilliant television producer-director, had created a methodology for inserting educational issues in an entertaining medium by designing positive, negative, and transitional role models for the educational values that were being promoted (Nariman, 1993). Population Communications International, a non-profit organization headquartered in New York, helped introduce Sabido's entertainment–education strategy to Doordarshan officials.

Some 156 episodes of *Hum Log* were broadcast in Hindi for 17 months in 1984–85. The television program promoted such social themes as gender equality, small family size, and national integration. At the end of each 22-minute episode, a famous Indian film actor, Ashok Kumar, summarized the educational lessons from the episode in an epilogue of 30 to 40 seconds. Kumar connected the drama to viewers' everyday lives. For instance, he might comment on a negative character who is drunk and beats his wife by asking: "Why do you think that people like Basesar Ram drink too much, and then behave badly? Do you know anyone like this? What can be done to reduce incidents of alcoholism? What can *you* do?"

Our study of *Hum Log*'s audience effects showed that a high degree of parasocial interaction occurred between the audience members and their favorite *Hum Log* characters (Singhal and Rogers, 1989). *Parasocial interaction* is the perceived face-to-face interpersonal relationship that develops between a television viewer and a media role model (Horton and Wohl, 1956). For example, many *Hum Log* viewers reported that they routinely adjusted their daily schedules to "meet" their favorite character "in the privacy of their living rooms" (ibid.). Many other individuals reported talking to their favorite characters through their television sets; for instance, "Don't worry, Badki. Do not give up your dream of making a career."

Hum Log achieved audience ratings of 65 to 90 percent in North India and between 20 and 45 percent in the main cities of South India. About 50 million individuals watched the average broadcast of *Hum Log*. One unusual aspect of this soap opera was the huge number of letters, over 400,000, that it attracted from viewers; so many that most of them could not be opened by Doordarshan officials.

■ The Arrival of Cable and Satellite Channels

While Doordarshan was expanding rapidly in the 1980s, the cable television industry was mushrooming in major Indian cities. The VCR greatly multiplied entertainment options for Indian audiences, providing alternatives to Doordarshan's single-channel programming.[8] Video viewing at home and in community-based video parlors increased rapidly. The video fare consisted mostly of film-based entertainment, both domestic and imported. By 1984, entrepreneurs in cities such as Mumbai and Ahmedabad had begun wiring apartment buildings to transmit several films a day. Within a few years, this phenomenon became widespread in other urban centers. The number of cable operators in India exploded from about 100 in 1984 to 1,200 in 1988, 15,000 in 1992, and to about 60,000 in 1999 (Kumar, 1998).

The Gulf War of 1991 (which popularized CNN), and the launching of STAR-TV in that same year by the Whampoa Hutchison Group of Hong Kong, signaled the arrival of private satellite channels in India (as we detail in the next chapter). STAR-TV, broadcast through the Chinese satellite ASIASAT 1, offered five 24-hour channels in 38 countries of Asia. In 1992, Zee-TV, a Hindi-based satellite entertainment channel, also began beaming programs to cable television systems in India. Many cable operators installed large satellite dishes to receive these private satellite channels, and offered them to cable subscribers, greatly multiplying the entertainment options. By 1995, over 12 million Indian households were watching cable and satellite channels; by 2000, this number had risen to over 35 million. Over 40 private cable and satellite channels were available to Indian audiences, including several that focussed exclusively on regional-language broadcasting like Sun-TV, Eenadu-TV, Udaya-TV, Raj-TV, and Asianet. By 2000, Zee-TV also launched several regional networks, broadcasting in Marathi, Bengali, and other languages.

Doordarshan, a monopoly until the early 1990s, had to respond to this challenge from the private television networks (S. Rao, 1998). Beginning in 1993, Doordarshan launched a second metro entertainment channel, several regional-language channels, an international channel, a sports channel, and a 24-hour news channel. Faced with audiences' growing appetite for entertainment programs and increased competition from private networks, its public service mandate increasingly took a back seat, and revenue maximization became the mantra. Doordarshan's rhetoric was consistent with the New Economic Policy of 1991: privatization, globalization, liberalization, and commercialization. To increase commercial revenues, Doordarshan sold the marketing rights of its most popular programs—like the Hindi feature films, *Chitrahaar, Rangoli*, and others—to private companies. Sponsored television serials, especially on the metro entertainment channels, were aimed at audiences with disposable incomes. Doordarshan's commercial revenues increased steeply from the *Hum Log* days to 1996–97, but thereafter began to decline as popular cable and satellite channels like Zee-TV, SONY, and STAR-TV began to acquire a larger share of the elite audience pie, cutting into Doordarshan's advertising revenues (see Figure 2.3).

In summary, since the onslaught of private cable and satellite channels, Doordarshan has been operating much like a commercial network with about 20 channels targeted to different audience segments, vying for advertising revenues with private television channels, measuring its success in terms of audience ratings, and producing very few programs of its own (S.C. Bhatt, 1994; Gupta, 1998). What happened to Doordarshan in the 1990s is reflective of the defeat of public broadcasting systems all over the world: BBC and ITV in England continue to lose ground to Rupert Murdoch's satellite channels; ARD and ZDF, two public service networks in Germany, lost 50 percent of their audience in the 1990s (Gupta, 1998). The global wave of private television is swamping public television broadcasting.

Television for Development: Missed Opportunities

Several decades ago, India was a world leader in experimenting with television technology for spurring national and local development. However, as was the case with AIR and radio farm forums (discussed previously), India failed to capitalize on the lessons learned from these early television experiments, frittering away a golden opportunity. The cases of SITE and the Kheda Communication Project are illustrative.

■ SITE

India was one of the first developing countries to experiment with satellite television, when in 1975–76 it launched the Satellite Instructional Television Experiment (SITE). Evaluations of SITE showed that its operational management, spearheaded by officials of the Space Application Center (SAC), was commendable. The hardware of satellites, earth stations, uplinks and downlinks, worked wonderfully. On a given day, more than 80 percent of the television sets worked to deliver television pictures to 2,400 villages.

With respect to software, however, SITE was a somewhat humbling experience. The key lesson learned was that engaging television programs produced in local languages and that were relevant to the needs and aspirations of rural people were needed (Mody, 1979). Further, to be effective, these programs needed to be

integrated with local audience activities. However, barring notable exceptions like the Kheda Communication Project (discussed
later in the present chapter), such locally based, engaging programs were rarely seen on Doordarshan.

When the Indian national satellite (INSAT) became operational
in the 1980s, the Indian government, through its various ministries
and rural development programs, installed community television
sets in several thousand Indian villages. However, no infrastructure was created to locally support the television messages. While
the strength of SITE was its detailed operational management
procedures and the committed leadership of SAC officials, the
agencies in charge during the INSAT period—state governments,
Doordarshan, and the Ministry of Rural Development—failed in
systems management. Responsibilities were not clearly delineated
and, thanks to bureaucratic restrictions and watertight compart-
ments among implementing agencies, the mission of using satellite television to address rural needs was all but run into the
ground by the 1990s. Community television died an untimely
death, much like the radio farm forums of previous decades.

■ The Kheda Communication Project

Another pioneering experiment in using television for educational purposes in India was the Kheda Communication Project
(KCP). Inspired by the lessons learned from SITE, KCP was a
decentralized experiment in community-based television (Kalwachwala & Joshi, 1990). The site chosen for the experiment was
Kheda district, an area near the SAC headquarters in Ahmedabad. What made the Kheda Communication Project especially
effective (see Contractor et al., 1988)?

1. The hardware consisted of one low-power transmitter located
   in Pij village, about 50 kilometers south of Ahmedabad,
   which was connected to a local studio, the local Doordarshan
   station, and to a satellite earth station in Ahmedabad. Thus
   KCP could broadcast either local television programs or
   national satellite television programs. Some 650 community

television sets were provided to 400 villages and installed in public places (frequently schools) where village audiences gathered in the evenings to view the broadcasts. Technicians periodically toured these villages to service and repair the television sets.

2. Kheda district comprises some 1,000 villages with over three million inhabitants. In recent decades, it has become a major center for milk production in India, as part of the so-called "White Revolution." The KCP collaborated with extension agencies working in dairying, agriculture, and health services, and with local banks, cooperatives, and employment exchanges. Thus, the development infrastructure in Kheda district was tapped to facilitate the use of information transmitted by the television broadcasts.

3. The Project was independent of commercial interests, as it relied mainly on government funds for financial support. Managed by the Space Application Center, it enjoyed a great deal of political autonomy from the national government, and the support of the state government.

4. The Project relied heavily on audience research by conducting needs assessments of village audiences and by carrying out formative and summative evaluations of Kheda television programs.

5. It promoted rural development and social change at the local level. Audience participation was aggressively encouraged at all levels. Villagers were involved as actors, writers, and visualizers in the production of television programs dealing with such local issues as exploitation, caste discrimination, minimum wages, alcoholism, cooperatives, and local and national elections. Television serials, puppet shows, folk drama, and other popular local formats were used to address issues such as family planning, gender equality, and village sanitation. *Chatur Mota* (*Wise Elder*) and *Nari Tu Narayani* (*Woman You Are Powerful*), for instance, were two popular entertainment–education serials produced by KCP with the active participation of its audience members (Mody, 1991). A campaign approach was followed, synchronizing television programs with local efforts by development agencies.

The Kheda Project represented a model of community-level, decentralized television broadcasting in India. It received the prestigious UNESCO Prize in 1984 for rural communication effectiveness. However, the Indian government did not replicate the KCP community-based television model in other parts of India. Instead, in 1985, when a high-powered transmitter was commissioned in Ahmedabad with a range that covered Kheda district, the government ordered that the Kheda transmitter be transferred to Chennai in order to facilitate a second entertainment channel for its urban residents.[9] Why spend money on running a rural community-based communication project when advertising incomes could easily be earned from metro audiences?

The failure to capitalize on the lessons of SITE and the Kheda Communication Project demonstrates missed opportunities in utilizing television for social progress.

❑ Chicken-Mesh Antennae and Ruggedized Television Sets

The Space Application Center (SAC) in Ahmedabad introduced several technological innovations in the SITE Project on satellite broadcasting to rural India. For instance, during SITE the Center used chicken-mesh antennae and ruggedized TV sets in the 2,400 Indian villages receiving direct television signals from the ATS-6 satellite.

The chicken-mesh antenna was made of aluminium, and resembled the wire mesh that is used in chicken houses. Aluminium is a good conductor of electricity and is light in weight, which made the antenna easily portable. The antennae used in SITE had a 3-meter diameter and cost 1,500 *rupees* (U.S.$35). They could be installed in a village in just a few hours. The mesh allowed strong winds to pass through, eliminating the need to build a strong support structure for the antenna. In later years, these antennae were designed as collapsible umbrellas, further enhancing their portability and reducing set-up time.

Ruggedized television sets were developed to meet the needs of harsh village conditions. These sets could withstand wide variations in voltage, vibration during transportation, and extreme conditions of heat, dust, and moisture. The Space Application Center designed ruggedized

> television sets with easily replaceable fuses, and sealed them to reduce problems of vibration during transportation and the penetration of dust and moisture.
>
> Chicken-mesh antennae and ruggedized television sets represent examples of how technology can be reconfigured to meet rural needs, benefitting the most disadvantaged audience segments.

The Scorecard for Indian Public Broadcasting[10]

The scorecard for India's public broadcasting service fares well with respect to the expansion of hardware, but is poor in terms of formulating a public service policy, and very uneven in terms of its implementation. Caught in a whirlwind of private competition and rising audience appetites for entertainment programs, public broadcasting has deviated from its stated mission of empowering and educating audiences.[11] Allocating government funds for expanding irrigation or adult literacy programs seems obvious, but such commitment has not been evident in expanding community-based public service broadcasting in India, such as the Kheda Communication Project.

1. Misplaced Focus The focus of Indian broadcasting has largely been on hardware expansion and on quantitative targets (for example, achieving the installation of 1,000 TV transmitters). While the expansion of television services to the rural hinterlands is laudable, little attention has been given to software, and to qualitative aspects such as program relevance, appropriateness, and effects. This neglect of program software has occurred despite the much-lauded P.C. Joshi Committee recommendations on revamping television software (*An Indian Personality for Television*, 1985). The story of public broadcasting in India is replete with incidents of governmental delays, political apathy, and missed opportunities.[12]

2. Whose Autonomy? All India Radio and Doordarshan, comprising the public broadcasting networks in India, were the arms of the Indian Ministry of Information and Broadcasting until

1997. In 1966, the Chanda Committee, followed by the Verghese Committee in 1978, recommended granting autonomy to AIR and Doordarshan and establishing guidelines for their role in public service (Akash Bharati, 1978). After that, dozens of committees explored this issue of broadcasting autonomy, often in response to imminent factors such as cross-border satellite broadcasting (Table 2.3). However, the government in power was reluctant to give away the political advantage gained through media control. Autonomy[13] to Doordarshan and AIR was officially sanctioned in 1997–98 in light of the landmark 1995 Supreme Court directive that the "airwaves belong to the public." Today, while All India Radio and Doordarshan are governed by an independent statutory body, the Broadcasting Corporation of India (Prasar Bharati), little else has changed. The advent of satellite and cable television created a de facto deregulation of Indian television broadcasting services, breaking the monopoly of Doordarshan, and making the issue of autonomy passé. The 31-year countdown to the granting of broadcast autonomy to AIR and Doordarshan, and the highly politicized process surrounding it, is reflected in Table 2.3.

3. Delhi-centric broadcasting   Public service broadcasting in India has remained Delhi-centric, and hence highly politicized. The rapid turnover of governments, ministers, secretaries, and director generals has subjected broadcasting to the whims and fancies of political expediency.

4. Hindi-centric broadcasting   Broadcasting in India has also been Hindi (North Indian)–centric, and the dominant worldview of the majority has taken precedence over regional needs and interests. However, this situation is changing. With increased competition from regional cable channels such as Sun-TV, Eenadu-TV, Udaya-TV, Raj-TV, and Asianet, Doordarshan has launched several regional-language channels. Even Zee-TV, which was launched in 1992 as a private Hindi channel, has expanded into regional-language broadcasts (for instance, Marathi and Bengali).

5. Urban–Rural Divide   With increased commercialization, programming decisions are heavily influenced to serve urban, elite

Table 2.3

Delays in granting broadcast autonomy in India

Year	Event
1966	The Chanda Committee recommends autonomy for All India Radio and Doordarshan.
1977	The Janata Party comes to power in the post-Emergency period, when press freedom in India was severely curtailed and the broadcast media serves primarily as propaganda tools for the Indira Gandhi government.
1978	The Verghese Committee, instituted by the Janata Party, recommends the establishment of a National Broadcasting Trust, an autonomous body for Indian broadcasting.
1979–80	The Janata Party loses power. Indira Gandhi's Congress government returns to power and shelves the Verghese Committee Report. Under the Congress government the broadcasting infrastructure in India expands rapidly in the 1980s.
1989	After the Congress Party loses power in 1989, the National Front government introduces the Prasar Bharati Bill in Parliament to grant autonomy to All India Radio and Doordarshan.
1990	After much political wrangling, a highly modified version of the Prasar Bharati Bill is passed by the Indian Parliament (it will be another eight years before this Act is implemented, when—given the onslaught of private cable, satellite, and services—the issue of autonomy has become passé).
1991–92	In the aftermath of the Gulf War, private cable and satellite channels flourish in India, competing for audiences with Doordarshan. STAR-TV, followed by Zee-TV, begins broadcasting in India from foreign sites. The Congress government, back in power, asks that the Prasar Bharati Act be reviewed in light of the new developments in cross-border satellite broadcasting. The Varadan Committee is established and makes additional recommendations. No action is taken.
1993–94	The Deodhar Committee is established to make recommendations about how to appropriate broadcast airtime in the context of competing channels, but is aborted by the government. In 1994, the Cable Regulation Act is promulgated by the Indian government, which "officially" recognizes the existence of several thousand Indian cable operators (some 10 years after cable operations began in India).
1995	The Supreme Court of India delivers its landmark judgement that the airwaves belong to the people, and recommends the establishment of an autonomous corporation to oversee the carrying out of this mandate. Meanwhile, the newly installed United Front government establishes the Paswan Committee to frame a comprehensive

Table 2.3 continued

Table 2.3 continued

Year	Event
	National Media Policy, going beyond issues of autonomy to include issues of programming, cross-media ownership, advertising, and others.
1996	The Sengupta Committee is established to revise the Prasar Bharati Act of 1990 and to suggest amendments.
1997–98	A new, comprehensive Broadcasting Bill is introduced in Parliament to address regulatory, administrative, and autonomy issues related to public broadcasting service (the Prasar Bharati Corporation), market-driven broadcasting services (including cable, satellite, and other private operations), and community service broadcasting services. The Pawar Committee is established to suggest amendments to this Bill. Meanwhile, the Prasar Bharati Act of 1990 is modified further and the Prasar Bharati Corporation, granting autonomy from the Ministry of Information and Broadcasting to both All India Radio and Doordarshan, is established. A Prasar Bharati Board is constituted.
1999–2000	The functioning of All India Radio and Doordarshan continues as before even though the two organizations now constitute an autonomous Prasar Bharati Corporation. The Prasar Bharati Board witnesses turnover of three CEOs in two years. The policy and legislative vacuum in Indian broadcasting continues.

Source: Singhal and Rogers (1989); Kumar (1998); http://www.ddindia/net/.

audiences (Pendakur, 1991). Middle-class and upper-middle-class city-dwellers constitute a majority of television viewers, and represent the individuals of greatest interest to advertisers (S. Rao, 1999). This audience wants entertainment programs rather than educational shows. Rural, poor viewers usually lose out, widening the existing information divide.[14]

❏ Jhabua Development Communication Project[15]

An innovative broadcasting experiment is presently under way in the rural, hilly hinterlands of Jhabua district in India's Madhya Pradesh state (Space Application Center, 1996). Some 85 percent of Jhabua's population is tribal, and its literacy rate is 15 percent. While the district is rich in natural resources, Jhabua's people are India's poorest. Agriculture is primitive, infant mortality rates are high, and transportation and communication facilities are poor.

The Jhabua Development Communication Project (JDCP) was launched in the mid-1990s by the Development and Educational Communication Unit (DECU) of the Space Application Center (SAC) in Ahmedabad (DECU implemented the Kheda Communication Project discussed previously). The purpose of JDCP is to experiment with the utilization of an interactive satellite-based broadcasting network to support development and education in remote, rural areas of India. Some 150 direct-reception systems (a satellite dish, TV sets, VCRs, and other equipment) have been installed in several villages of Jhabua, which receive television broadcasts for two hours every evening from DECU's Ahmedabad studio, uplinked through satellite. In addition, 12 talkback terminals have been installed in each of the block headquarters of Jhabua district, through which village functionaries ask questions, provide feedback, and report on progress.

The evening television broadcasts, on topics such as health, education, watershed management, agriculture, natural forestry, and local governance, are designed to be entertaining and educational. The programs are made with the active participation of the local people of Jhabua (as was the case in the Kheda Communication Project). In the afternoons, interactive training programs are conducted (through the talkback terminals) with a variety of village functionaries like teachers, anganwadi workers, handpump mechanics, and local panchayat members. Information flows in JDCP are thus both downward and upward, connecting the rural audience of Jhabua with media producers in Ahmedabad in an ongoing loop of feedback and feedforward.

To facilitate sustainability of the project, JDCP was implemented by DECU in cooperation with state government departments, local NGOs, and officials of the Jhabua district administration. A mid-term evaluation of the Jhabua Project conducted in 1988 showed that the poor people of Jhabua district had made significant knowledge gains in several lifeskills areas, enhancing the quality of their life and of the environment surrounding them (Kasturirangan, 1999).

Can the Jhabua Project experience be scaled up to address the development and communication needs of other rural hinterlands in India? Or, like the radio farm forums, SITE, and KCP, will it represent another missed opportunity? Only time will tell.

■ Contentious Policy Issues

Some of the contentious policy issues concerning public television in India are:

1. To what extent does Indian television serve educational/development goals?

    In the early decades of government television in India, consistent with the socialist policies of the Nehruvian era, Doordarshan broadcast many educational and development-related programs, although of mixed quality. But in the early 1990s, in the wake of liberalization and globalization, when private television networks arose and competition sharpened, Doordarshan became more and more like the private commercial networks in order to compete for mass audiences and for advertising revenues.

2. Does the commercialization of Indian television propagate consumerism and other Western cultural values?

    The major increase in the size of the television audience in India since the mid-1980s has triggered the commercialization of Doordarshan. *Commercialization* of the mass media is the production and transmission of media products intended to attract large audiences and thus to generate large profits from advertising sales. The commercialization of television in India escalated during the 1990s with the rise of the 40 private television networks (Chapter 3). Much of the privatization and commercialization has been accompanied by imported Western programs, or Indian versions of such programs, inevitably with the values of consumerism and capitalism represented therein. The proliferation of consumer brands and the rise of conspicuous consumption in Indian cities and villages reflect this trend (Johnson, 2000).

3. Does Indian television encourage unity in diversity?

    A national television system in a culturally diverse country can promote a national identity for its people. One important function of Doordarshan until the early 1990s was to encourage national identity. But the rise of private television networks during the 1990s forced Doordarshan to launch a metro channel and 15 regional channels; a number of the private networks were also regional (broadcasting in Telugu, Tamil, Bengali, and Punjabi, for example). So a greater linguistic and cultural plurality is evident in Indian mass media programming. Nevertheless, the nationwide television signal of Doordarshan has continued to attract a large audience, indeed the largest audience of any single television network in India (consisting of about two-thirds of all television viewers).

To perceptually counter the Westernization of television in India in the 1990s, many private, foreign-owned networks have consciously adopted a "nationalistic" stance in order to boost their audience appeal. For instance, MTV India uses the colors of the national flag for its on-screen MTV logo. The number of patriotic advertisements broadcast on Indian television networks has increased in recent years, especially during the celebration of 50 years of India's independence in 1997. Projections of national pride increased in intensity, especially on the private networks.[16]

Conclusions

A phenomenal expansion of radio and television audiences has occurred in India in the past few decades. These millions and millions of new radio and television viewers offer a tremendous potential for development communication and social change. However, the scorecard of Indian public broadcasting in promoting literacy, limiting family size, preventing HIV infection, or improving nutrition and health is dismal (notable exceptions include the radio farm forums, entertainment–education radio and television serials, and the Kheda Communication Project, among others). Public broadcasting failed to realize its full potential in India because no clear-cut, long-term broadcast policy existed, and because political interference, apathy, and missed opportunities were characteristic of both AIR's and Doordarshan's expansion.

Indian television, during its first 30 years, attempted mainly to perform a public service function, to serve as the mouthpiece of the government in power, and to encourage national integration. Until the 1970s, and even during the early 1980s, Doordarshan was not very commercialized. However, beginning in the mid-1980s with the broadcast of an extremely popular entertainment–education soap opera (*Hum Log*), Doordarshan earned advertising sales that demonstrated the profit-making potential of television. As program choices multiplied and television productions became slicker, viewers' appetites were whetted and Doordarshan was forced to change. During the 1990s, with the rise of private television broadcasting in India, Doordarshan became more and more a commercial television system.

Notes

1. This chapter draws upon Singhal and Rogers (1989, 1999), and Singhal, Doshi, et al. (1988). For more information on public broadcasting in India visit the All India Radio Web-site at http://air.kode.net/, or the Doordarshan Web-site at http://www.ddindia/net/.
2. Doordarshan has 27,000 employees, compared to BBC's 20,000 and NHK's 12,000.
3. In addition, five princely states of India had private radio stations.
4. These numbers are based on the National Readership Survey (NRS) 1999; the figures were provided to us by the Center for Media Studies, New Delhi.
5. The transcreation process for *Tinka Tinka Sukh* in the four South Indian states, as well as the design of the original Hindi broadcast, was carried out by All India Radio with technical cooperation from Population Communications International, a New York–based non-governmental organization.
6. This case draws upon Singhal and Rogers (1999), and Papa, Singhal, et al. (2000).
7. Our research team spent an average of 20 person-days per year in Lutsaan.
8. This channel mostly carried educational content, particularly during the daytime hours. This type of programming created an entertainment vacuum that cable operators could fill with their pirated video fare.
9. Entertainment and commercial lobbies were, in part, influential in limiting the national replication of the Kheda Communication Project. The costs associated in maintaining KCP were high and expenditures involved in scaling up were prohibitive. What if communities all across India starting demanding such community-based television initiatives?

10. This section is informed in part by our personal conversation with Dr N. Bhaskara Rao, Chairman, Center for Media Studies, New Delhi, on 12 August 1999.

11. While a non-lapseable revolving fund was created so that Door-darshan could plow back its advertising dollars to produce high-quality programs for public service, it was rarely used. Under the NEP, the Ministry of Information and Broadcasting cut budgetary grants, forcing Doordarshan to "earn" its advertising revenue. Door-darshan's purpose shifted from serving "society" and "citizens" to serving "markets" and "consumers."

12. Lack of a broadcast policy, coupled with delays and apathy in formu-lating and implementing broadcast policies, denied India the op-portunity to be a global media force. With supportive government policies and the resources of a vibrant film industry, India had the prerequisites for being a major regional/global media player (much like the Indian computer software industry).

13. On paper, from the structural control of the Ministry of Information and Broadcasting.

14. While the urban bias of public television is understandably problem-atic, Doordarshan's programs, relative to previous decades, increas-ingly reach rural, poor, and female audiences.

15. This section draws upon Space Application Center (1996).

16. For instance, in the highly rated Zee-TV music program *Sa Re Ga Ma*, nationalistic pride is often displayed in the commentary provided by the popular host, Sonu Nigam, and in the songs that are sung by the participants, judges, and invited guests.

3 The private television revolution[1]

"MTV has built a strong connection with the Indian youth—we are the *dhadkan* (heartbeat) of the youth."

> SUNIL LULLA, Vice-President and General Manager, MTV India (quoted in http://www.ipan.com/press/99jan/2801mt.htm).

"These poor kids will never know Indian culture. See what trash we now get on cable television."

> A school teacher in Sonepat, Haryana (in a personal interview, 3 December 1998).

"Five years ago, no one thought of the Internet through television, or cable carrying Internet or telephone. Now satellites are joining in, telecom wants the data game, and data wants telecom. This is convergence."

> VIJAY BHATKAR, Chairman of Dishnet, an Internet service provider building a nationwide Internet and cable network (quoted in Halarnkar and Ramani, 1999, p. 37).

I n the 1990s, the nature of Indian television changed in a very important and dramatic way. Indian television suddenly became much more entertainment-driven, like the Hollywood-produced television fare in America. Western programs and Indian-produced programs that conveyed consumerist and material values predominated on the new private television channels. The new television atmosphere was made possible by satellite and cable technology. A host of private television networks like STAR-TV, Zee-TV, SONY, and MTV began broadcasting in India. Even the relatively staid Doordarshan was forced to change its programming in order to retain its dominant market share and its advertising revenues (Chapter 2). But the private networks dominated among the urban elite audiences in India, the market particularly desired by advertisers because it yields more advertising income per rating point. Urban elites have the expendable income with which to purchase the products and services advertised on television; these people possess the ideal "demographics" that are desired by television advertisers.

How did this fundamental change in Indian television come about? Why did it happen during the 1990s? What role can cable and satellite television technology play in the convergence of the Internet, telecommunications, and entertainment industries?

The Birth of Private Television

In 1990, the only television broadcaster in India, by law, was the public broadcasting system, Doordarshan. No other television system was permitted to broadcast from Indian soil. But this situation was totally changed by a faraway event, the Gulf War, which began with Iraq's invasion of neighboring Kuwait in 1990 (Lahiri, 1998). Many Indian families had relatives working in the Gulf states, and they were desperate for news from the region. In January 1991, warfare began between Iraq and America and other allied military forces. In cities across India, people huddled around television sets in the lobbies of the Taj Group and other five-star hotels (like the Oberoi) that subscribed to CNN and various international television news networks (S.C. Bhatt, 1994).

Thus was born the idea of satellite television networks broad-casting into India, with programming uplinked to satellite transponders from Hong Kong, Singapore, Moscow, or other sites outside of India. Until late 1998, each private network in India sent videos by courier to one of these sites, and its programming was then uplinked for satellite transmission to India.[2] Thus it circumvented the Indian government's prohibition of broadcasting from Indian soil. Today, private networks in India can uplink their programs from Indian soil.

The first private network to capitalize on the opportunity provided by direct broadcast satellite (DBS) was STAR-TV, headquartered in Hong Kong. "STAR" stands for Satellite Television for the Asian Region. The network, originally owned by the Hutch Vision Group of Hong Kong, was founded in 1991, and then acquired for $871 million by Rupert Murdoch's gigantic News Corporation in 1995. STAR-TV targets urban elites in Hong Kong, Taiwan, South Korea, Indonesia, India, and 50 other nations from Japan to the Middle East (Bansal and Carvalho, 1998). India soon became STAR-TV's priority audience, and STAR began broadcasting in Hindi as well as in English.

STAR-TV shocked many Indian middle-class parents by broad-casting sexually explicit music videos, first on MTV, and then on its Channel V launched in 1994.[3] While STAR-TV was the catalyst for direct satellite broadcasting into India, its example was rapidly followed by Indian-owned private networks like Zee-TV, and by foreign-owned broadcasters like SONY. By the late 1990s, more than 40 private television channels were available to Indian audiences. It was estimated that by 2000 India would have the world's largest cable and satellite markets with cable connectivity to 35 million homes, comprising some 150 million cable viewers (Mohan, 1997).

■ The Cable Television Wars

The private television revolution in India in the 1990s could not have occurred without an important development on the ground, coupled with direct broadcast satellites (DBS). An entirely new industry of cable television operators arose in India. This

groundswell began when many small-time entrepreneurs established cable television operations, typically by renting movies and
television serials from video stores. The entrepreneur usually set
up a small control room in the basement of an apartment block,
wired to each apartment in the building. Each household paid a
small monthly fee. Under the outdated Indian Telegraph Act of
1885, it was illegal to form such video distribution systems, but the
government looked the other way. Much of the programming
consisted of Hindi films, pirated copies of prime-time American
television shows like *LA Law* or *Three's Company*, or Hollywood-
produced films. Occasionally the police, perhaps tipped off by a
competing cable operator, raided the control room of the cable
television system, confiscated the pirated videos, and fined the
operator. Sometimes the operator was jailed.

Once satellite channels began broadcasting in India, cable operators realized that they could install satellite-receiving dishes to
catch the signals of CNN and STAR-TV (Plate 3.1). The operators
typically charged their customers Rs 75 to 150 (two to four dollars
at the time) per month. Thus the cable television systems evolved
out of the already established cable systems for videos. The next
step was for the cable television systems to expand, often by string-
ing wires from rooftop to rooftop to rooftop. Local "wars" occurred between rival cable operators as their elaborate fiefdoms came
into conflict (Malhotra, 1999).

With the rise of additional private television broadcasters, these
networks began to compete for cable operators, as most Indian
television sets have only eight to 14 channels. The private television networks purchased partial ownership in cable systems, so as
to guarantee that their networks would be carried by a cable system. In some cases, a private television system purchased a number of cable television systems and consolidated them into one
larger network. An example is Siticable, a cable television network
owned by Zee-TV.

The cable television systems were operated in an everything-
goes manner, as they were completely unregulated by the Indian
government (Pathania, 1998). Unlike most other countries, cable
television proliferated in India as a completely "illegal" activity.
Expansion occurred in the 1990s at such a furious rate that the

Plate 3.1: Satellite dishes on top of an office building which houses ACN (Agra Cable Network), the largest cable operator in Agra

Satellite dishes connected to Indian homes through cable have spurred a revolution in private television networks in India. Some 35 million households watched cable television in 2000, comprising about 150 million viewers.

Source: Saumya Pant (used by permission).

THE PRIVATE TELEVISION REVOLUTION   111

government watched helplessly; no policies were established until 1995 (Figure 3.1). Cable wires were strung across houses, lamp-posts, and trees, and cable systems soon covered much of urban India, most market towns, and even many villages (S.C. Bhatt, 1994). During the 1990s, the national ruling political party in Delhi changed numerous times. This revolving-door style of gov-ernment, replete with political uncertainties, weakened national policy-making in India and further served to discourage the implementation of regulations governing the exploding cable TV industry. Finally, the Cable Television Regulation Act of 1994 was promulgated, requiring cable operators to register their "exist-ence" at local post offices, follow an advertising code,[4] carry at least two Doordarshan channels, and pay a 40 percent entertainment tax on their sales. Most cable operators minimized their tax bills by under-reporting the size of their customer-bases (Crabtree and Malhotra, 2000).

■ Star-TV

Rupert Murdoch's huge News Corporation stands behind STAR-TV in India, giving it certain advantages in competing with Zee-TV and other Indian-owned television networks. Murdoch has very deep pockets. So where financial resources are involved, STAR-TV has a big advantage. Another benefit STAR-TV enjoys in the vicious competition within the private television industry in India for imported programs is its access to programs like *X-Files*, *Baywatch*, and *Ally McBeal*, which News Corporation produces for its Fox Network in America. Executives at STAR-TV have a free hand in developing indigenous programs in India, but even in this case the parent media company provides production tech-niques, consulting, and finances.

By late 1999, STAR was broadcasting several channels in addi-tion to the five channels with which it started the STAR-TV net-work: (*a*) STAR Plus, which originally broadcast only in English; (*b*) STAR Sports; (*c*) Channel V, a music channel (originally, STAR-TV broadcast MTV on its platform); (*d*) BBC; and (*e*) STAR Man-darin (aimed at Chinese viewers). STAR soon added STAR Movies. In 1997, STAR provided news broadcasts focussed on the Indian

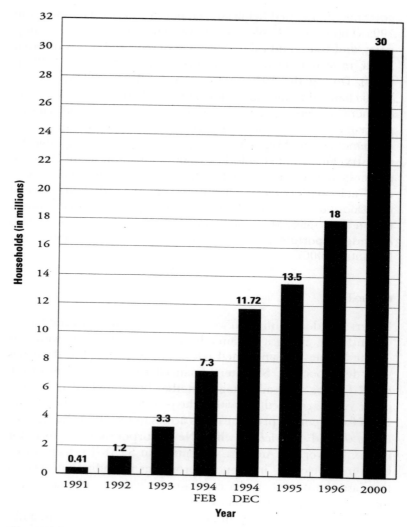

Figure 3.1: The rapid growth of cable television in India

A private television revolution occurred in India during the 1990s as over 40 private television broadcasters began operations. Typically, a private network like STAR-TV, Zee-TV, or SONY produced its programs in India, couriered them to Hong Kong or some other place for uplinking to a satellite, and then beamed them to cable television operators who distributed them locally.

Source: Cable Quest (1998).

region. In 1998, STAR World was launched; it became the channel for English-language entertainment programs. STAR Plus greatly increased its Hindi-language programming, and in 1999 this channel was gaining audience loyalty. In 2000, STAR-TV's hit program *Kaun Banega Crorepati?* (*Who Will Become a Multimillionaire?*) attracted a record audience of 100 million cable viewers. Thus, STAR-TV has emerged as a very major force in Indian television.

■ Zee-TV

Zee-TV started in late 1992, and has enjoyed phenomenal success, surpassing STAR-TV and Doordarshan with certain audiences. It consistently dominates the 10 highest-rated television shows in India, in a manner somewhat akin to that of the Fox Television Network in the United States. Zee-TV excels at populist-type television programming.

In the late 1990s Zee-TV had advertising sales approximately equal to those of Doordarshan (Figure 3.2), even though the public broadcasting network attracted an audience that was four times larger (advertisers are willing to pay higher advertising rates to Zee-TV because it reaches an audience with greater spending power).

Through its wealthy owner, Subhash Chandra, Zee-TV has considerable political clout with the Indian government.

❑ **Subhash Chandra: India's Media Mogul[5]**

When a communication revolution, like the private television revolution, occurs in a nation, economic opportunities often present themselves, and immense fortunes can be made. Subhash Chandra, the wealthiest of India's media moguls, is a multibillionaire (Plate 3.2). His net worth was estimated in 2000 at $9.7 billion, ranking him second to Wipro's Azim Premji (see Chapter I) (*India Abroad*, 2000, p. 38). Chandra's Zee-TV has more than 200 million viewers worldwide (most are in India). In 2000, some 65 percent of all South Asian homes in the U.K. subscribed to Zee-TV. Zee-TV has a tremendous brand equity in India: in the past five years, over 100 million audience members

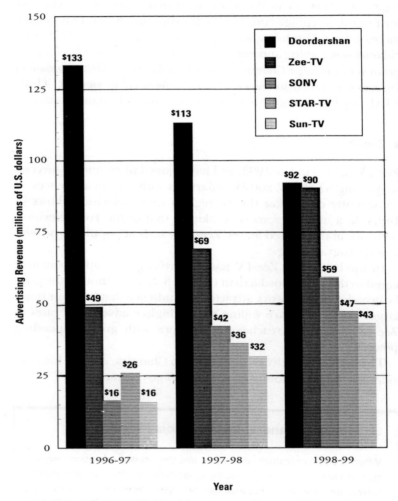

Figure 3.2: How cable and satellite channels are eating into Doordarshan's advertising revenues

During the 1990s, Doordarshan lost part of its dominance in television advertising revenues to such private television networks as Zee-TV, SONY, STAR-TV, and others. These private television networks, featuring imported American programs and Indian-produced American-style programs, attracted the urban elite audiences in India, which advertisers covet because of their consumer buying power.

Source: Nimbus Research/DD Handbook.

have written to Zee-TV in appreciation of its programming, or to participate in its various popular programs (such as *Sa Re Ga Ma*, a highly interactive television program that includes a music competition). In 1998–99, Zee-TV earned the highest advertising revenues of all satellite channels in India, almost equaling the advertising revenues of Doordarshan despite the latter's much larger viewership (see Figure 3.2).

Plate 3.2: Subhash Chandra, Chairman of Zee-TV

Chandra launched Zee-TV in 1992 when many Indians were eager to obtain news of the Gulf War. The huge audiences attracted by Zee-TV and by Chandra's related companies helped boost his net worth to billions of dollars.

Source: http://www.india-today.com/ctoday/19990916/buzz3.html#Subhash (used with permission).

However, Zee-TV is only one member in Chandra's family of companies, which includes Zee Cinema, a movie pay-channel; Zee Music, which markets cassettes; Zee Education (ZED), a computer training company; Zee Multinational Worldwide, a Mauritius-based company; Siticable, a cable television company; and Zee Telefilms, the flagship company that produces the television programming. Chandra has also teamed up with his main competitor in private television broadcasting, Rupert Murdoch who owns STAR-TV, as part of his News Corporation. Chandra and Murdoch own equal shares in Asia Today Ltd (ATL), a Hong Kong–based broadcasting company that provides television programming to broadcasting stations.

Chandra, who only completed high school, began his entrepreneurial career as a rice trader in Hissar. He became wealthy by exporting rice to the Soviet Union. In the 1970s, he entered the packaging business; his Essel Packaging Company was started by making laminated covers for the Food Corporation of India, to store surplus agricultural harvests. Chandra invested his profits in land, on which he built Esselworld, a 753-acre popular amusement park in Mumbai. The next logical step was Zee-TV. As Chandra says: "Some people do not want to travel three hours for entertainment" (Lahiri, 1998). The idea of Zee-TV took shape during the Gulf War, when Chandra was watching CNN in the office of Ashok Kurien, an advertising executive who was marketing Esselworld. Kurien recalls how Chandra asked him whether launching a private television channel like CNN was possible in India. Kurien replied that Chandra could make it happen, and that he would help him. Thus, Zee-TV was born.

In 2000, the Zee group of companies was positioning itself to tap the tremendous business opportunity offered by digital communication services in India. For instance, Chandra's Siticable Company, which he owns jointly with Rupert Murdoch, is gearing itself to transmit voice, video, and data for entertainment and e-commerce purposes. When that happens, Siticable, with six million subscribers in 2000, will become the biggest provider of cable Internet services in India. Chandra is also launching a $755 million satellite telephony venture called Agrani (Sanskrit for "staying ahead"), establishing a Zee Internet portal, and building 18 multiplex theater-cum-entertainment centers—called E-Citi—in six states in India at a cost of over $100 million (Ratnesar, 2000). Chandra's vision is to turn his broadcast software operations into a media, entertainment, and telecommunications conglomerate.

Fond of *beedis* (hand-rolled Indian cigarettes), Chandra is a low-key, media-shy individual, who understands the importance of building a high-quality media conglomerate. While some perceive his business style as being a traditional Marwari one, he was the first in the television industry to introduce employee stock options. The value of Zee's stock rose by a whopping 15,000 percent in seven years after the company went public in 1993, making it the fastest-rising Indian stock of all time. Chandra's Essel group of companies is headquartered in a nondescript, two-storied building in the Mumbai suburb of Worli, but he has a rooftop office in Mumbai's prestigious Oberoi Towers (Bansal and Carvalho, 1998). From here, Chandra rules the world of laminate packaging, supplying over 1,200 million laminated tubes annually to the likes of Colgate Palmolive and Hindustan Lever, and, on the side, beams programs to an audience of over 200 million people worldwide.

■ SONY

SONY (its full name is SONY Entertainment Television) is owned by the SONY Corporation of Japan. It began broadcasting in India in 1995, being one of the later entrants to the private television revolution. SONY rose rapidly to become the second most popular private channel, behind only Zee-TV, and bypassing STAR-TV.

By 2000, several private networks were in financial difficulty, and some private networks had gone bankrupt. With their focus on Hindi-language-based entertainment programming, Zee-TV and SONY continued to grow rapidly, with both networks generating a profit. Zee-TV and SONY programs are watched in over 75 percent of homes with cable television in Mumbai and Delhi (Figure 3.3). Other private networks are targeting their programs to reach specialized audiences. Examples are Eenadu-TV that targets Telugu speakers in South India, and SUN-TV that broadcasts mainly in Tamil.

■ MTV India[6]

A 24-hour music channel, MTV India is targeted to young Indians between the ages of 15 and 24. Beamed into India via PanAMSat 4,

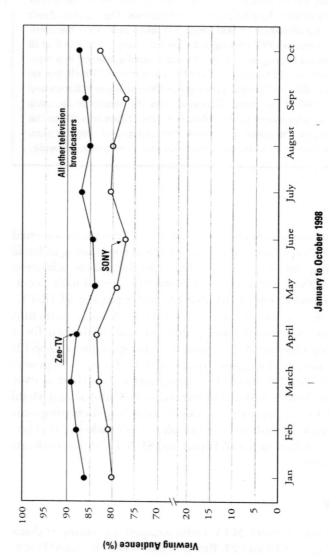

Figure 3.3: Viewership of Zee-TV and SONY in cable and satellite homes in Mumbai and Delhi

Two private television networks, Zee-TV and SONY, dominate the television ratings in Mumbai and Delhi. Here we see how private networks have taken the urban elite audience away from Doordarshan.

Source: Cable Waves (1998).

MTV India was viewed in 12 million Indian cable households in 2000.[7] MTV India is one of Music Television's (MTV) 14 international networks which have an audience of 350 million households, one quarter of all households worldwide. MTV, which began in the United States in 1981, is essentially an endless series of popular music videos aimed mainly at teenage viewers, and usually noted for its sexually explicit content.

MTV India represents a fascinating case of how a foreign, private channel transforms itself to create a hybrid identity that appears Indian, but embodies Western traits. MTV India's logo uses the tricolors of the Indian national flag, and its fare comprises 70 percent Indian film and popular music, and 30 percent foreign, Western music (Dey, 1999). MTV India employs 10 Indian video jockeys (VJs), and has used audience research to create 21 India-specific music shows including interviews with popular artists, coverage of music concerts, viewer contests, film countdown shows, and variety, request, and talk shows. Popular MTV programs in India include *MTV House Full*, *MTV Ek Do Teen*, *MTV India Hit List*, *MTV Select*, *MTV Hipshakers*, *MTV Filmi Fundas*, *Made in India*, *MTV Fresh*, *MTV Bollywood in Control*, *MTV Cricket in Control*, *MTV Chill Out*, and others.

South Asia is a big market for MTV, and its viewership levels in Asia are among the highest in the world. Over 125 companies with youth-oriented products such as Pepsi, Colgate, Levi's, Candico, Phillips, Perfetti, Archies, Coca Cola, Dabur, and Elle 18 advertise on MTV India, or sponsor its popular music shows. Further, MTV India strategically partners with various companies to build its brand. For instance, it partnered with Colgate for the Colgate Gel & MTV Fresh VJ Hunt, with Pepsi for the Pepsi Dance Connection in Association with MTV, and with Chiclets for the Chiclets & Club MTV Dance Blasts. At the Chiclets & Club MTV Dance Blast in Bangalore in 1999, over 8,000 young people partied for 16 hours. Further, in association with SONY Music, MTV India brought Western pop idols (like Diana King and Ricky Martin) to India. MTV India also promoted the Walk For Life and The Race Against AIDS campaigns in Mumbai and Delhi, attracting thousands of participants to these charity events. During election time in 1999, MTV India launched a Rock the Vote–style campaign, encouraging the Indian youth to vote (Dey, 1999).

In 1998, MTV India received the Most Outstanding Brand of the Year Award at the All India Advertising Awards ceremony. To capitalize on its brand equity among youth, MTV India, at the turn of the century, was launching pagers, a clothing and accessories line, and branded credit cards (Anjan Mitra, 1999). Prior experience in the Philippines and Singapore shows that such MTV-branded products constitute a hip fashion statement for the youth who adopt them.

What lies ahead for MTV India? At the turn of the century, MTV India was syndicating its programs for the expanding FM radio services in India, and also venturing into regional-language music television broadcasts in Tamil, Telugu, Kannada, Malayalam, and Bengali (Dey, 1999). Plans were under way for MTV India to expand its reach into neighboring countries such as Nepal, Bangladesh, and Sri Lanka, and to offer programs for the 20 million Indians in the global diaspora.[8]

MTV India is a much-loved *and* much-hated channel in India: it is widely popular among the urban Indian youth, but not among parents and elders who worry about the harmful effects of its fast, racy, and sexually suggestive content. MTV India symbolizes the struggles of Indian society, caught off guard by the forces of Westernization and Americanization.

■ Discovery Channel[9]

The Discovery Channel, headquartered in Bethesda, Maryland, began operations in India in 1995 and reached 10 million households four years later, which is approximately 25 percent of Discovery's reach in the U.S. market (Mohan, 1997). By 2002, Discovery expects its India operations to double to some 20 million households, comprising about 100 million cable viewers. Discovery's rapid penetration in India, even though it is a subscription channel (meaning that households must pay an extra fee each month above their basic subscription fee),[10] is attributed to its culturally neutral content. It has something for everyone as a provider of wholesome "edutainment."

While the Discovery Channel is watched in more than 100 million homes in 90 countries, its India operations are part of its corporate push to globalize. India seemed a natural venue for the education-oriented content of the Discovery Channel, given "the strong culture and social ethos that makes education such an important thing here," according to Kiran Karnik,[11] Managing Director of the Discovery Channel in India (quoted in Mohan, 1997, p. 30). The Discovery Channel carved out a unique educational niche among other entertainment-oriented channels like Zee-TV, STAR-TV, and SONY.

The Discovery Channel astutely focussed on expanding its viewership among children,[12] sponsoring various interschool quiz programs, and launching educator guides to help teachers use the channel as an educational resource. To widen its subscriber base, Discovery customized its programs in India by either dubbing them in Hindi or providing Hindi voiceovers.

The experience of the Discovery Channel in India demonstrates that a substantial number of viewers will consume educational content, provided that it is of high quality and in their own language.

Impacts of Private Television on Doordarshan

Despite the inroads made by the private television broadcasters, Doordarshan still has 500 million viewers, compared to 150 million for the private broadcasters. The private television networks, however, skim off the urban elite audience that is most desired by advertisers, leaving Doordarshan with an audience of villagers, small town people, and a share of the urbanites (about 70 percent of India's total population lives in villages).

The threat from the private television networks forced Doordarshan to make several important changes. During the 1990s, Doordarshan launched Doordarshan Metro (DD-2) aimed at urban audiences, 15 regional channels, a sports channel, a 24-hour news channel, and an international channel, Doordarshan-International. Doordarshan also began broadcasting 2.5 hours of Music Television on DD-1, along with such other American imports as *Dynasty* and *Dallas*. Doordarshan agreed with CNN to exchange programs and to purchase staff training and technical assistance (this latter agreement was terminated due to political opposition).

In general, competition from private networks forced Door-darshan to edge away from its role as a public broadcaster devoted to the rhetoric of education and development, and to become primarily a commercial broadcaster (Pathania, 1998). During the 1990s, Doordarshan placed decreasing emphasis on acting as a catalyst for social change, promoting national integration, enhancing maternal and child health, and boosting literacy. Instead, it became increasingly concerned with maintaining the steady flow of advertising dollars into its coffers, and underwent a facelift (slicker graphics and glamorous productions) to withstand the competition from private networks.

In addition to these impacts of the privatization of television on Doordarshan, the film industry was hard hit. For example, attendance at movie theaters dropped precipitously in the early 1990s as cable television spread in metropolitan areas. A similar displacement of film attendance by commercial television occurred in the United States during the 1950s, the decade when most American households purchased television sets. However, the Indian film industry in the late 1990s adopted a new style, including the use of exotic locales and mega dance sequences that require viewing on the big screen. Moviegoers are thus increasingly returning to the theaters.

Impacts of Private Television on Indian Audiences

The private television networks in India encourage commercialization and consumerism through the advertisements they carry, and through the products that actors and actresses in entertainment programs, especially imported Western programs, wear and consume. The privatization of Indian television in the decade of the 1990s acted to Westernize Indian society in several important ways, an inevitable consequence of living in a global village.

■ Consumerism

Consumerism is the orientation of individuals toward purchasing products and services. The growth of the private television networks benefitted from, and contributed to, India's new economic policy (NEP) launched in 1991. This policy of openness to American and other foreign companies was initiated by the then Finance Minister Dr Manmohan Singh in the face of a severe foreign exchange crisis. Nike, Puma, Kentucky Fried Chicken, McDonalds, AT&T, and other foreign companies sold their products and services in India and advertised on Indian television channels and in other media.

At about the same time, urban professionals began to command higher salaries. These concurrent changes meant that an Indian consumer might view a television advertisement for a pair of expensive Nike shoes, see a pair of these shoes in a neighborhood store window, and have the disposable income to purchase them (Malhotra, 1999). Here we see how the rise of private cable and satellite networks, the New Economic Policy, and the consequential availability of foreign products and services, all acted in concert to encourage consumerism on the part of the Indian people.

■ Conservative Nationalism

Just as 200 years of British rule in India aided the initial development of Indian nationalism leading to independence, imported Western television programs such as *Baywatch* and *Lifestyles of the Rich and Famous* and American icons such as McDonalds and Coca Cola during the 1990s posed the threat of cultural loss to many Indians. This threat of Westernization, coupled with other political and social complexities, may have indirectly encouraged the acceptance of conservative political movements like that of the Bharatiya Janata Party (BJP) in India (Malhotra, 1999). The rapid Westernization of Iran in the 1970s by the Shah led to the religious/political conservatism expressed in the Iranian Revolution of 1979, and to consequent changes in women's dress, attitudes toward the United States and other Western nations, and other aspects of society. The rise of political and religious conservatism has also been observed in several other nations, like Afghanistan under the rule of the Taliban. India's brand of conservative nationalism is, however, quite different from that of Iran or Afghanistan.

■ Changing Female Images

One of the most notable changes in Indian society, to which private television has contributed, is with respect to the images of women. A content analysis of the 10 most highly rated television programs on the private networks in 1997 by Malhotra (1999) showed that women appeared in approximately equal numbers as men. This 50:50 ratio contrasts with American prime-time television programs in which men appear about twice as often as women.

How were women portrayed on Indian television? Krishnan and Dighe (1990) found that the television image of woman depicted on Doordarshan was one of a home-bound individual who derived her meaning in life through her husband and children. Women were shown mainly in passive, subordinate roles, defined only in relation to men. Public television could have been a powerful force for bringing reality more closely into line with the legal rights of women.[13]

Private television programs in the 1990s began to depict a more plural, career-conscious and independent female image (Malhotra, 1999; Mankekar, 1999). Women were portrayed as lawyers in *LA Law* and *Street Legal*, as policewomen in *Picket Fences*, and as working women in *Grace Under Fire*. These female television characters are assertive and independent, and work outside of the home. At the same time that these Western images began to be broadcast in India, many opportunities for women to work outside the home were being provided by the Indian economy. Not only did women on television work, they might also be the boss as in *Tara*, one of the highest-rated Zee-TV shows which revolves around a strong-willed woman executive (somewhat like the strong female character portrayed by actress Joan Collins on *Dynasty*) (Malhotra and Rogers, 2000).

Television images of women shown on private networks are more openly sexual. The ideal depiction of women shifted from motherhood to womanhood. The physical image of women, especially on MTV and Channel V, changed from a voluptuous body to a more Western image of Twiggy-like thinness. This image did not match the reality of women's bodies in India (Malhotra and

Rogers, 2000). Anorexia and bulimia began to be reported in India, especially among the urban affluent class, and a sharp increase occurred in plastic surgery for enlarged or smaller breasts, fat removal, and nose operations (Chopra and Baria, 1999).

How did the Indian government react to these social changes brought about by private television in India during the 1990s? While debates on regulating private broadcasting raged in the Indian Parliament, there was no mechanism to legislate public consumption patterns. Audiences welcomed the diversity of media channels and the ever-expanding program choices. The central government was rather weak during this period, with numerous changes of ruling party. Given this political uncertainty, India's leaders chose to ignore the rising influence of private television. Further, the owners of the private networks and their advertisers represented considerable economic and political power in India, and thus acted as an opposing influence on any kind of regulation.

When the cable television industry began to proliferate in India in the 1990s, primarily as a programming alternative to Doordarshan, few could imagine that it would hold the key to India's informatization progress in the new millennium.

Cable Television: The Backbone of Digital Convergence

The rapid spread of cable television in India, covering over 35 million homes in 2000 and expected to reach 60 million homes by 2010, has positioned India as it has enabled no other developing country to capitalize on the revolution in digital communication services. The convergence of computers, mass media, and telecommunications now makes it possible for the local *cablewallah*, if the Indian government will allow, to offer Internet, telephony, videoconferencing, home-shopping and other interactive media services through a family's home television set. Ordinary telephone lines are incapable of handling the huge amounts of digital traffic that these new services generate; the favored route in India is cable wire, which can carry voice, video, and data at speeds up to 500 times faster than the normal telephone line (Halarnkar and Ramani, 1999).

Heavy investments are being made in India to capitalize on the existing cable infrastructure and to build digital pipelines to make possible the delivery of video, audio, and data to an ever-widening base of potential subscribers. The Zee Network plans to invest over $500 million between 1999 and 2004 to capitalize on this digital convergence, in order to become a media-entertainment-communication giant. Internet service provider Dishnet, run by the former head of the Center for Development of Advanced Computing, Vijay Bhatkar, is investing over $100 million in building a nationwide Internet and cable network. Even the government-run VSNL has signed a $300 million deal with the Power Grid Corporation of India to use its 45,000 kilometer length of high-tension transmission lines to build a nationwide fiber optic network of high-capacity digital pipes (Halarnkar and Ramani, 1999).

In Bangalore, 20,000 homes are already connected to the Cable TV–based Home and Office Interactive Services (CHOIS), an experimental service begun by technology-savvy entrepreneur Mohan Tambe of Innomedia Technologies, which allows a home TV set to become an intelligent, interactive machine through a set-top box. Services offered on CHOIS include shopping, pay-per-view, video-on-request, rail and bus bookings, Internet services, email, voice-mail, and others (Shekar, 1999). Tambe, a graduate of IIT Kanpur, holds several patents and works relentlessly with 50 young engineers in Innomedia's Bangalore offices to develop a range of interactive media technologies suitable for Indian consumers. Tambe's underlying mantra for CHOIS, as the service is being commercially launched through cable operators across India, is "infotainment," that is, provide viewers a wholesome and healthy dose of entertainment and offer educational opportunities, public services, and information services to improve the quality of life of audience individuals (Tiwari, 1999).

What does this digital convergence of cable, telecommunications, computers, and the Internet mean for India's informatization? Consider the following. In 2000, only 1 percent of Indian households owned a personal computer; more than 20 percent had cable connections (see Figure 1.1). Furthermore, for every household adopting a personal computer, some 25 households adopt cable television (that is, the number of households acquiring cable television is increasing 25 times faster than the number of households acquiring personal computers). By providing digital Internet connectivity to tens of millions of Indian households with access to cable television through a home-based TV set, India can leapfrog over the traditional, less efficient mode of Internet connectivity through telephone lines and personal computers.

Through serendipity, cable television in India has become the giant lever capable of propelling the nation along its informatization path. Favorable government policies, and new accompanying "mindsets" among media operators and audiences, can help India rapidly expand its digital communication infrastructure.

Conclusions

If we had predicted in our earlier book about India's information revolution written over a decade ago (Singhal and Rogers, 1989) that the following decade would see the rise of private television in India, we would have been regarded as crazy. But this has indeed occurred. How did the process of commercialization of television begin?

McDowell (1997) identified the beginnings of private television in India as occurring in 1984 with *Hum Log* and the attendant commercialization of Doordarshan. At that point, India's Ministry of Information and Broadcasting had developed the satellite technology of broadcasting from about 200 ground stations, without a corresponding concentration on software (that is, television programming). Thus, Doordarshan was forced to involve private television producers of programs that would attract large audiences. The episodes of *Hum Log* were produced by a private company at hired studios in Gurgaon and then sold to Doordarshan for broadcast. Such private program production in the 1980s was a precursor to the establishment of private television networks in the 1990s.

A theme of this chapter has been the struggle of the private networks and Doordarshan for audience ratings, and competition for the choice audience demographics of urban, well-educated viewers who have the disposable income to purchase advertised products. The disparity between the average income of the mass of poor villagers and that of urban educated elites is especially pronounced in India. The financial attractiveness of the urban audience encouraged television broadcasters to air imported Western programs, and also Indian television programs that explicitly promoted consumerism and new, svelte female images. Overall, within the bounds of the patriarchal tradition, a new, more assertive, independent, and modern image of women began to appear on Indian private television channels.

Private television broadcasting in India during the 1990s provided a kind of natural laboratory for understanding the nature of social change as a nation pursues a strategy of informatization. Furthermore, India's cable television industry, with its reach of 35 million households, is ideally placed to capitalize on the market for digital communication services. If government policies are favorable, the cable wire, because of its higher bandwidth and speed, is likely to emerge as the conduit for the proliferation of voice, video, and data traffic in India, further speeding up India's informatization.

Notes

1. The authors express their special gratitude to Dr Sheena Malhotra, whose 1999 Ph.D. dissertation provided many of the important ideas cited in this chapter.
2. However, news programs of private networks were allowed to uplink via the government's VSNL facility in India.
3. When STAR-TV was launched, it carried MTV. When the contract term expired, MTV did not renew its agreement with STAR-TV. So, in 1994, STAR-TV created Channel V, modeled after MTV. Eventually, MTV was relaunched in 1996 as its own network in India.
4. The cable TV operators had little control over the ads that were broadcast, once again demonstrating the out-of-touch nature of government policy-making.
5. This case draws upon Lahiri (1998) and Bansal and Carvalho (1998).
6. This section draws upon press clippings on MTV India, accessible at the following Web-site: http://www.ipan.com/press/99jan/2801mt.htm.
7. First beamed into India in 1992 as part of STAR-TV (see note 3), MTV later became an independent channel in 1996.
8. The satellite-beamed Asia TV, targeted to the South Asian diaspora in the U.S., often carries MTV India broadcasts.

9. This section draws upon Arvind Singhal's personal conversation with Mr Kiran Karnik, Managing Director of Discovery Channel in India, on 11 August 1999.

10. Often, a *cablewallah* works this fee into his total customer fees so that a household does not fully realize that it is paying an extra fee for Discovery.

11. Karnik is a noted development communication practitioner who previously headed the Development and Educational Communication Unit (DECU) at the Space Application Center, which managed the Kheda Communication Project in Gujarat (see Chapter 2).

12. While children's programming exists on Indian channels through the Cartoon Network, Nickelodeon, and STAR-Children, there is very little locally produced programming.

13. The Indian constitution guaranteed complete equality to women. The reality, however, is quite different. Although child marriage is illegal (the legal age at marriage in India is 18 for women), it is widespread. The payment of dowry by a bride's family (also illegal under Indian law) is common. While Indian women won the legal right to abortion in 1971, the reality is that many women have little control over their reproductive lives, which are dictated by their husbands and family elders (Bumiller, 1990).

4 Rising Technopolises

"Silicon Valley is a land of opportunities and is the place where legends are created every day. I wanted to start a company of my own and pursue some of my dreams."

> SABEER BHATIA, co-founder of Hotmail (quoted in Sreenivas, 1998, p. 1).

"I tell people that once you get this nuclear reactor going—of entrepreneurs producing energy and wealth—so much surplus energy is produced that it uplifts everybody including the guys who were in it for social service."

> KANWAL REKHI, President of The Indus Entrepreneurs and a highly successful Indian venture capitalist in Silicon Valley (quoted in http://www.tie.org/0999timescomputing.htm).

"My vision of Andhra Pradesh is a State where poverty is totally eradicated, where every man, woman, and child has access to not just basic minimum needs, but to all the opportunities for leading a happy and fulfilling life; a knowledge and learning society built on values of hardwork, honesty, discipline, and a collective sense of purpose."

> CHANDRABABU NAIDU, Chief Minister of Andhra Pradesh and a champion of India's informatization strategy (quoted in the Andra Pradesh Web-site http://www.andhra-pradesh.com/cm/avisiona.html).

A s mentioned previously, a *technopolis* is a geographically con-centrated high-technology complex characterized by a large number of entrepreneurial spin-off companies. A technopolis is not only a center of technological innovation, it also acts like a mint for producing great wealth. By 1980, Silicon Valley, the most famous technopolis in the world, had created over 15,000 million-aires in its first 20 years of growth. In 1999, Silicon Valley was cre-ating 63 millionaires a *day*, some 23,000 per year (Nieves, 2000). Many of these new millionaires were Indians. A technopolis is somewhat like a gigantic money machine. One can easily under-stand why many nations desperately want to grow a technopolis. India is one such nation, and Bangalore and Hyderabad are its main technopolises.[1]

Not only are technopolises emerging in India, but Indian tech-nologists and entrepreneurs are playing a major role in techno-polises like Silicon Valley, Route 128 (near Boston), and Austin, Texas. During the 1990s a cadre of young Indians became sud-denly rich by converting brainpower and hard work into high-tech companies that rested on cutting-edge technologies in com-puters, software, or Internet-related businesses. Is there something about Indian culture that fits naturally with high-tech entrepre-neurship?

The Technologies underlying Technopolises

The communication revolution occurring throughout the world today is the result of advances in microelectronics technologies which are then applied to bring about social changes. Microelec-tronics is a sub-industry of electronics centered on semiconductor chips and their uses in computers, telecommunications, and many other types of electronic equipment. A semiconductor is a solid-state device which controls the flow of electricity so as to boost, or amplify, an electrical signal. Semiconductors act like miniature valves in the flow of small electrical currents. A computer is essen-tially composed of millions of such on–off switches. As a result of semiconductors, computers over the past 55 years have shrunk in size and cost, and become enormously more powerful.

One illustration of this trend is the shrinking of computers from mainframe computers that filled a room, to laptop computers that fit in a briefcase, to palmtop computers that fit in a purse. While the mainframe computer typically cost several million dollars, today's laptop can be purchased for a few thousand dollars. And it may be more powerful than the world's first mainframe computer built in 1945.

What is distinctive about microelectronics technologies is that they are continuously changing, an advance brought about by skilled, highly intelligent individuals who have been well trained at research universities. They engage in R&D to develop new applications for cutting-edge information technologies which create the opportunities for start-up companies. These new companies commercialize technological innovations, new products, and services by selling them in the marketplace. The result can be a sudden financial bonanza, and the entrepreneurs who launched the new companies at great risk are, a few years later, multimillionaires (and in a few cases billionaires). We tell the story of several such Indian entrepreneurs here: Lata Krishnan, Vinod Khosla, Sabeer Bhatia, and others.

Of course, only a small proportion of all high-tech start-up companies succeed. Despite the backbreaking work of their highly intelligent founders, most start-ups are *not* successful. Perhaps many go bankrupt because technical benchmarks cannot be met. The new company might be wiped out by the predatory tactics of its parent company or a competitor, or it might be acquired by a larger competitor. Many high-tech start-ups continue for several years but do not grow past a handful of employees. These too are considered failures in a technopolis. Only about one in 10 high-tech start-ups becomes highly profitable within five years of being launched. So there is no certainty of success in the high-technology industry. It is a high-stake gamble.

What is High-Technology?

A *high-technology industry* is an industry at the cutting edge of technology whose core technology changes rapidly. Microelectronics and biotechnology are two leading high-tech industries. A high-tech industry is typically characterized by (a) a high proportion of scientists and engineers in total employment, often about 1:10; and (b) up to 10 percent of sales being spent for R&D (compared to only 2 or 3 percent for non-high-technology industries). The basis of competition in a high-technology industry is continuous technological innovation. For a high-tech company to stay ahead of its rivals, it must keep coming up with new products. Intel, the famed Silicon Valley microprocessor company, is noted for its ability to succeed through continuous innovation. Most high-tech industries operate in a global, highly competitive market, in part because the products are usually small-volume and lightweight, so that the cost of shipping is a small fraction of the eventual selling price.

Any location, including India, must have a competitive advantage in order to grow a high-technology industry. For certain high-tech products, India's competitive advantage is its huge domestic market. In certain other industries, India has an advantage in its large pool of skilled computer engineers who work for salaries that are well below those of comparably skilled professionals in the United States, Europe, or Japan. For example, Indian universities graduate a total of 150,000 engineers each year, one of the largest pools of engineers produced in any country. One result of this is India's booming exports of computer software.

How can a nation encourage the rise of high-technology industry? By funding research at universities or in government laboratories, and by improving the quality of its universities, especially in providing graduate-level education. Essentially, high-tech industry rests on brainpower, hard work, and risk-taking. It is a quite different ball game from the industrial manufacturing basis of competition that predominated in the past.

The key role that high-technology companies play in economic development in the United States is indicated by the finding that *65 percent* of the economic growth of metropolitan centers in the 1990s was explained by high-tech activity (DeVol, 1999). High-tech start-ups, in turn, were incubated by universities and other R&D institutions. Policy-makers in the U.S. realized that investing in research universities like MIT, Stanford, Carnegie-Mellon, and the University of Texas at Austin was the direct route to a booming local economy.

❑ High-Technology and the New Economy

Economist Brian Arthur (1996) feels that high-technology industry represents a New Economy in which a fundamental shift has occurred from a principle of diminishing returns to a principle of increasing returns. The case of coffee production exemplifies diminishing returns. Say that an increase in coffee prices occurs and a coffee plantation expands its production. Ultimately, it would plant coffee on land less suited for coffee, and run into diminishing returns. Bringing another acre of land into coffee production would eventually not be matched by increasing profits. So further expansion halts. This principle of decreasing returns dominates economic thinking, and is indeed a sound basis today in agriculture and in manufacturing industries. But not so for high-tech industry, where the principle of *increasing* returns is dominant.

In the early 1980s, three operating systems for personal computers existed: CP/M, DOS, and Apple Macintosh. Eventually, Microsoft's DOS became dominant, in part due to its acceptance by IBM, a major manufacturer of personal computers. DOS was not technically the best, but Microsoft became the market leader (Arthur, 1996). By getting ahead and gaining an initial advantage, Microsoft's DOS was further adopted by software developers and hardware manufacturers, which helped it get even *further* ahead. This is a case of increasing returns. The result was fat profits for Microsoft, and Bill Gates was on his way to becoming the richest man in the world.

An increasing returns scenario means that one product or service wins, and wins big. Competition is based on achieving the largest installed base, not just on gaining dominant market share. The name of the game in the New Economy is to capture as many customers as possible, and create a database of customers' needs, interests, and preferences. This customer information can directly translate into sales dollars (Gladwell, 1999). Consider the case of giant e-retailer Amazon.com as another example.

Say that you have purchased 10 books from Amazon.com, a company with an installed customer base of 20 million individuals located in many countries. Suppose that several of these books are mystery novels and others are military history and travel books. Amazon's computer aggregates you with its thousands of other customers who have book-buying profiles similar to yours, and then sends you an email message alerting you, for instance, to a new history book about

Alexander the Great. The email contains reviews of this book by professional book reviewers and by readers. It is your choice to buy or not, of course, but you are probably likely to do so. After all, as Amazon.com knows, you like to read military history books. Amazon will offer you a discount bargain price on the book selection, and will deliver to your doorstep within three or four days. This new type of marketing rests on Amazon's possessing a very large installed base of book buyers, one that is continuously growing (Hegel and Singer, 1999).

The bottom line in the new high-tech economy is to achieve a large base of users, which makes increasing returns possible (as we demonstrate later with the Hotmail case).

■ Spin-offs

A *spin-off* is a new company that is created (*a*) by individuals who leave a parent organization, (*b*) around a technology that these entrepreneurs bring with them from the parent organization. So the new company literally "spins off" the parent institution in a kind of centrifugal process. Spin-offs are one of the main engines of growth in a technopolis, and are the principal means by which jobs and wealth are created. The parent organization from which the spin-offs arise may be a high-tech company, a research university, or a government research institute.

A newborn company is very fragile, and can only survive in a protective cocoon. A spin-off often needs help from the parent company in order to survive. In some cases, the parent company, especially if it is in the same industry as the spin-off, tries to destroy its progeny, for instance by filing nuisance lawsuits concerning trade secrets.

Technopolis

"Silicon Valley" in Northern California is practically synonymous with "technopolis," although there are a number of other technopolises around the world, including several emerging technopolises in India such as Hyderabad, Pune, and especially Bangalore. Other well-known technopolises are Austin, Texas; Route 128 in the Boston area; Cambridge, England; and Tsukuba Science City north of Tokyo. Many others are emerging in Israel, Taiwan, and Egypt.

What do these technopolises have in common? The most important element in a technopolis is the *entrepreneurial spirit* of the individuals who launch new companies around a technological innovation. As an Indian software engineer in Silicon Valley, Manish Mehta, told us in a research interview: "When I go to a party where everyone is talking about their start-up company, I want to tell them about *my* dot-com company. It is a great thrill to start a new company." Entrepreneurial fever leads to the founding of new high-tech companies; such spin-offs drive the growth of a technopolis. This entrepreneurial quality is indeed a fever in that it is highly contagious. Once an individual like Bill Gates or Azim Premji becomes a billionaire, many other individuals think *they* can start new high-tech companies and quickly become wealthy. Successful role models help spread entrepreneurial fever. In the Austin technopolis, for example, Michael Dell, a dropout from the University of Texas who started selling computers out of his dormitory room and who now presides over Dell Computer, serves as a much-admired role model for many other aspiring entrepreneurs (Dell, 1999). Sabeer Bhatia, the founder of Hotmail, which he sold to Microsoft for $400 million in 1998, is a role model for many Indian entrepreneurs.

Venture capital is money invested in new high-tech companies with a high potential for growth. Venture capitalists provide the funding for new start-ups so that they can purchase land, build plants, and hire employees, and thus outgrow competitors. In exchange for the infusion of capital, an entrepreneur must usually give up 51 percent of ownership, and thus majority control, of his/her start-up company. So the venture capital is an investment, not a loan, made on the basis of the start-up company's potential profitability. Loans are made on the basis of a company's collateral which an entrepreneur does not possess, other than a nebulous vision of his/her company's technology-based product or service. Visions are not worth much to bankers providing loans, but, when packaged in a business plan, an entrepreneur's vision may attract a venture capital investment of a million dollars or more.

The entrepreneur is typically an engineer, physicist, or some other type of technologist who initially lacks business management training or experience. The venture capitalist supplements this deficiency of the entrepreneur by providing business management advice, often on a daily basis. This need for regular contact is why a venture capitalist must be geographically close to the new company in which he invests. In the United States, it is often said that "venture capital only travels up to 50 miles." For example, most of the venture capitalists who invest in Silicon Valley spin-off companies are officed in one building, located at 3000 Sand Hill Road in Menlo Park, California, near the northern end of Silicon Valley. Some 40 venture capital firms are housed in this structure. This building's parking lot is filled with Jaguars, Mercedes Benzes, Bentleys, BMWs, and other sleek, expensive cars.

A typical venture capitalist reviews the business plans for many hundreds of proposed new ventures each year. Perhaps only a handful are selected for funding by the venture capitalist. Some 80 percent of these start-ups fail or are acquired by larger companies within the first five years of their life. But about one in 10 of these new ventures repays the venture capitalist in a big way, perhaps at the rate of a $100 return for each dollar invested. This profit is realized when the new company "goes public" by selling its stock on the stock market, or when it is acquired by a large company. At this time, the venture capitalist and the entrepreneurs may become overnight multimillionaires. This is how wealth is created in the technopolis, at least on paper. The wealth is produced by the promised *future* sales of an innovative product or service, not by actual profits already made. But the dollars in the entrepreneur's bank account are real.

Technology is defined as information that is put to use in order to accomplish some task. An *innovation* is an idea perceived as new (Rogers, 1995). The sources of technological innovations are R&D institutions such as government research institutes, research universities, and corporate R&D laboratories.

Defense-related technologies are particularly difficult to commercialize. For example, two weapons laboratories in New Mexico, Los Alamos National Laboratory and Sandia National Laboratories, conduct $2 billion worth of R&D per year, but the research results are not easily converted into civilian products that can be sold in the marketplace to consumers. Similarly, several of the government-funded research institutes in Bangalore are defense-related, which makes technology transfer more difficult.

Quality-of-life factors make a location attractive to high-tech entrepreneurs. Climate, cultural and recreational opportunities, and infrastructure are the usual quality-of-life factors. Bangalore is often called the "air-conditioned city" due to its pleasant, high-altitude climate, which is one reason why it is a paradise for pensioners (Stremlau, 1996). Other technopolises also have a relatively high quality of life, although the specifics of the quality factors may be different in each technopolis. For example, Austin is located in the Texas hill country, which is perceived by many people as a rather ideal place in which to live. Silicon Valley in Northern California was thought to be a perfect location in the 1960s and 1970s when it was getting under way, but since the 1980s this overcrowded technopolis has been choked with traffic and its atmospheric pollution rivals Los Angeles's smog. Nevertheless, Silicon Valley is attractive to many entrepreneurs and high-technology workers who migrate here from other places. For example, some tens of thousands of Indian citizens live and work in Silicon Valley. Taiwanese, Koreans, and people of other nationalities are also well represented in Silicon Valley.

One paradox of the technopolis is that it may grow so explosively that it destroys the quality-of-life attractiveness that originally helped it evolve. For example, both Silicon Valley and Silicon Hills (Austin) have become traffic-clogged. The cost of housing in Silicon Valley is exorbitant: the median price of a home here is $410,000, twice that in the rest of the country. Many people with jobs in the $50,000 per year range are homeless (Nieves, 2000). Bangalore has become a very polluted city, so much so that some of its high-technology companies are moving to Hyderabad or other high-quality-of-life sites. Once a community's quality of life is lost, it is not easily regained.

■ Agglomeration

A technopolis represents an agglomeration of high-tech companies. *Agglomeration* is the degree to which some quality is concentrated spatially in one area. High-technology companies are not the only kind of industry that agglomerates, of course. The American automobile industry is concentrated in Detroit, for example, and film production companies are centered in Hollywood and in "Bollywood." So agglomeration of similar companies in the same community is a natural process, caused by the tendency of similar companies to exist in close proximity. This spatial closeness allows company officials to form a network of networks, so that information is easily exchanged to the benefit of everyone in the agglomeration.

Why do high-tech companies agglomerate? A basic reason is that a technopolis grows mainly by means of start-up companies, which tend to remain very near their parent organization. When an entrepreneur leaves a parent company in order to launch his or her spin-off, the entrepreneur seldom moves to another part of the country or overseas. In Silicon Valley, when the founder of a new spin-off goes to work the next morning, he or she just turns into a different driveway. Usually, the new location is very close to the entrepreneur's previous place of work. It night be just across the street. So once a technopolis begins to grow through spin-offs, it tends to agglomerate. The agglomeration process is greatly accelerated in an emerging technopolis once the number of high-tech companies reaches a critical mass.

Another reason for the agglomeration of high-technology companies is the availability of infrastructural factors such as venture capital, skilled personnel, and entrepreneurial role models. In Silicon Valley, where many semiconductor companies are concentrated, pipelines that deliver nitrogen gas run under the streets in certain areas (where the semiconductor companies are concentrated). This specialized service has contributed to the agglomeration of the U.S. semiconductor industry in Northern California over the past decades. The concentration of semiconductor companies in this area has meant that personal computer start-ups, laser companies, and biotechnology spin-offs have also tended to locate themselves in Silicon Valley. The agglomeration process, which began in the 1960s, has continued and intensified in following decades.

California's Silicon Valley

Prior to 1960, Santa Clara County in Northern California, stretching between San Francisco and San Jose, was the "prune capital" of America. This 10 by 20 mile area was covered with plum trees, and was rather sparsely inhabited. Today the plum trees have all been bulldozed, and the main products from Silicon Valley are microcomputers, semiconductors, computer peripherals, lasers, and Internet-related products and services. The open spaces had disappeared by 1980, and since then Silicon Valley has become much more crowded, with frequent traffic jams and pollution problems and unbelievable real estate prices. However, Silicon Valley is still "the world capital of the Information Society" (Rogers and Larsen, 1984).

The key institution in a U.S. technopolis like Silicon Valley is the *research university*, defined as an institution of higher education whose main functions are to conduct research and to train graduate students in doing research. Stanford University played a major role in launching the Silicon Valley technopolis.[2] It was the Valley's seed institution. Professor Frederick Terman, Vice-President and Provost of Stanford University in the 1950s, envisioned a West Coast electronics industry, and devoted his efforts to making it happen. Terman lent two of his graduate students in electrical engineering, Dave Packard and Bill Hewlett, $538 to enable them to start their company in 1938. They launched their electronics company in a garage behind the rooming house in which they lived in Palo Alto, CA (one can still visit the garage, at 517 Addison). Today, Hewlett-Packard is a major high-technology company, with over 100,000 employees, operating in the global marketplace. It is the most admired company in Silicon Valley.

Eventually, by about 1960, more electronics companies spun off Stanford University, and spin-offs from spin-offs began to occur. Soon, a critical mass of such high-tech firms had formed. By then, there were thousands of microelectronics companies, many of them small firms with less than 15 employees. Once the entrepreneurial fever had caught on, it began to feed on itself, and to grow in a self-sustaining process. A key factor in this development was the Stanford Industrial Park, located on the campus of Stanford

University, which provided a locus for agglomeration. Hewlett-Packard's world headquarters, Xerox PARC, and more than 60 other high-technology companies are located in the Stanford Industrial Park. It formed an early nucleus for the agglomeration of high-tech companies that were beginning to assemble in Northern California.

Silicon Valley is noteworthy for the ease with which technical information is exchanged here, facilitated by the close proximity of several thousand high-tech companies and their approximately one million employees, and by bars and restaurants which are favorite places to talk shop. The oldest and most famous of these informal gathering places is the Wagon Wheel Bar and Restaurant, where old friends who may have worked previously for the same company (but who then became employees of competing companies) meet in order to swap information about bits and bytes. The cocktail napkins at the Wagon Wheel are intentionally large-sized, and many business plans for new ventures are sketched on them. Today, Silicon Valley is so large that dozens of favorite meeting places exist, and they are constantly changing. In 2000, the Coffee Society in Cupertino and Birk's Restaurant just north of San Jose International Airport were favorite places for making deals. But the main lesson here is that a technopolis is an information-exchange network. In fact, it is a network of networks.

One can see the importance of interpersonal networks in the way that entrepreneurs secure venture capital. For instance, Nitin Parekh, President and CEO of Sapphire Software in Fremont, California, tells of an Indian friend from the Boston area who moved to Silicon Valley to start his own company. Parekh invited a dozen people to his home for brunch with the newly arrived entrepreneur. Two hours later, after the entrepreneur had explained his business proposal, a quarter million dollars in venture capital were promised.

Sanjay Gangal, Vice-President for Marketing of Internet Business Systems, a 1999 start-up in Silicon Valley, obtained a venture capital investment through his business partner, who is Jewish. The partner's small son attends a Hebrew school; the father of the son's best school-friend learned about the start-up, and decided to invest. Thus, social networks in Silicon Valley are a route to scarce resources. Many Indians find jobs in high-tech companies through IIT batchmates, family relatives, or other types of acquaintance.

By 1980, all but two of the 80 major semiconductor companies in the United States were headquartered in Silicon Valley. Many spun off of Fairchild Semiconductor, the first semiconductor company in Silicon Valley, and the "mother hen" of the semiconductor industry. This spin-off process was facilitated by venture capitalists who provided the investment funds to launch new companies. Then, during the early 1980s, the microcomputer industry, which uses semiconductors, also got under way in Silicon Valley. About this time, an informal association of microcomputer nerds (including the famous pair of Steve Jobs and Steve Wozniak who co-founded Apple Computer in the Jobs family garage), called the Home Brew Computer Club, was formed. This association met monthly in order to facilitate information exchange among computer technologists, many of whom (like Jobs and Wozniak) were counter-cultural hippies. Some 45 microcomputer companies were founded by members of the Home Brew Club in the 1960s and early 1970s (Rogers and Larsen, 1984).

Eventually, after about 1980 when all of the available space in Silicon Valley had been taken up, only company headquarters and the R&D function were located in this technopolis. Manufacturing facilities for Silicon Valley companies may be located in Austin, Albuquerque, Portland, or in such overseas locations as Penang, Guadalajara, or Singapore. So Silicon Valley fever has spread throughout the world, cloning technopolises here and there. And the communication technologies that Silicon Valley companies produce have changed almost everyone's lives, wherever they live. Since the late 1990s, an entrepreneurial buzz in Silicon Valley has been characterized by the "dot-com" Internet companies. Indians and Chinese immigrants to California play a dominant role in these new ventures.

■ The New Gold Rush

A new gold rush got under way in California's Silicon Valley in the late 1990s, centering around 24 new *billionaires* many of whom reached their pinnacle during the 12 months of 1999 via their

❑ Epinions.com: The Mother of All Shopping Services

Silicon Valley is the mother hen of "dot-com" companies. Indian entre-preneurs have played a key role in launching many of them.[3] A well-known example is Junglee.com, a company started by four ex–IIT engi-neers—Anand Rajaraman, Asish Gupta, Rakesh Mathur, and Venky Harinarayan—to provide virtual database technology for the World Wide Web. Founded in 1996 with an initial investment of $60,000, Junglee.com was acquired by the mighty Amazon.com for $180 mil-lion, making each of the four young founders a multimillionaire (N. Sharma, 1998). The success of Junglee.com inspired many Indians in Silicon Valley to launch dot-com companies.

A more recent dot-com company in Silicon Valley is Epinions.com, headquartered in Mountain View, CA (Dutt, 1999). The company is the brainchild of Naval Ravikant, Nirav Tolia, and Ramanathan Guha—all top-grossing, Indian-American Net whizzes who left high-paying jobs and stock options to provide consumers with the mother of all shopping guides, an on-line service called Epinions.com.

Guha, a graduate of IIT Madras, earned a Ph.D. in computer science at Stanford University, and guided the development of Net browser Navigator 5 at Netscape Communications (founded by Jim Clark, as we discuss later in this chapter). Ravikant, who came to the U.S. from India with his parents at age 7, earned degrees in computer science and economics at Dartmouth College before co-founding GenOA Cor-poration, a telecommunications start-up. Tolia, also of Indian origin, worked at Yahoo! Inc. where he was a brand manager of Yahoo! Visa and Yahoo! Shopping. He earned degrees in biology and English litera-ture at Stanford University, and then co-founded Round Zero, a non-profit organization of Silicon Valley entrepreneurs, venture capitalists, and technology professionals. Round Zero, which began with five members in 1997, had a membership of 1,000 enthusiastic individuals two years later. Tolia met Ravikant at Round Zero, where the idea of Epinions.com was born. They raised over $25 million in venture capital in order to launch their company.

By spring 2000, Epinions.com had generated one million page views a day and boasted more than two million users a month, earning a place among the 200 most-visited Web-sites (Dutt, 2000). So if you are shopping for a camera, a car, a book, or a computer, you no longer need to check with a friend about where to buy the product. Epi-nions.com creates a similar experience on-line, transcending the limits of space and time in seeking opinions about a certain customer product.

Internet-related companies.[4] Most of these new billionaires are of Indian or Chinese ancestry, having emigrated from India, Taiwan, or Hong Kong. Most have Ph.D. degrees. None of their Internet-related companies has yet made a profit; the escalating net worth of these companies is due to the investing public's confidence that these ventures *will* be immensely profitable. So investors bid up the stock-market prices of these companies. For example, the share price of Exodus Communications, a company founded by Indian expatriate K.B. Chandrashekar, exploded during 1999 (see Chapter 1).

The American stock market is thus creating a new class of super-rich people in Silicon Valley. Here, brains, business ability, and entrepreneurial risk-taking are rewarded with a gigantic pile of green dollars. Having 24 new billionaires in their community has changed the way that Northern Californians think about money and what it can buy. For instance, one of the Silicon Valley billionaires, a Taiwanese engineer who founded an Internet company, wanted to buy a tract of land for his new house. A 60 foot by 100 foot lot in a choice location had recently been purchased for $1 million. A month later, the cyber czar offered the land-owner $3 million, explaining that he did not want to argue through a bothersome negotiation process. The new Asian-American owner then had the existing structure bulldozed, so that his dream house could be built on the lot. When an individual is extremely wealthy, a million dollars here or there really does not matter much.

The Merril Lynch financial office in Palo Alto, California (the money capital of Silicon Valley) has one of the greatest volumes of financial transactions of any of the hundreds of Merril Lynch offices worldwide. The Palo Alto office has an unbelievable 500 individuals with at least $50 million invested with Merril Lynch. This office has several customers who are among the new billionaires, and many of these Merril Lynch customers are Indians or Chinese.

Silicon Valley is putting on an Asian face. Santa Clara County, California, an area that is essentially coterminous with Silicon Valley, increased its Asian population by 405 percent from 1980 to 2000. One out of three residents in Santa Clara County is foreign-born, with India, Taiwan, and Hong Kong being the main sources of the new migration stream. These individuals, highly mindful of money matters, display an aggressive entrepreneurial "wheeling and dealing" acumen. Coming from relatively modest backgrounds back home, they are highly motivated to work hard and take chances, and many have a high level of technical expertise. Taiwan will not allow students to migrate to the U.S. until they have completed Bachelor's degrees at Taiwanese universities. So many Taiwanese, as well as Indians, come to America to earn Master's and Ph.D. degrees, often in engineering, computer science, or other technical fields in which numeracy skills are particularly valuable.

About one-third of the scientific and engineering workforce in Silicon Valley comprises immigrants, and two-thirds of these immigrant technologists are either Indians or Chinese (Saxenian, 1999). A common saying in Silicon Valley is that this technopolis is "built on ICs." But in the late 1990s, the meaning of ICs changed from "integrated circuits" to "Indians and Chinese." Some 32 percent of the Indians and 23 percent of the Chinese in Silicon Valley have postgraduate degrees, compared to only 11 percent of the European Americans (ibid.). Up until the mid-1990s, Indians strongly felt that a "glass ceiling" blocked their advancement. As an Indian engineer noted: "When I left the company after 5 years, I was doing functions of Level 4 (the highest level to which a software engineer can progress), but not given salary, or acknowledgement, or recognition deserved. I was static in Level 2 of the organizational chart" (quoted in Fernandez, 1998, p. 143). At that time, if an Indian submitted a business plan for a start-up company to a venture capitalist in Silicon Valley, it went to the bottom of the stack. Today, the Indian business plan is likely to go to the top of the stack.

❑ How Indians Get Rich in Silicon Valley

The process through which Indian engineers become multimillionaires in Silicon Valley is best understood by analyzing an actual case of a start-up company, Healtheon. This Internet-based venture went public (that is, first sold shares on the New York stock market in an IPO, or initial public offering) in mid-February 1999. An IPO in Silicon Valley is a day of high drama, as vast fortunes may be made by the new company's employees who own stock. Or the IPO may be a day of vast disappointment as high expectations are dashed. Healtheon's 600 employees gather in the company's recreation room at 5.30 A.M., which, due to the difference of time zones, is 8.30 A.M. in New York (the stock exchange opens at 9.30 A.M.). Five million shares of Healtheon's stock, about 8 percent of the company, are to be offered. The employees who have gathered in the rec room control 15 million shares, so the stock price established in New York will determine how much they are worth.

Pavan Nigam, who organized the company and recruited its first employees, is on a cell-phone connected to New York. At 9.30, he begins calling off the numbers: "21-and-a-half." The employees go wild. They are worth $300 million! (Lewis, 2000, p. 243). "28." "34-and-a-quarter." The company is now worth $2.2 billion, and Nigam is worth $33 million! When the stock market closes for the day, he returns to his office cubicle. His body is shaking, as the reality sets in that he is now rich.

A few months later, in spring 1999, Healtheon's stock shot up to $105 per share,[5] and the company was valued at $16 billion, even though it had not yet shown a profit. Such wealth is created by the *promise* of Healtheon's technology, which interconnects medical doctors with patient records, drug prescriptions, and other information in the vast U.S. health care system. Each connection that is made earns Healtheon a few cents. The company handled five million such connections in 1998, 500 million in 1999, and 1.5 billion transactions in 2000.

The imagination behind Healtheon was that of a fabled Silicon Valley wizard, Jim Clark, former Stanford University professor of computer science and founder of Silicon Graphics, his first billion-dollar company. Clark believes that the success of his ventures rests on attracting a small team of very bright engineers. Pavan Nigam is from Kanpur, and attended IIT Kanpur. He arrived in Silicon Valley in 1980, and went to work for Silicon Graphics. Nigam in turn hired Kittu Kolluri in 1990. They were writing software code in Nigam's cubicle one day when Jim Clark strolled in. Clark said, "Pavan, we got to get some more Indians around here" (quoted in Lewis, 2000, p. 69).

Clark holds that Indian brainpower was essential to converting his visions into technological reality. "The Indian engineers had the lust for the kill that Clark loved. They were ferociously, relentlessly competitive" (Lewis, 2000, p. 120). Just how competitive Nigam and Kolluri are is illustrated by the way that Nigam reminds Kolluri that he finished 250 places behind him in the national engineering exams in India. Both Nigam and Kolluri finished in the top one-hundredth of 1 percent of the 150,000 bright young Indians who sit for the two-day exam each year, a batch that perhaps represents the top one-hundreth of 1 percent of brainpower nationally (ibid.). The 2,000 Indians with the highest scores on the engineering exam are admitted to the IITs. They are further ranked according to their scores on the test, with the toppers getting their choice of department at an IIT. The computer science department at IIT Kanpur was a top choice in 1975; so Nigam, who finished 91st nationally, chose to study there.

Kolluri remembers the defining moment when he decided to become an engineer. His cousin from Mumbai, a pretty young woman, came to visit his family in Hyderabad one summer when he was in sixth grade. She was in love with a complete geek. "She talked about how she loved his *brain*. He went to an Indian Institute of Technology. That was the first time that I ever heard of an IIT" (quoted in Lewis, 2000, p. 118). Kolluri knew from that time on that he wanted to go to an IIT and be an engineer. A year later, he finished first in the seventh-grade tests administered in Andhra Pradesh, a state with 80 million people. He became obsessed with gaining admission to an IIT, often studying until 3.00 A.M.. Like Nigam, immediately after graduating from IIT, he departed for graduate school in a U.S. university, and then on to Silicon Valley.

The two Indians missed out on an opportunity to become rich quickly when they opted to remain at Silicon Graphics in 1994 when Jim Clark founded Netscape. However, Nigam had purchased stock in Netscape at its IPO, leaving a buy order with his stockbroker before he got on a flight to India. He figured that anything in Jim Clark's world would turn to gold. His stock quickly jumped from the $50 per share that he had paid to $171 per share. He was visiting his family in Kanpur at the time, in 1995, and only learned of his new wealth when he read *USA Today* in Delhi. Netscape was the first big Internet-related company, and the first Silicon Valley company to go public before it made a profit. Until Netscape, high-tech business wisdom said that a company should have at least a year of solid profits before its IPO. Netscape was only 18 months old when it went public in August 1995, and it had not made *any* profit. So Netscape set the stage for the IPOs of many later

Internet-related companies. The investor community learned to buy them on promise.

Nigam did not intend to miss out on the next Jim Clark venture. So when Clark telephoned him with an invitation to be the first employee of Healtheon, he quickly jumped ship at Silicon Graphics. That same day he invited Kittu Kolluri for a walk along Shoreline Boulevard, near San Francisco Bay, where they could not be overheard. They wished to avoid a run-in with the lawyers at Silicon Graphics over the issue of raiding key employees. Kolluri immediately decided to join Healtheon. "No freaking way I was going to miss this one" (quoted in Lewis, 2000, p. 121). Then Kolluri talked with Jim Clark about salary and stock options. Clark told him to get over his habit of thinking in *thousands* of dollars, and instead to think about *millions* (ibid., p. 122).

Nigam resigned from Silicon Graphics to join Healtheon on a Friday in February 1995. The word spread quickly that Jim Clark was launching a new company. No one knew exactly what it was, but they wanted to get on board. When Nigam arrived at his home, applicants began ringing his telephone off the hook. By Monday morning, 300 resumes had been faxed to his home machine. He only needed a dozen top engineers, but they had to be really brainy, the very best. "After Kittu he picked Shankar. After Shankar he picked Motasim..." (Lewis, 2000, p. 123). One was Chinese, two were Italians, most were Indians.

They moved into a tiny office in Palo Alto and set to work, trying to convert Clark's vague vision into an actual company. Healtheon took shape bit by bit. The team had high morale, and worked long hours. Often they slept on cots in their cubicles. One morning Clark dropped in early to find one of the engineers hunched over a computer work station. Clark said: "You're here early." The engineer looked up and said, "I never left," and went back to writing code (Lewis, 2000, p. 124). Clark was seldom involved with the new company, leaving the details to what he called his "horde of Indians." He was not adept as a manager or executive. Clark worked mainly on his completely computerized yacht, a sailboat that was being built for him in the Netherlands. The *Hyperion* had the tallest mast and the largest sail of any sailboat. But its most amazing quality was that it only required a crew of one, plus, of course, 14 computers. In fact, Clark could sail it on San Francisco Bay from his office in Silicon Valley.

His successful entrepreneurial start-ups, Silicon Graphics, Netscape, and Healtheon, have made Jim Clark a billionaire several times over. He was one of the 465 billionaires listed in the July 1999 issue of *Forbes* magazine. His wealth gives him the resources to sail his computerized sailboat from the Netherlands to San Francisco, or to go up in his helicopter. Like other Silicon Valley tycoons, he enjoys the "toys" that come with technological/entrepreneurial success.

Kittu Kolluri still lags behind his Indian friend and co-worker. In late spring 1999, Pavan Nigam was worth $85 million. Kolluri was worth "only" $30 million.[6]

The Indian Diaspora

The approximately one million Indian citizens living in the United States today represent the immigrant group with the highest average income in America. Some of these overseas Indians eventually return to India, where they make major contributions to the communication revolution. One example is Sam Pitroda (see Chapter 5). Many others help establish their foreign company's business offices in India, create joint ventures, provide venture capital, facilitate technology transfer, and maintain close social and economic ties with India. The young Indian transplants in America are not only smart, but entrepreneurial. Alluding to the many founders of high-tech start-up companies in Silicon Valley who are Indians, one observer noted: "The definitive smell inside a Silicon Valley start-up was of curry" (Lewis, 1999). With the "death of distance" by advances in telecommunications and the Internet, the term "brain drain" is considered passé. Indian computer software engineers worked on Y2K problems for an American company from their offices in Bangalore in 1999, with software code transmitted via the Internet. The brain drain of the past has become a "brain circulation" today, with money and talent moving between the U.S. and India.

At the turn of the century, some 20 million Indians lived in the global diaspora (Padmanabhan, 2000a). Several thousand Gujaratis, many of them Patels, were transported by British colonialists to South Africa and East Africa, Jamaica and the Caribbean, and to Malaysia. Their descendants long ago left the unskilled occupations in which their forefathers had gained entrance to these scattered locations, in order to become businessmen and/or to migrate to other places with greater opportunities. So Indians in Kenya, Uganda, and Tanzania migrated to England, from there to Canada, and then to the United States. Most of the small hotels and motels in the United States are today owned and operated by Patels.

In more recent decades, Indian workers have migrated to Kuwait, Saudi Arabia, and to the Gulf states, while Indian doctors and engineers have moved in large numbers to the United States (Khadria, 1999). Silicon Valley has become a primary destination in recent years, with over 80,000 Indians working in this technopolis in 2000. In fact, Silicon Valley has become a kind of alumni club for India's IITs. At the Oracle Company's cafeteria in Silicon Valley, for example, sambhaar–rice is a standard menu item. Indian restaurants, grocery stores, Hindu temples, Hindi movie houses, and schools of Indian dance and music now dot the landscape of Silicon Valley. The festivals of Diwali and Holi have become important celebrations in Sunnyvale and Fremont, California.

On 21 September 1995, when it was reported in Delhi and other Indian cities that the Hindu deities were drinking milk, this unusual news event immediately diffused worldwide throughout the Indian diaspora. Within a few hours, long queues of Indians were lined up at temples in Toronto, San Francisco, Kingston, and Kuala Lumpur. Milk-feeding spread around the globe, following lines of telecommunications and time zones. This news event helped demonstrate the nature of the global village, and the wide distribution of individuals of Indian ancestry (Singhal, Rogers, et al., 1999).

Migrants from any culture are highly untypical of those people who do not leave (Bhagwati, 2000). America, a land of immigrants, is an example of this point. The individuals who pulled up stakes in Europe to travel to America were the desperate and the highly motivated, people who wanted a better life, and who were willing to take chances to get it. Some, like the Jews, fled religious persecution in Europe. Others, especially after World War I, the rise of Hitler's fascism in the 1930s, and World War II, left their European homelands in order to gain political freedom. Many European migrants to America came in search of economic opportunities; for example, in the 1850s, several million Irish people moved across the Atlantic in order to escape the widespread starvation caused by the Potato Famine.

Most Indians migrated to the United States in pursuit of economic opportunity. In the global society, brainpower flows relatively easily across national boundaries, seeking promising opportunities. Many Indians migrate on educational visas in order to enroll for graduate degrees, and then stay on to work in high-tech industries, as professors, or as medical doctors. They might start up new entrepreneurial ventures. Some return to India after reaching middle age, bringing new ideas, capital, and expertise with them (Murthy, 2000). Many Indians in Silicon Valley return to their motherland every year or two, in order to visit their families, to get married, or to stay in touch with Indian culture.

At the turn of the century, the Indian migrants to the U.S. wielded enormous economic and political clout. Professor Jagdish Bhagwati of Columbia University calls Indian-Americans "the 'next Jews' of America: a highly successful, intellectually eminent and economically prominent group that has all the networking advantages that a merit-based immigration-oriented society such as the American society offers" (Bhagwati, 2000, p. 32).

☐ Lata Krishnan: Successful Woman Entrepreneur[7]

Indian *women* entrepreneurs are increasingly making a dent in Silicon Valley. Notable role models include Vani Kola, CEO of Right Works Corporation, a leading Silicon Valley company in the e-procurements business; Anu Shukla, CEO of RubricSoft, a leading software company; and Lata Krishnan, a highly successful woman entrepreneur and one of the highest-paid female executives in Silicon Valley.

Krishnan co-founded SMART Modular Technologies with her husband, Ajay Shah, and their friend, Mukesh Patel. Krishnan was born in Kerala, raised in Kenya and England (where she attended the London School of Economics), and worked in finance and accounting for English companies, before moving to Silicon Valley in 1987. With experience of four continents, Krishnan symbolizes the global spread of the Indian diaspora.

Krishnan's first company, a semiconductor export business, was a failure. But she gained useful business experience, and her second company, SMART, became a leading designer and manufacturer of memory modules, memory flash cards, and other high-performance computer products. In 1999, SMART merged with Solectron, the world's largest provider of customized electronics manufacturing solutions, in a $2-billion deal (Pais, 1999).

Until 1988, Krishnan's husband, Shah, worked for Samsung Semiconductors, but his employer was not interested in memory modules manufacturing. So Krishnan wrote the business plan for SMART. The proposed new company was turned down by venture capitalists in Silicon Valley. So Krishnan and Shah turned to a family friend, Mukesh Patel, who helped raise $120,000 from friends and family, and SMART was launched in 1988. By 1999, SMART had grown to 1,700 employees, and sales of $700 million per year. The company had manufacturing plants in Fremont, CA (in Silicon Valley), Puerto Rico, Scotland, and Malaysia. SMART has design centers in Bangalore and in Fremont, CA.

SMART's employees, like its co-founders, are multicultural. As Shah (who was born in Uganda and studied in India and the U.S.) said: "We are an international company, manufacturing in many locations. Our customers are all over the world and they should feel comfortable with us. So it is advantageous to have a multicultural, cosmopolitan team of employees" (J. Rao, 1999, p. 1). SMART sells components to Intel, Microsoft, Hewlett-Packard, Motorola, IBM, Nokia, and other large electronics companies, who use these components in digital cameras, mobile phones, and other products.

Krishnan and Shah maintain such a degree of professionalism that many of their employees do not know, and few care, that the two top officials in the company are married. Shah specializes in marketing, Patel is the technologist, and Krishnan is the finance expert, who also serves as vice-president for human resources. In 1999, she arranged for SMART to donate thousands of dollars worth of computer equipment to Irvington High School in Fremont, the California city where SMART is headquartered. She stated: "SMART felt it was important to contribute something to the area in which so many of our employees have their homes" (cited in http://www.smartm.com/news/html, p. 1). The donation of "the computer lab gives SMART the opportunity to contribute to the education of the children who will shape the future of this community—an investment more important than the value of the actual equipment," she said.

> Vani Kola, Anu Shukla, and Lata Krishnan symbolize excellence in high-tech entrepreneurship in Silicon Valley, demonstrating that this is not exclusively the domain of their countrymen.

■ Successful Indians in Silicon Valley

Of the approximately 80,000 Indians who work in Silicon Valley, one of the most famous is Vinod Khosla, son of an Indian Army officer, who earned his Bachelor's degree at an IIT (Plate 4.1). He enrolled for a Master's in biomedical sciences at Carnegie Mellon University in Pittsburgh, and went on to earn an MBA degree from Stanford University. Having first co-founded Daisy Systems, an electronic design automation company, Khosla joined several of his classmates in 1982, at age 27, to launch Sun Microsystems, named "Sun" for Stanford University Network. Sun work stations became the industry standard for a new era of powerful computers, and the company grew rapidly to one billion dollars in sales by 1988. Khosla served as Sun's CEO until he retired at the ripe age of 30 to become a partner at a prestigious venture capital company, Kleiner Perkins Caulfield & Byers, in San Francisco. From here, Khosla has backed several highly successful start-ups, including Cerent Corporation,[8] which was acquired in 1999 by Cisco Corporation for $7 billion, netting Khosla over a billion dollars. Other high-flying companies backed by Khosla include Juniper Networks and Siara Networks. Khosla is today one of the richest Indians in America. His widely known success has inspired many other Indians in Silicon Valley.

As noted previously, some 40 percent of all start-ups in Silicon Valley today have Indian co-founders (Krishna, 1999b).[9] Jim Clark, founder of Silicon Graphics, Netscape, and Healtheon, three successful Silicon Valley companies, said: "As a concentrated group they [Indians] are the most talented engineers in the Valley...and they work their butts off" (Lewis, 1999). In 1999, nearly half of all temporary work visas issued by the United States government went to Indians, many of whom are engineers or scientists (Richter, 2000). This means that American captains of high-technology

Plate 4.1: Vinod Khosla, co-founder of Sun Microsystems and one of the richest Indians in Silicon Valley

Khosla co-founded Sun Microsystems in Silicon Valley with his Stanford classmates in the early 1980s; this entrepreneurial venture made him very wealthy at an early age. He then joined the San Francisco–based venture capital company, Kleiner Perkins Caulfield & Byers. Khosla is a role model for many Indians in Silicon Valley.

Source: Vinod Khosla (used with permission).

industries highly value the technological/entrepreneurial abilities of young Indian men and women, whose temporary visas they sponsor.

Sabeer Bhatia is a prototypical young Indian in Silicon Valley, who grew up in Bangalore (Plate 4.2). Bhatia earned a Bachelor's degree from Caltech, a Master's degree in electrical engineering from Stanford University, and worked with Apple Computer and

FirePower Systems, a start-up company in Silicon Valley, before launching Hotmail with two friends. Hotmail, a Web-based email company, provides email addresses to individuals that they can access wherever they are in the world. Hotmail is free to the user (and can be adopted via the Internet). During the late 1990s, the number of users rapidly cascaded into many, many millions (the co-authors of this book both use Hotmail). And Bhatia's net worth cascaded into many millions of dollars.

Plate 4.2: Sabeer Bhatia, co-founder of Hotmail

Bhatia was raised in Bangalore, educated in California, and worked for Apple Computer. He co-founded Hotmail in 1997, which was sold to Microsoft for $400 million 18 months later. Bhatia was 31 years old in 2000.

Source: Sabeer Bhatia (used with permission).

One of the radically new ideas embedded in the Hotmail innovation was that of giving it away "free." Near the bottom of the computer screen, when one accesses a Hotmail address, appears this instruction: "Get your free Web-based email at Hotmail.com." A click on this tag line takes a user into the Hotmail Web-site, where securing an email account takes about two minutes. The tag line means that Hotmail involves its customers in marketing the innovation to others. This strategy made for a very rapid rate of diffusion. On 4 July 1996, when Hotmail was launched,[10] there were zero users. Some 18 months later, on 31 December 1997, when Bhatia and his co-founders sold Hotmail to Microsoft for $400 million, there were an unbelievable 12 million users, and new subscribers were coming on board at the rate of 150,000 per day! The diffusion curve kept right on marching up like a hockey-stick; by January 2000, some 25 more months later, Hotmail had about 50 million users worldwide,[11] more than the populations of 202 countries. Here is a rate of technological diffusion that is unmatched in human history.

At first glance it would seem that by giving away Hotmail for "free," the company would not have a revenue base. Of course, Hotmail is not really "free." In order to secure a "free" Hotmail address, an individual must provide certain socio-demographic information, providing an opportunity for Hotmail to target various segments of Hotmail users for special advertisements, transmitted via the Internet. So the name of this game is the installed base of users. An individual "buys" a Hotmail email address for the cost of providing personal information about himself/herself. Notice the economic value of this personal information. The Hotmail success story was quickly followed by similar Internet-based companies: ICQ, Onelist, and All Advantage. None of them, however, matched Hotmail's overnight success.

Bhatia, 31 years old in 2000, is one among many Indians who have made it big in Silicon Valley. After selling Hotmail in 1997, Bhatia became an Internet strategist for Microsoft Corporation before launching an electronic commerce company on the Internet named Arzoo! Inc.[12] He lives in a skyscraper apartment in San Francisco with smashing views of the entire San Francisco Bay area.

Another Indian success story in Silicon Valley is Juniper Networks. This company was co-founded in 1996 by Pradeep Sindhu, with an investment of $200,000 in venture capital from Kleiner Perkins Caulfield & Byers (KPCB), after Sindhu pitched his idea to KPCB partner Vinod Khosla (mentioned earlier). Sindhu immigrated to the U.S. from Haryana in 1974 and has a doctorate in computer science from Carnegie Mellon University (Springer, 1999b). Sindhu's stake in Juniper Networks in 2000 was estimated at about a billion dollars.

Indians are highly regarded in Silicon Valley as technologists and, especially in recent years, as business entrepreneurs, as they crack the "glass ceiling" (Fernandez, 1998). Five Indians were among Silicon Valley's 100 highest-paid executives in publicly held companies in 1999. The annual salaries of these five Indians ranged from $11.5 million (for 15th-ranked Mukesh Patel) to $3.8 million (for 73rd-ranked Prabhat Goel).

Indians have organized in professional forums such as the Silicon Valley Indian Professionals Association (SIPA) and The Indus Entrepreneurs (TiE) to provide opportunities for networking and support services to Indian entrepreneurs, and to facilitate Indo–U.S. joint ventures. Founded in 1992, TiE is headed by Kanwal Rekhi, a highly respected venture capitalist in Silicon Valley and previously co-founder of Excelan, which he sold to Novell for $250 million. By 1999, TiE's 200-plus charter members, including luminaries like Vinod Khosla, Gururaj Deshpande, Suhaas Patil, and K.B. Chandrasekhar, had invested over $100 million of personal funds in Indian high-tech start-ups in Silicon Valley, and raised over $400 million in venture capital from other sources (Springer, 1999c). As a ready source of venture capital, business expertise, and entrepreneurial mentorship, TiE has played a key role in fueling start-up fever among Indians in Silicon Valley.[13] Now with several regional chapters in the U.S., in the U.K., and in India (for instance, in Mumbai, Delhi, and Bangalore), TiE is playing a key role in India's progress toward informatization.

One type of network connection exists among Indians who have attended IITs. The number of IIT graduates in Silicon Valley is actually a rather small proportion of all Indians in this technopolis. Remember that the IITs only graduate about 2,000 engineers per year, and perhaps about half migrate to America (and not all to Silicon Valley). Then why are the IIT alumni associations so important in U.S. high-tech start-ups? In the first place, being selected at an IIT builds self-confidence in an individual, as well as labeling him or her as brainy. As Raj Baronia, an IIT Kanpur graduate and President and CEO of Indolink, an Internet portal company in Silicon Valley, told us in a research interview: "One feels that if one is good enough to get admitted to an IIT, one can really do anything." Having a high level of self-efficacy is important in launching a start-up. If an individual does not believe in himself/herself and in the new business venture, how could its vision be sold to venture capitalists and to the key employees who must be recruited? Further, having attended an IIT means that a newcomer to Silicon Valley arrives with an already established set of networks.

Indians in Silicon Valley have also begun to "give back" to their homeland, making the earlier debate about the "brain drain" passé. Kanwal Rekhi of TiE, for instance, donated $2 million to his alma mater, the Indian Institute of Technology in Mumbai. Rekhi now heads a campaign to raise over a billion dollars from successful Indians (many thousands of whom are based in Silicon Valley) to institutionalize cutting-edge teaching, research, and consulting in high-tech business at the five Indian IITs. Various others individuals, including Narayana Murthy of Infosys, Arjun Malhotra of Techspan, and Suhas Patil of Cirrus Logic, have contributed generously to their respective IIT alma maters. Others have endowed chaired professorships in Indian universities, previously a rare occurrence.

Indians like Lata Krishnan, Vinod Khosla, Sabeer Bhatia, Pradeep Sindhu, and Kanwal Rekhi represent a new kind of Indian. Their parents' generation, at home in India or abroad, highly valued job security. The old-fashioned goal was to obtain a position with a bank or some other established business, or in the government bureaucracy. The "new" Indians enjoy taking chances, facing risk, and dealing with uncertainty. The high-tech start-up "game" thus fits perfectly with their "risk-taking" migrant values. They are willing to work long hours; the average professional in Silicon Valley works 60 hours per week, and during "crunch time" when a start-up is getting under way, the entrepreneurial team may work 16 or 18 or even 20 hours per day, perhaps for six months! An individual who lives through a crunch may appear to have aged eight to 10 years by the experience. So the high-tech start-up game is for the young and the ambitious. Burnout at age 30 is not uncommon.

A keen observer of Silicon Valley, economist Brian Arthur, was in an airplane that was circling to land at San Jose Airport. He looked down to see a cricket match under way. All the players were Indians. Silicon Valley is increasingly acquiring an Indian face.

❑ Malaviya and Deshpande: Success on Boston's Route 128

Outside of Silicon Valley, Indian entrepreneurs have also excelled in other American technopolises, such as Boston's Route 128.[14] However, not all Indian entrepreneurs experience the rocket-like success of the Sabeer Bhatias and the Vinod Khoslas; for many, the pay-off comes after several years of hard work. Consider the case of two entrepreneurs in the Boston Route 128 technopolis: Atin Malaviya and Gururaj Deshpande. Malaviya tasted success with a 1998 start-up. Deshpande, with several start-ups, is a "serial" entrepreneur.

Atin Malaviya (Plate 4.3) was born in the U.S. in 1966, while his father, a medical doctor, was studying at Tufts University. His parents moved back to India when he was a year old. He attended Modern High School in New Delhi, an elite private school, prior to arriving in the U.S. to earn a Bachelor's degree in computer science (in 1990) from the University of Massachusetts at Amherst. Then Malaviya spent four years writing software for Intermetrics Inc., a U.S. defense contractor. In order to "become a part of the telecommunications revolution," Malaviya left Intermetrics in 1994 and joined Natural Microsystems (NMS), a small, fast-growing company that designed and manufactured computer hardware to connect PCs with telecommunications devices (personal conversation, 3 November 1999). Appointed a junior software programmer, Malaviya rose rapidly to become principal engineer at NMS and, more importantly, a member of a four-person core group responsible for designing the next generation of software products for the company. Malaviya considers this R&D experience as being "invaluable for what was to follow" (ibid.).

Plate 4.3: Atin Malaviya, who tasted financial success in 1999 when his company, Redstone Communications, was acquired by Siemens

Malaviya, born in the United States of Indian parents, was a computer software writer for Redstone Communications, an entrepreneurial start-up on Boston's Route 128 technopolis. He was paid with stock options, which led to his becoming a millionaire when Redstone was acquired by the German electronics company in 1999.

Source: Atin Malaviya (used with permission).

In 1997, a co-member of Malaviya's four-person group, Michael Lipman, left NMS to join Arris Networks, a high-tech start-up company in the Boston area. Lipman was hired at Arris Networks by a former NMS employee, Steve Morss, who in a farewell speech at NMS said: "Either I will lose my shirt at this, or I will buy you all shirts." Morss and Lipman did not lose their shirts: Arris Networks was acquired for

$165 million by Cascade Communications (a company co-founded by Gururaj Deshpande, as we discuss later). Inspired by Morss's and Lipman's success, Malaviya was rapidly catching start-up fever. If his ex-colleagues could be successful entrepreneurs, why couldn't he?

After his success at Arris Networks, Morss joined another start-up company in the Boston area called Redstone Communications as its Director of Hardware, and brought Lipman aboard. Redstone was founded by two experienced entrepreneurs, Jim Dolce (previously Vice-President of Sales at Arris Networks) and Kurt Melden (a co-founder of Cascade Communications). Redstone Communications, which raised $6 million in venture capital from Matrix Partners, needed several software engineers to get under way, and Lipman thought of Malaviya, with whom he had worked previously at NMS. "I was a young guy and nobody knew me," said Malaviya. "It was Lipman who convinced the people at Redstone that I was the right person for the job" (personal interview, 3 November 1999). Here we see the importance of personal networks in a start-up's recruitment efforts. The new company must quickly attract high-quality relevant expertise.

Redstone began with some 20-odd software/hardware engineers, of which three (including Malaviya) were from Indian backgrounds. They were handpicked; each brought a unique expertise to the new venture. "All of us were very motivated to get the product out of the door," recalls Malaviya. "Salary-wise, the move was lateral... we were making the same salary as in our previous jobs, but we were given generous stock options. We knew that if Redstone was successful, we would be rich."

Malaviya began work at Redstone Communications in early 1998. The company designed and manufactured state-of-the-art Internet equipment to efficiently route data traffic. The pressure to deliver a working product was intense: "The workdays were long, often stretching 10 to 14 hours, from Monday through Saturday, and sometimes spilling over on Sundays," said Malaviya (personal interview, 3 November 1999). In order to devote even more time to his work, Malaviya rented a small apartment close to his office. On Sundays, he commuted back to Cambridge to be with his wife, Tina, who was earning a Ph.D. in computer science at MIT. "It was a lot of work but we knew we were in a 'hot' market and we had a good product...we just had to get the product done in time," recalled Malaviya. Compared to the standard 40-hour work week in America, the Redstone engineers were working 70 to 80 hours per week. High-tech entrepreneurs call this intense period the "crunch." Individuals may work until they see spots; then they nap for 30 minutes on a cot in their office and go right back to work. Veterans of high-tech start-ups say that going through a "crunch" ages them considerably. But the rewards that come with company success can be very sweet.

Some 19 months after its inception, Redstone Communications, in mid-1999, was acquired for $500 million by Siemens, the gigantic German electronics company, making the co-founders and the initial team of engineers, including Malaviya, millionaires. Along with Redstone Communications, Siemens acquired two other start-ups in the Boston area—Argon Networks and Castle Networks—whose products were complementary to Redstone's. Siemens merged the three acquisitions into a new company called Unisphere Solutions to design the next generation of Internet routing products. Why did a large company like Siemens pay such a huge sum of money for Redstone Communications? It wanted to acquire the promising new technology and the skilled employees, which allowed it to enter a new technology area. Malaviya and his Redstone colleagues received generous stock options at Unisphere Solutions. If Unisphere becomes successful, it will go public, bringing in a second round of riches for Malaviya and his colleagues. Here we see an example of how wealth is created by high-technology start-ups. The entrepreneurship process converts successful technological innovations into dollars, lots of dollars.

How has Malaviya's lifestyle changed? He and his wife have bought a new home in an affluent Boston suburb, and Malaviya has replaced his 10-year old Geo with a new Audi sports car, which blends with the BMW and Mercedez Benz cars in the parking lot at Unisphere. Malaviya spends more time at home on weekends and has resumed his art classes. When asked by one of the present authors if he was considering retirement at the ripe age of 33, Malaviya responded: "This isn't enough. There is more to go."

Entrepreneurs like Malaviya, once they have experienced success with a start-up company, often continue on this fast track. Boston area entrepreneur, Gururaj ("Desh") Deshpande (Plate 4.4), exemplifies this brand of "continuous" entrepreneurship. A 1973 graduate of IIT Madras, Deshpande is one of the richest Indians in the U.S. Deshpande displays a Midas touch in founding high-tech start-ups, which have either been acquired or have gone public (that is, been listed on the stock exchange for the public to invest in), making Deshpande a billionaire. Start-ups founded by Deshpande include Coral Networks (in 1987), Cascade Communications (in 1990), and Sycamore Networks (in 1998).

Plate 4.4: Gururaj "Desh" Deshpande, co-founder of several start-ups on Boston's Route 128 technopolis

Deshpande, an IIT Madras alumnus, co-founded Coral Networks, Cascade Communications, and Sycamore Networks in the Boston area. All of Deshpande's start-ups were highly successful, making Deshpande a multibillionaire.

Source: Sycamore Networks (used with permission).

All of Deshpande's start-ups were founded on his belief that "Computers will have no value unless they connect to every other computer in the world." Cascade Communications, which began in 1990 with a venture capital investment of $3.5 million from Matrix Partners (the venture capitalist who also funded Redstone Communications), designed and built state-of-the-art data transmission switches, which form the backbone of Internet traffic. Seven years later, in 1997,

Cascade Communications was acquired by Ascend Communications for $3.7 billion, making Deshpande a rich man. In 1998, Deshpande and Dan Smith (a co-founder of Cascade Communications) joined hands with two MIT professors, Rick Barry and Eric Swanson (whom they met at a Christmas party), to found Sycamore Networks,[15] with $20 million in venture capital from Matrix Partners. A year later, when Sycamore went public, the stock gained 386 percent in value on its first day on the NASDAQ stock exchange, making Deshpande very rich.

Deshpande is an inspiration to young Indian entrepreneurs in the Boston area, showing how brainpower and entrepreneurship are combined to generate substantial wealth in a short time. Deshpande holds a three-hour "open house" in his Boston home each Sunday, mentoring aspiring high-tech entrepreneurs from the Indian subcontinent. Furthermore, Deshpande has contributed generously to his alma mater, IIT Madras, noting: "Once you feel that you are successful, you first want to help those who helped you" (quoted in Lakshman, 1999, p. 1).

Austin's "Silicon Hills"

Of the various technopolises around the world, the technology city with the closest similarity to Bangalore is Austin, a rapidly growing city nestling in the Texas hill country. Like Bangalore, Austin is a computer software center, and has risen as a technopolis during the same time frame, although its growth has been fueled by other factors than those that led to the rise of its Indian counterpart.

Until 1983, Austin was mainly known as the capital of its state, the home of the University of Texas, and as the world center for country music. Willie Nelson and a host of other country music stars were its leading citizens. This cowpoke image changed after May 1983 when the Microelectronics and Computer Technology Consortium (MCC) chose Austin as the headquarters for its 500 R&D workers and $75 million per year effort to compete with Japan's fifth-generation computer project. The MCC is a consortium composed of about 20 leading U.S. electronics companies that joined together to compete more effectively with Japan by conducting collaborative R&D (Gibson and Rogers, 1994). The choice of Austin as the MCC headquarters site set off a building boom in 1983–85 in this Texas city, which was accompanied by rapid population growth and by a quickening rate of high-tech spin-off companies. As a Texas official remarked, "The rocket took off."

By 2000, Austin's population had doubled to 1.2 million people, many of whom worked in the city's 1,800 high-technology companies. Some 20 percent of the workforce is employed in high-tech jobs, with 35 percent indirectly employed (represented by the people who work for the travel agencies, restaurants, and other suppliers of services to the high-tech companies). Austin experienced a 35 percent rate of increase in gross regional product (the total earnings in the region), about 2.5 times the growth rate of the booming U.S. economy during the same period. Austin became the number one U.S. city in semiconductor manufacturing, and also in computer manufacturing (mainly due to one local start-up, Dell Computer). The Silicon Hills technopolis ranked number four in computer software development in the United States, with some 450 software companies employing about 30,000 workers.

Much of the growth in the Austin technopolis has been fueled by start-up companies during the 1990s decade. The number of new high-technology companies established in Austin per year keeps increasing: from 119 start-ups in 1994, to 141 in 1995, to 163 in 1996, to 178 in 1997, to 203 start-ups (some 70 percent of which are software companies) in 1998. Once Silicon Hills passed the critical mass point in the late 1980s, further growth of the technopolis increased at an increasing rate, and this entrepreneurial expansion became self-sustaining. Venture capital companies, originally very scarce in Austin, were soon attracted to Texas by the lure of promising investments. By 2000, 27 local venture capital companies provided $1.3 billion in investment funding.

Unfortunately, the Austin technopolis grew so rapidly that roads and highways and other public facilities could not keep up with the rapid population growth. Traffic is hopelessly congested, and people complain about the hours they waste every day in stalled traffic. The MoPac, one of the main superhighways through Austin, has become a 10-mile long parking lot in the morning and evening commuting periods. Air and water pollution is becoming problematic. High-tech companies pay relatively high wages, so the cost of living in Austin has increased. Here we see a common problem of a fast-growing technopolis: an attractive quality of life leads to skyrocketing growth, which in turn destroys much of the original quality of life.

What lesson can be drawn from the case of the Austin technopolis (and of similar technopolises)? *The main factor in economic development in an information society is the entrepreneurial process through which research-based technological innovations are commercialized in high-technology spin-off companies.*

❏ *Sulekha*: The Global Web Magazine from Austin

Begun in 1998 by an Indian-American couple living in the Silicon Hills around Austin, *Sulekha* (literally "good writing") has become a highly popular global Web magazine. In mid-1999, *Sulekha* (www.sulekha.com) recorded over 3,000 hits a day with visitors from 60 countries, and with its traffic increasing 25 to 30 percent per month. The aim of its founders, Sangeeta Kshetty and Satya Prabhakar, a computer scientist, is for *Sulekha* to become "the most popular writer-oriented culture magazine and community resource for Indians around the world" (Easwaran, 1999, p. 43).

Sulekha encourages the latent writing talents of thousands of Indians and other people of South Asian origin, offering a forum where non-resident Indians (NRIs) can publish their work, and provide insights into their experiences in a foreign land. This on-line publication appears daily. Each writer has a home page, complete with biographical sketch and a list of their published articles. One of the most popular forums on *Sulekha* is "Coffeehouse," where visitors can chat about any topic of their choice. Another site, called "*Sulekha* for Kids" was launched recently to encourage creative writing by the younger generation of Indians around the world.

Sulekha earns revenues by providing direct Web links to its e-commerce partners such as Amazon.com, Barnes and Nobles, and other relevant Internet sites (including locations where Indian groceries can be purchased). Like other Internet ventures, *Sulekha* has the ability to remove the effect of physical distance from human communication. Given the widespread scattering of Indians in their global diaspora, *Sulekha* is a unifying literary force.

Bangalore: India's "Silicon Plateau"[16]

Bangalore is India's most well-entrenched technopolis (Figure 4.1). Some call Bangalore "Silicon Plateau," referring to the city's location at some 3,000 feet above sea level, which gives it a pleasant climate throughout the year (Singhal and Rogers, 1989; S. Rao, in press). The story of Bangalore's rise as a technopolis begins several hundred years ago.

Figure 4.1: Location of the Bangalore and Hyderabad technopolises

Two Indian cities have emerged in the 1990s as technopolises (technology cities). The rapid growth of the high-technology industry in both cities has been fueled by computer software start-ups.

■ **Historical Background of Bangalore**

Bangalore was first settled in 1537, when Kempegowda I, the ruler of Yelahanka, built an expansive mud fort; its four watch towers signified the boundaries of "Bengalooru" township. The British took a particular fancy to Bangalore, after defeating the armies of Hyder Ali and his son Tipu Sultan in the Anglo-Mysore Wars of the late 1700s. Charmed by the landscape of the high plateau country, its hills and valleys, its salubrious climate, and its strategic military location in south-central India, far removed from the sea, the British made Bangalore the home of their military garrisons in 1809. From a city of mud forts, small markets, and military hamlets, Bangalore rose to become a modern British military cantonment city in the mid-19th century, complete with army barracks, parade grounds, and officers' clubs. During the era of Mark Cubbon, the British Commissioner of Mysore from 1834 to 1861, some 1,600 miles of new roads and 309 bridges were built, connecting Bangalore with all of the district headquarters in the state. Telegraph lines were strung and a rail link was established with neighboring towns, making Bangalore the nucleus of trade routes in South India.

In the 1880s, the British government restored the princely state of Mysore, with the Maharaja as its ruler. Aided by the progressive vision of rulers like Maharaja Krishnaraja Wodeyar IV, who ruled from 1900 to 1940, and his able *dewans* (prime ministers) Seshadiri Iyer, Sir M. Visvesvaraya, and Mirza Ismail, a number of scientific and technological institutions emerged in Bangalore, including the Indian Institute of Science (IISc), India's first privately established research university. Several engineering colleges, polytechnics, and vocational training centers were established to fuel high-tech development.

After independence, Bangalore became a center for defense-related R&D laboratories and defense industries because of its key location in South India, far from Pakistani bombers, and because of its network of scientific and technological institutions. The Indian National Aeronautics Laboratory, the Indian Space Research Organization (ISRO), and the Electronics and Radar Development Establishment are located in Bangalore. The main operations of Hindustan Aeronautics (the manufacturer of supersonic MIG aircraft for India's Air Force) and Bharat Electronics Limited (BEL), a defense contractor, are also located in Bangalore. Bharat Electronics Limited has been a "mother hen" to many of the high-tech spin-off companies in Bangalore; every year, some 10 to 15 percent of BEL engineers leave the company to join other electronics firms. Although only a few become entrepreneurs and start their own companies, ex–BEL engineers add to the pool of skilled technical personnel in Silicon Plateau.

This city of six million people, with one of the fastest economic growth rates in India, is the scientific and technological capital of India. Its premier research university, the Indian Institute of Science (IISc), was founded by visionary industrialist Sir Jamsetji Tata on land gifted by Maharaja Krishnaraja Wodeyar IV. Modeled after the California Institute of Technology, IISc was home to India's Nobel Prize–winning physicist, C.V. Raman, and was also a major influence on Homi Bhabha, founder of India's atomic energy program, and Vikram Sarabhai, who founded India's space program and the Indian Institutes of Management (IIMs). Both Bhabha, who taught theoretical physics at IISc, and Sarabhai, then a graduate student, helped establish the Cosmic Ray Research Laboratory at the IISc in the 1940s. They conducted cosmic shower experiments at heights of over 35,000 feet with the help of U.S. Air Force planes stationed in Bangalore during World War II.

While technology transfer from the IISc has not played a particularly important role in the rise of the Bangalore technopolis, the Institute conducts cutting-edge research in the basic and engineering sciences. Bangalore is also the site of numerous engineering colleges, which produce many of the technical professionals employed in its growing technopolis.[17]

❑ The Mysore Military Rockets

Previously a part of the princely Mysore state, Bangalore has been at the cutting edge of military defense research in India, especially in avionics and rocketry. Both Hindustan Aeronautical Limited (HAL) and the Indian Space Research Organization (ISRO) are headquartered in

Bangalore. However, Bangalore's fame in rocketry goes back several centuries.

Hyder Ali, who ruled Mysore from 1761 to 1782, and his son Tipu Sultan, ruler of Mysore from 1782 to 1799, gained international recognition for their stubborn military opposition to British rule in India. In fact, Tipu's story became the subject matter of a highly popular historical television serial, *Tipu Sultan*, broadcast on Doordarshan in the early 1990s. However, the contributions of Hyder Ali and Tipu Sultan to military rocket technology are relatively less known.

Hyder Ali was a champion of military technology, and his engineers were the first to develop gunpowder-propelled rockets using metal cylinders. Higher pressure was achieved in the metallic cylinders, representing a major innovation over the shellac-coated and paper-wrapped Chinese rockets and the heavier German rockets made of wood and glue-soaked sail cloth. The Mysore rockets, mounted on long bamboo sticks and fastened with leather thongs, had a range of up to 1 mile, and were particularly effective against enemy cavalry when hurled into the air or when skimmed along the ground.

Tipu Sultan, an innovator and a technology buff, improved on the rocket design by using pure iron castings, which allowed for higher thrust and a greater range (up to 1.5 miles). Tipu created a military division exclusively for his rocket troops, boosting their strength from 1,200 to 5,000 men. His rocket army, wielding 3-meter-long bamboo poles on which the metal cylinders were mounted, wreaked havoc on the British army during the Anglo-Mysore Wars of 1792 and 1799. While Tipu eventually lost the battle, the British were so impressed with the high quality of Tipu's rockets that they invested heavily in developing military rockets. The British rockets, patterned after Tipu Sultan's rockets, helped the British to battlefield success during the Anglo-French Napoleonic Wars (1806) and the Anglo-American War of 1812. In World War I, the Allies used the "Bangalore torpedo" to destroy German barbed wire and other defense installations in the trench warfare in France. And in the 1944 Normandy landings, Allied troops used Bangalore torpedoes to blast German fortifications, as they successfully invaded the coast of France.

■ Bangalore Becomes Silicon Plateau

The turning point in Bangalore's rapid growth as India's Silicon Plateau occurred in 1986 when Texas Instruments (TI) established a computer-aided design center in Bangalore for semiconductor chip design. The TI design center employed over 400 employees in 2000, and is equipped with a satellite dish which connects the Bangalore design team with other TI semiconductor design engineers at the company headquarters in Dallas. Each evening, at the end of the work day in Bangalore, the computer code written that day is relayed by satellite (via London) to Dallas, where the TI Dallas team then continues the effort. Thus, two days' worth of computer code can be produced in each 24-hour period thanks to the time zone differences. Importantly, TI India was incorporated under Indian law as a 100 percent software export organization.

G.R. Mohan Rao, the Indian-born vice-president of Texas Instruments, accompanied his company president from Dallas to India in 1983. They noted the high caliber of Indian engineers, the much lower salaries for skilled brainpower (about 10 percent of comparable salaries in the United States at that time), and the attractive climate of the "air-conditioned" city. The TI officials met in Delhi with then prime minister Rajiv Gandhi, who promised them that cumbersome government restrictions on the electronics industry were in the process of being removed. Richard Gall, the manager of TI India, stated: "We came because of the amount of talent that was available here. We could not hire enough software designers in Europe to meet demand, and India was producing more than it could use."

Once TI began operations in Bangalore, many other American high-tech companies quickly followed: DEC, 3M, Hewlett-Packard, and Motorola, for example. By 2000, some 82 multinational companies engaged in computer software operations were based in Bangalore; most had headquarters in the U.S. Many of these U.S. companies already employed Indian citizens at their American headquarters. Indians working in Silicon Valley played an important role in urging their companies to locate R&D or manufacturing operations in Bangalore.

Next, a wave of Indian high-tech companies were established in Bangalore as the agglomeration process got under way. Wipro, a leading Indian computer company headquartered in Mumbai, located its computer design and manufacturing operations in Bangalore. Another major Indian company, Infosys Technologies, specializing in high-end software solutions, is centered in Bangalore, and is an anchor tenant of the rising technopolis.

One function of a technology park in a technopolis is to facilitate the communication networking advantages of the agglomeration of high-tech companies. The proximity of the new ventures in a technology park encourages their entrepreneurs to share their business experience and technologies. Many technopolises have established technology parks in order to jump-start the growth of high-tech agglomeration. Bangalore has several technology parks, including the International Tech Park and the Electronics City, both located a dozen miles outside the city limits.

Bangalore, with about 500 high-technology companies, has a long way to go before rivaling such big-league technopolises as Boston (with about 3,600 high-tech companies), Washington, D.C. (with 3,000 companies), or Seattle, the Microsoft city with 2,500 high-tech companies. Silicon Valley has over 5,000 high-tech companies, with several more being born every day. So Bangalore is a promising technology city at the early stages of rapid growth. If it develops in a fashion similar to Silicon Valley, Bangalore will soon have several thousand high-tech companies, each with 10 or 20 or 50 employees, all trying to crowd out rivals and to grow larger so as to dominate their technology niche. It is unclear at present whether a high rate of high-tech spin-off is occurring in Bangalore. Such start-ups are fundamental to creating self-sustaining growth in a technopolis.

The Bangalore technopolis may choke on its own growth. The city's population doubled from three million to six million over the past two decades, bringing with it "more dirt, higher rents, and deteriorating electric and water supplies" (Niejahr, 1997, p. 32). Bangalore's air is now worse than Bangkok and Mexico City, cities that are notorious for their pollution. Bangalore's once-pleasant climate, its main attraction, is changing. Many companies use their own petrol generators to compensate for power outages, raising the city's temperature (ibid.). Motorola is one of the most important of the 130 foreign companies located in Silicon Plateau, employing 600 scientists and engineers in its Bangalore computer design center. However, in 1999, when Motorola wanted to expand its India operations, it decided to start a separate R&D

center in Hyderabad, given the pollution and traffic problems in Bangalore.

Hyderabad: An Emerging Technopolis[18]

While Bangalore was the first technopolis in India, its lead has since been followed by several other "wanna-be" technology cities.[19] One of these emerging technopolises is Hyderabad, the 400-year-old seat of the Nizams,[20] and at present the capital of the State of Andhra Pradesh. The visionary of a New Hyderabad is Chief Minister Chandrababu Naidu, who is commonly referred to as the "CEO of Andhra Pradesh Inc.," "Pentium Premier," and "Cyber Minister." He travels with his ubiquitous IBM Thinkpad computer to the United States and other high-tech nations in order to attract foreign companies to his ancient city. His Thinkpad was used to make a multimedia presentation to Bill Gates during the Microsoft chairman's 1998 visit to India, and when Naidu visited Gates in Seattle in 1999 (Plate 4.5). Naidu made a similar presentation to Bill Clinton when the U.S. president visited Hyderabad in spring 2000.

Naidu followed his father-in-law, N.T. Rama Rao, as chief minister of the state of Andhra Pradesh. Rao had become well known for playing "god" in various Indian movies. Rao was an old-style politician, handing out special benefits to the needy. The 49-year-old Naidu has an entirely different agenda, centering on computers and high-technology growth. Every morning, Naidu boots his IBM Thinkpad to check the water levels in the state reservoirs, power-generation statistics, progress on the state's infrastructural projects, and the number of files cleared by the state bureaucrats. Bottlenecks are identified, and Naidu uses his cell-phone to call the erring official with his signature line: "This is Chandrababu Naidu speaking." Naidu, perhaps more than any other Indian politician, realizes the importance of information technology in governance, and of building a technopolis as a means of regional economic development. He holds regular videoconferences with district collectors of Andhra Pradesh, pursuing his IT vision with a vengeance. Naidu stated: "I want to make Andhra Pradesh the best investment destination in the new millennium."

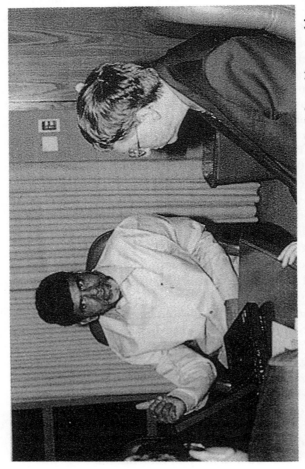

Plate 4.5: Andhra Pradesh's chief minister Chandrababu Naidu (left), making a multimedia presentation on his laptop computer to Microsoft Chairman Bill Gates, in his Seattle office

Hyderabad, the capital city of Andhra Pradesh, is fast rising as a technopolis under the visionary leadership of Naidu. The Microsoft Corporation has operations in Hyderabad's HITEC complex, and participates in the Indian Institute of Information Technology, which trains technologists. Naidu, more than any other Indian political leader, understands the informatization strategy for development.

Source: http://www.andhrapradesh.com/. (used with permission).

Naidu envisions his city, Hyderabad, as the computer capital of India, with particular emphasis on computer software. He knows that relatively little infrastructure is required for software development, in comparison with computer hardware, semiconductors, or biotechnology. All that is needed to start a software company is lots of brainpower, plus a couple of powerful computers. Andhra Pradesh is well positioned for software development because such a high proportion of Indian software engineers are Andhrites. A further advantage of the computer software industry is that the product is in demand worldwide, so that much of the software sales from India are for export, bringing in foreign exchange. Finally, as pointed out previously, the English-language ability of educated Indians gives them a software advantage in global competition, as does the much lower salaries paid to software professionals. So India offers high-quality software products at a lower price; this advantage translates into the stock formula for a successful technological innovation: better, quicker, cheaper.

Naidu knows that to attract U.S. company officials and motivate them to locate their companies' R&D operations in Hyderabad, the city's rundown appearance must be refurbished. Traffic snarls must be remedied, and potholed streets repaired. So a massive clean-up and road construction campaign was launched in the late 1990s. Eighteen fly-overs were constructed to ease road traffic. Each fly-over was built in less than one year, as Naidu had boasted they would be. Some infrastructural improvements have been funded by a huge World Bank loan, particularly the computerization of all government offices in Andhra Pradesh.

Naidu calls his high-tech dream "Vision 2020." One component of this plan is the Hyderabad Information Technology and Engineering Consultancy (HITEC) City, a 10-story modernistic complex with an uninterrupted power supply and high bandwidth telecommunications facilities. The HITEC complex, opened in 1998, attracted Microsoft, Oracle, and Metamor Global Solutions as its residents. Naidu understands the importance of well-trained technologists, so he created the International Institute of Information Technology (IIIT), which has university status. Private companies like Microsoft, Motorola, and IBM are encouraged to provide training courses at the IIIT, which has helped get this new institution off to a fast start.

Naidu states: "My dream is to make Hyderabad a 'Cyberabad,' and bring Silicon Valley down here." Clearly, here is a government official who understands the informatization strategy of economic development.[21] The Chief Minister dispatched a dozen study groups of 25 MLAs from all political parties on nine-day tours of Malaysia, Singapore, and China, in order for these Andhra politicians to better understand what it takes to win in the global game of high-technology.

Hyderabad positions itself as an attractive alternative to Bangalore, which is suffering from overcrowding and a lessened quality of life. For example, Wipro Infotech, located in Bangalore, placed its large software facility in Hyderbad in 1998. Other hightech companies that are headquartered in Bangalore are opening branches in Hyderabad. By 2000, some 300 computer software companies had established operations in Hyderabad. The rapidly deteriorating quality of life in the Bangalore technopolis makes Hyderbad look better and better by comparison. Shrewdly, Naidu priced the cost of floor space in his HITEC City at about half that of Bangalore's Technopark.

Government Policies toward High-Tech Development

Several government policies are intended to help Bangalore and other rising technopolises grow rapidly, especially in the computer software industry. For example, in 1999, the Indian government established a $25 million venture capital fund especially to encourage software start-ups. The annual government budget for 2000–01 also included several fiscal incentives to promote the venture capital industry. Venture capital investments in Indian hightech companies grew from $20 million in 1996 to $750 million in 2000, and are expected to rise steeply to $10 billion by 2008 (Padmanabhan, 2000b). Overall, the free-market policies of the NEP eased government controls on importing technology, foreign currency, and on raising capital. The NEP also invited competition for Indian companies from multinational corporations.

State government policies, such as those of Chief Minister Chandrababu Naidu in Andhra Pradesh, may be at least as important as national government policies in building technopolises.

For example, Naidu supplied the vision of Hyderabad as a technopolis, and then pursued policies and actions to make this dream come true. An elected politician is vulnerable in leading a technopolis, as there is always the chance that he or she might not be re-elected. In 1998 when Naidu invited Bill Gates, President of Microsoft, to inaugurate HITEC City in Hyderabad, Gates deferred his visit to the year 2000 (after the 1999 political election in Andhra Pradesh). Naidu told Gates, "Don't worry, I'll be there." He was indeed re-elected as chief minister of the state.

While government policies can play an important role in building a technopolis, the experience of technopolises around the world indicates that collaboration between government, private companies, and research universities (or other R&D institutions) is essential. *Collaboration* is the process through which each unit in a system voluntarily agrees to unite with other units to pursue common goals. The basis of collaboration is identifying and pursuing win/win opportunities for mutual gain. For example, the Austin technopolis arose because leaders in the Texas state government, at the University of Texas, and in private companies agreed to collaborate in building a technology city (Gibson and Rogers, 1994).

Wealthy individuals and corporations provided $60 million for the construction of a building for the Microelectronics and Computer Technology Consortium (MCC) on the University of Texas Balcones Research Park. Several dozen endowed professorships in electrical engineering and computer science were created at the University of Texas. Some 20 U.S. electronics companies collaborated in providing several million dollars each per year, as also contributing their most talented R&D workers to their jointly owned R&D consortium in Austin. The result, several years later, was the Austin technopolis, which benefitted all of the collaborating organizations.

So one of the important lessons learned about growing a technopolis is the crucial value of collaboration. Is this value a part of Indian culture? How could government policies be designed to encourage collaboration for high-technology economic development? The answers to these questions are not yet clear, at least in the context of India.

One problem is that high-tech businesses are regulated locally or nationally, but in today's world they compete *globally*. This fundamental fact is one factor that forced India to adopt the NEP. Further, the enthusiastic efforts of Bangalore, Hyderabad, and other Indian technopolises to attract the Microsofts, Motorolas, and Texas Instruments compels the Indian government to prune its cumbersome regulations so as to give the invisible hand of the marketplace greater freedom. Thus is India entering a prominent place on the world stage of high-technology.

■ Problems in Paradise

While technopolises are centers of wealth creation, and might appear to represent a kind of economic paradise, they are also characterized by a high degree of socio-economic inequality, and by other troublesome social problems. Top executives in Silicon Valley corporations, for instance, annually earn as much as 200 times an average production worker's salary. Some 20 percent of all the jobs pay less than a living wage for a single adult, and nearly 55 percent of Silicon Valley jobs pay too little to support a family of four (Mendoza, 1999). In fact, the hourly wages of 75 percent of Silicon Valley workers were actually lower in 1996 than in 1989. These skilled manual workers, employed in highly monotonous assembly-line jobs, make up about half of the Silicon Valley workforce of 500,000 individuals. In 2000, *The New York Times* published a photograph of people sleeping on a bus; they were employed but homeless, earning annual incomes of $50,000, which is insufficient to own or rent decent housing in Silicon Valley where, as noted previously, the median price of a home is an astronomical $410,000. So people are forced to buy a bus ticket for the two-hour ride around Silicon Valley; then they must exit, buy another bus ticket, and go to sleep again (Nieves, 2000).

On the south-western outskirts of Bangalore, where the International Tech Park was built, some 3,500 day laborers, many of them women, toiled daily for 10 to 12 hours, earning $1 a day. They built India's most modern office buildings, with glass facades, by ferrying large wooden bowls full of concrete on their heads. The engineers who design software in these swank offices earn incomes that are 30 to 40 times the wages of the day laborers. A technopolis is characterized by extreme inequality between the technologists and other upper-middle-class professionals, and the skilled proletariat workforce and daily wage laborers. Viewed from the underside, neither Silicon Valley nor Bangalore looks much like paradise. When young, middle-class Indians in a Bangalore cyber cafe surf the Net and sip cappuccino, the view through the cafe's tinted windows is one "of rickshaws, cows, and emaciated beggars" (Niejahr, 1997, p. 31).

The exploitation of the underprivileged sections of society is often legitimized by offering the success stories of the newly wealthy few as "carrots." This problematic dynamic should be understood as a dominant characteristic of free-wheeling capitalism as expressed in contemporary technopolises. However, growth with equity, or at least with a conscious concern for equity, is possible (as illustrated in the next chapter by the case of the Grameen Bank telephone ladies in Bangladesh).

The experience of Silicon Valley, Bangalore, and several other technopolises suggests that as a technopolis experiences very rapid growth, one should expect more traffic jams, higher levels of atmospheric pollution, a heavier burden on the public and civic infrastructure, a higher cost of living, and greater socio-economic inequality: the so-called "price of progress."[22] Perhaps these social problems can be minimized through their anticipation and amelioration, but inevitably the once high quality of life suffers. Thus the golden goose of high-tech wealth creation fouls its own nest.

Conclusions

While India is for the most part a developing country characterized by poverty, poor health, and illiteracy, this huge nation also contains a number of "hotspots" of rapid economic development. One of these is Bangalore, a technopolis specializing in computer software, much of it for export sale. Bangalore is not the only aspiring technopolis in India, with Hyderabad rising as a rival center for high-technology companies. There are also several others. Here, famous foreign firms like Microsoft and Motorola come together with Wipro and Infosys, sparking high-tech spin-offs that create an Indian-style technopolis.

As defined previously, a *high-technology industry* is one whose core technology changes rapidly. Microelectronics, the industry based on the applications of semiconductor chips, is of main interest in India, especially computer software. A *technopolis* is a geographically concentrated high-tech complex characterized by a large number of entrepreneurial spin-off companies. A *spin-off* is a new company that is created (*a*) by individuals who leave a parent organization, (*b*) around a technology that these entrepreneurs bring with them from the parent organization. *Agglomeration* is the degree to which some quality is concentrated spatially in one area. Spin-offs tend to agglomerate in Bangalore, Hyderabad, or other technopolises.

Technopolises like Bangalore and Hyderabad are extreme illustrations of India's informatization strategy. Here, vast fortunes in individual and corporate wealth are created, and new jobs generated, as Indian brainpower competes with the best and brightest of Europe, America, and the rest of the world. Indian technologists and entrepreneurs excel not only in Bangalore, Hyderabad, and other technopolises in India, but also in Silicon Valley and in technopolises around the world.

Perhaps Indians have a unique ability to flourish in high-technology entrepreneurship. Some part of this success may be traced to the excellent engineering education provided by India's IITs and to the management skills imparted by the IIMs. Although these educational institutions were created in another time and for a different purpose, today they place India in an advantageous position, globally, for informatization. The long tradition of India's merchant class, now expressed in a quite different arena, helps contribute to intense entrepreneurial fever. So do the role models provided by Vinod Khosla, Sabeer Bhatia, Atin Malaviya, and Gururaj Deshpande.

Notes

1. As noted in Chapter 1, we prefer, for simplicity, to use "technopolises" as the plural form of technopolis.

2. The University of California at Berkeley, a premier research university in the U.S., also fueled the rise of Silicon Valley, although not to the extent that Stanford University did.

3. MedBookStore.com, co-founded by Sundeep Bhan and three other Indians, is another well-known "dot-com" company that offers medical books, CD-ROMs, and other related products on-line (Dolan, 1999). The 1999 sales of this Manhattan-based on-line retailer were about $10 million, up 300 percent from the previous year.

4. One reason why Indian entrepreneurs in Silicon Valley are increasingly involved in start-ups is that the Internet represents a "new" area of business opportunity, where they have an "equal" opportunity to compete with others. In contrast, in the personal computer business, a start-up would need to compete with highly entrenched companies.

5. By spring 2000, Healtheon's stock was trading between $30 and $35, down from its 1999 highs.

6. A year later, in spring 2000, Healtheon's stock was down to its IPO levels (see note 5 above), substantially reducing the net worths of Nigam and Kolluri. However, they were still multimillionaires.

7. This case draws upon Pais (1999) and J. Rao (1999).

8. Rajvir Singh, a veteran of several high-tech start-ups in Silicon Valley (including Fiberlane, Stratum One, Siara, Advancel, InterHDL, and Roshnee Corporation), also played an important role in the co-founding of Cerent Corporation. He is a role model for many Indians.

9. Analysts estimate that, in 1999, some 70 percent of the business proposals made to Silicon Valley venture capitalists were from Indians.

10. Hotmail was launched consciously on 4 July, the U.S. Independence Day, to symbolize "freedom." A Hotmail user was not tied to a particular Internet service provider, and could freely access his/her account from anywhere in the world.

11. America Online, the world's second leading email service provider, has over 20 million members.

12. Bhatia and K.B. Chandrasekhar, founder of Exodus Communications (see Chapter 1), serve on a committee of the Securities and Exchange Board of India (SEBI) whose mission is to fuel the growth of India's venture capital industry.

13. Another Silicon Valley venture capital firm, Draper, specializes in U.S./India start-ups.

14. Indians now hold senior management positions in U.S. high-tech corporations like Microsoft, Yahoo!, Cisco, and Intel. Arun Netravalli is head of Bell Labs; Srinija Srinivasan is Editor-in-Chief of Yahoo!;

Anil Kripalani is Senior Vice-President of Qualcomm, and Rajiv Gupta is chief of Hewlett-Packard's e-services program. Indians are also well known in U.S. academic and policy circles relating to high-tech. For instance, Raj Reddy, the Herbert A. Simon University Professor at Carnegie Mellon University and world-renowned for his research in artificial intelligence, was appointed in 1999 by President Clinton as the co-chairman of the President's Information Technology Advisory Committee (PITAC). This committee's purpose is to accelarate the development and adoption of information technologies vital for American prosperity in the 21st century.

15. Sycamore Networks is a leader in the area of optical transmission and switching technologies, which transmit voice, text, or video through photons (not electrons), thus greatly enhancing bandwidth.

16. This section draws upon Singhal and Aikat (1993).

17. In the 1980s and 1990s, various new private engineering and medical colleges were established in the city of Bangalore, and more generally in the State of Karnataka.

18. For more information on the rise of Hyderabad as a technopolis, and Chandrababu Naidu's IT–friendly policies, visit http://www.andhra-pradesh.com/.

19. Other emerging technopolises in India include Hyderabad, the Mumbai–Pune Knowledge Corridor, Thiruvananthapuram, NOIDA, Gurgaon, Chennai, Calcutta, Bhubaneshwar, Mohali, Indore, and Coimbatore (Dutta, 1999).

20. The Nizams were the Islamic rulers of Hyderabad and its surrounding area; they lived fabled lives of luxury with multiple wives and impressive palaces.

21. In the World Economic Forum's *World Link* magazine survey, Naidu was selected as a member of the 15-person "dream" cabinet of outstanding world leaders (sharing the honors with British prime minister Tony Blair, New Zealand foreign minister Don McKinnon, and others).

22. The public works infrastructure of most Indian cities is highly inadequate, a problem compounded by the influx of migrants from rural and other areas. Bangalore, perhaps more than any other Indian city in recent decades, has witnessed a massive influx of people from outside the state, overburdening its infrastructure. Some two decades ago, the ratio of Kannadigas (natives of Karnataka state of which Bangalore is a part) to non-Kannadigas was 70:30. By 2000, this ratio had been reversed.

5 The telecommunications revolution

"Telecommunications is still the most confused policy issue in India. It has resulted in almost as many committees as new telephone lines."

RAJADHYAKSHA (1999).

"In India, to touch the roof, one needs to aim at the moon."

SAM PITRODA (1998), the visionary leader of India's telecommunications revolution.

T hirty-five years ago, one of the present book's authors was walking down the corridor of a government ministry building in New Delhi, when he overheard a snatch of telephone conversation while passing an open office door. An Indian official was shouting in an irritated voice: "But Madam, I *am* speaking English!"

This event would be less likely to occur today, as telephone service has markedly improved in both urban and rural areas. A basic reason for this improvement in telephone quality is the national government's realization that a reliable telecommunications infrastructure is essential for socio-economic development. Until recent decades, the telephone was considered a luxury good, and thus given low priority by government officials (McDowell, 1997, p. 2). This mistaken perspective was replaced, beginning in the 1980s, by a view that telecommunications services are essential for business, industry, and economic development. This newer policy is, of course, an informatization strategy of development. By improving telephone services, all types of business transactions become more efficient, as do government operations. The economy is thus able to operate more effectively, bringing benefits to many.

The telecommunications revolution began in the mid-1980s under the leadership of Prime Minister Rajiv Gandhi, India's "high-tech" national leader, and Satyen ("Sam") Pitroda, a U.S.–returned expatriate Indian. The revolution gathered momentum in the 1990s, spurred by the sweeping economic reforms of then finance minister Manmohan Singh, aided by visionary bureaucrats such as N. Vittal, technocrats such as T. Hanuman Chowdary, and others.[1] This vast improvement in telephony has reached out to India's villages and market towns, thanks to the establishment of digital automatic exchanges and 650,000 public call offices (PCOs), which were located everywhere in India by 2000 (Plate 5.1).

What are telecommunications? They include all of the means of communicating at a distance (thus, *tele-communications*). So telecommunications, which originally meant mainly telephone services, in recent years have also come to include satellite transmission as well as telephone lines, and computer communication like that occurring via the Internet (which occurs by means of telephone lines and satellites).

The purpose of the present chapter is to describe the revolutionary changes occurring in India's telecommunications sector,

Plate 5.1: A PCO operator in New Delhi, who offers telephony, Internet, email, courier, fax, and photocopying services

Cyber cafes like this one in an urban area provide the public access to the new communication technologies for a small fee. In rich, industrialized nations like the United States, and for urban elites in India, a high degree of individual ownership of such telecommunications equipment occurs, and public access is much less important. However, for the middle class and the relatively economically disadvantaged sections of Indian society, such access is crucial.

Source: Personal files of the authors.

including the expansion of its infrastructure, its reformist policies, the possibilities of telecommunications-led rural development, and its coming of age with the new telecommunications technologies of the Internet which are revolutionizing business, industry, and other sectors of Indian society.

India's Telecommunications Expansion

When India gained independence in 1947, the new nation had 84,000 telephone lines for its population of 350 million. Thirty-three years later, by 1980, India's telephone service was still "wretched," with only 2.5 million telephones and 12,000 public phones for a population of 700 million; only 3 percent of India's 600,000 villages had telephone service. However, in the late 1990s, a sea change occurred in the telecommunications scenario: by 1999, India had an installed network of over 25 million telephone lines, spread across 300 cities, 4,869 towns, and 310,897 villages, making India's telecommunications network the ninth largest in the world (Bahadur, 1999). Especially notable is the fact that more than 80 percent of this national telecommunications infrastructure, approximately 20 million telephone lines, was added in the 1990s alone (Figure 5.1). How did this telecommunications revolution take place?

The numbers show that a telecommunications revolution of mammoth proportions is under way in India: between 1988 and 1998, the number of villages with some kind of telephone facility increased from 27,316 to 300,000 villages (this is half of all of India's villages). By 2000, some 650,000 public call offices providing reliable telephone service, where people can simply walk in, make a call, and pay the metered charges, had mushroomed all over India, including the remote, rural, hilly, and tribal areas (Plate 5.2).

The emergence of PCOs satisfies the strong Indian sociocultural need of keeping in touch with family members. Much like train travel in India which is often undertaken to celebrate marriages, visit relatives, or attend funerals, the telephone is also viewed as a way of maintaining close family ties. Not surprisingly, most advertisements for telephony service show mothers talking

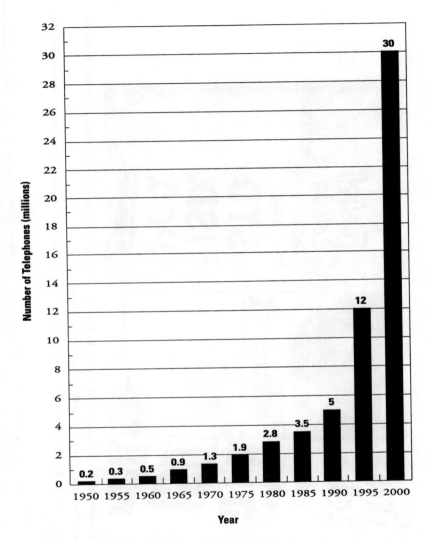

Figure 5.1: Growth in the number of telephones in India

A huge increase occurred in the 1990s in the number of telephones, due (*a*) to important advances in adapting telephone technologies to India's conditions; and (*b*) to increasing involvement of private operators and companies in manufacturing the equipment and providing telephone services.

Source: Singhal and Rogers (1989); Bahadur (1999).

Plate 5.2: A PCO operated by a village shop-owner in Kheda district of Gujarat state, offering subscriber trunk dial (STD) and international subscriber dial (ISD) telephony services

About 650,000 public call offices like this one have sprung up in India since 1988, reaching remote, rural, and tribal areas, creating jobs and income for the family that operates the PCO.

Source: Personal files of authors.

to their sons and daughters, or grandparents talking to grandchildren. Telephone expansion in India thus serves a strong sociocultural function for its users, in addition to a commercial one.

A staggering 117 billion metered calls were made in India from these PCOs in 1998 (Bahadur, 1999). Revenues of the Department of Telecommunications (DoT), the state-run telecommunications operator, increased from $790 million in 1988 to $4.3 billion in 1998, a five-fold increase in 10 years (Bahadur, 1999). Over the next several years, India plans to add four to five million digital telephone lines to increase its telephone density from 2.5 per 100 people in 1999, to 7 per 100 people by 2005, and to 15 by 2010.[2] So, by 2005, the number of telephones in India will rise to 75 million; projections for 2010 are pegged at 150 million. Massive investments running into billions of dollars (installing each telephone line costs about $750) are needed for this expansion, so private sector involvement will intensify. Mobile telephony represents one telecommunications sector where private sector involvement is especially important.

■ The Rise of Mobile Telephony

About 163 million mobile phones were purchased wordwide in 1998,[3] an increase of 51 percent over the previous year (Kaur, 1999b). Mobile telephone subscription is projected to increase from 46 million subscribers in all Asia–Pacific countries in 1996 (with 50 percent of these in Japan), to about 410 million subscribers in 2006. The two countries where most of this growth is projected to occur are India and China (Cable Waves, 1997). By 2001, China will have an estimated 30 million mobile phones, as compared to India's roughly 10 million. So while mobile telephones are becoming numerous in India, the rate of increase in China is rising much faster.

Mobile telephony services were introduced in India in 1995 along with pager services. By 1998, India had one million cellphone users in its four metropolitan cities, with 45 percent in Delhi followed by Mumbai (35 percent), Calcutta (12 percent), and Chennai (8 percent) (Cable Waves, 1997). Another 500,000 or so cell-phone users existed in other towns and cities, a number

190 INDIA'S COMMUNICATION REVOLUTION

that is rapidly climbing. Some analysts feel that mobile telephones would have diffused more rapidly in India if the cost of the handsets had not been so high.[4] While prices came down somewhat, a reasonably priced handset in 2000 still cost $250, compared to about $50 in the U.S.

In the late 1990s, adopters of mobile telephones in India were primarily urban elites: corporate leaders, businessmen, professionals, and upper-income families. The penetration of mobile phones in rural India, while small in number, was growing among village elites, primarily because mobile telephones circumvent the infrastructure needed for fixed telephone service, such as expensive digital exchanges or a regular power supply. For instance, Jagbir Singh, a brick kiln owner in Mohana village, Haryana, purchased five cell-phones for his staff because there was no fixed telephone in a 5-kilometer area. Well-to-do farmers in India often own mobile telephones, keeping in touch with block- and district-level officials, checking market information, scheduling transportation, pick-ups, and so forth (Plate 5.3). Many rural entrepreneurs sell mobile telephone services to truckers who travel on the highways near their village (Mishra, 1999).

So a telecommunications revolution is gathering momentum in urban and, to a lesser extent, in rural India. Here we highlight the various influences that have shaped India's telecommunications policy.

Changing Telecommunications Policies

Telecommunications services began in India in 1851 when a telegraph service became operational between Calcutta, then the seat of the British colonial government, and Diamond Harbor 21 miles away, a trading post of the British East India Company (Saran, 1997). The telegraph, and later the telephone (introduced in India in 1882), were viewed by the British as tools of command and control, essential to maintaining law and order in the country (Mody, 1997). For instance, India's attempt at challenging British rule in 1857, referred to as the "Sepoy Mutiny," was suppressed through the use of telegraph lines connecting the British rulers in India and their armies (Chowdary, 1998). In 1883, the British

Plate 5.3: A farmer using a mobile phone in Punjab state of India as he travels with his family by bullock cart

Mobile telephones have increased rapidly in number since their introduction in 1995, mainly in metropolitan areas. They are also used in rural areas where fixed-line service may not be available.

Source: India Today (used with permission).

merged the telegraph services with postal services to further increase their command and control in India. Runners, stationed at telegraph offices, carried telegrams to remote post offices, thereby linking the British rulers with even the most distant pockets of India (Mody, 1997).

After gaining independence from Britain in 1947, the national government continued the colonial legacy, organizing post and telegraph services exclusively in the domain of the state. Nehru's post-independence socialist policies committed India to state-run, state-owned monopolies in various sectors, including telephony (Chowdary, 1998). Managed by a slow-moving, overstaffed government machinery under the aegis of the Ministry of Posts and Telegraphs,[5] the performance of India's telecommunications sector was abysmally poor until the mid-1980s. The main reasons for this poor performance included (a) an official view that telephones were a "luxury" rather than a "necessity", (b) the dominance of the state-run telecommunications monopoly with no competitive pressures for innovation in telecommunications products, services, and pricing; (c) the absence, in the government telecommunications operation, of shareholder pressure for efficiency, profitability, sales growth, or market capitalization, (d) a bureaucratic, top–down telecommunications organization without delegation, initiative, or accountability, (e) an overstaffed structure of tens of thousands of telecommunications employees with inadequate job challenges or training, (f) strong unions of workers with considerable political clout, which led to skewed telecommunications policies to the benefit of employees while ignoring the needs of customers; and (g) the total dependence of the telecommunications sector on another state-owned monopoly, the Indian Telephone Industries (ITI), for the procurement of switches and telephones (Athreya, 1996).

Unfortunately for India, the Ministry of Posts and Telegraphs[6] focussed on improving the delivery of telegrams and telexes while other countries were embracing digital telephony and facsimile machines. India missed the opportunity of bypassing obsolescent technologies: telephone exchanges were slowly converted from crossbar to Strowger, and then even more slowly to digital; copper cables were first replaced by jelly-filled cables and then slowly by fiber optics. In essence, India missed the telecommunications boom of the 1970s and 1980s, which spurred the economies of Taiwan, Korea, Hong Kong, and Singapore.

■ Rajiv Gandhi: Sowing the Seeds of Social Change

The telecommunications sector got a shot in the arm when the "tech-savvy" Rajiv Gandhi became prime minister in 1984, and when Satyen (Sam) Pitroda, a U.S.–based Indian expatriate and a telecommunications wizard, returned to India to shake up a reluctant, monolithic, government monopoly. Rajiv Gandhi had been a professional airline pilot, used a laptop computer, and, during his administration, various structural and institutional changes occurred in the telecommunications sector. In Gandhi, India finally had a national leader who understood the informatization strategy of development. He unleashed the Indian potential in telecommunications.

In 1985, the Ministry of Post and Telegraphs was reorganized and a Department of Telecommunications (DoT) was formed under a new Ministry of Communications to focus exclusively on the telecommunications sector. In 1986, two new corporations, the Mahanagar Telephone Nigam Limited (MTNL) and the Videsh Sanchar Nigam Limited (VSNL) were established: MTNL to serve the lucrative subscriber markets of Delhi and Mumbai, and VSNL to provide overseas telecommunications services. More importantly, MTNL and VSNL introduced a market orientation into the telecommunications sector.[7]

Satyen Pitroda (see our illustrative case which follows), who established the Center for Development of Telematics (C-DOT) in New Delhi in 1984, was appointed by Prime Minister Rajiv Gandhi to head the Department of Telecommunications (DoT). Under Pitroda's leadership, various technology missions were formed,[8] including in telecommunications, identifying this sector as one of top national priority. Pitroda further established the Telecommunications Commission under the umbrella of DoT to speed up telecommunications decision-making and licensed private vendors to manufacture C-DOT's digital automatic exchanges, EPABXs, and telephone equipment, breaking for the first time the government's monopoly in telecommunications equipment production. Long-distance direct dialing services were introduced at a frenetic pace in major cities, towns, and district headquarters, and public call offices were established throughout India increasing telecommunications access for the common people while at the same time boosting DoT's revenues (Athreya, 1996).

India's telecommunications revolution was thus instigated by a technology-minded politician working closely with a visionary technologist.

❑ Sam Pitroda: Telecommunications Visionary for the Informatization Strategy

Satyen "Sam" Pitroda was born in the village of Titilagarh in the state of Orissa (Plate 5.4). The village's 6,000 people did not have central station electricity, running water or telephones. Pitroda majored in physics and electronics at the Maharaja Sayajirao University in Baroda, and earned a Master's degree in electrical engineering at the Illinois Institute of Technology in Chicago. Pitroda then worked for General Telephone Company (GTE) in Chicago, where he helped develop digital electronic switching systems. The advantage of this technology over analog switching equipment is that it has no electromechanical moving parts, uses semiconductor chips, and requires less space.

In 1974, Pitroda and two other entrepreneurs founded Wescom Switching Inc. to make telecommunications switches. Six years and a dozen patents later, Wescom was acquired by Rockwell International, Pitroda received $3.5 million, and became a Rockwell executive at $550,000 per year. One might imagine that Pitroda was fixed for life. Not so. At Rockwell, Pitroda became a keen observer of telecommunications problems in developing nations. Most telecommunications technology came from the industrialized countries, and did not suit the conditions of Latin America, Africa, and Asia, where dust, humidity, and an unreliable electrical supply were major problems for telephone service (Pitroda, 1993). Pitroda became convinced that India must develop an indigenous telecommunications industry if it were ever to become developed. He foresaw that communication technology was at the heart of the development process. In short, Pitroda was a visionary for the informatization strategy.

Plate 5.4: Sam Pitroda, the expatriate who returned to India to revolutionize telecommunications services

Satyen "Sam" Pitroda returned to India from the United States, where he had become a successful telecommunications technologist and entrepreneur, in the mid-1980s. He led C-DOT in developing improved telephone technologies for Indian conditions, and spearheaded government efforts in an informatization strategy for development. In 1995, Pitroda established WorldTel to assist developing nations in improving telecommunications services. WorldTel projects include the establishment of Internet community centers using local-language databases and applications software in six Indian states.

Source: WorldTel (used with permission).

In 1981, Pitroda traveled to India at his own expense, in order to present the idea of establishing the Center for Development of Telematics (C-DOT) to Prime Minister Indira Gandhi and her son Rajiv.

Pitroda argued that Indian telecommunications were characterized by high traffic, low density, and extreme climatic conditions unlike the industrialized countries of the West. India needed to achieve self-reliance in developing appropriate telecommunications technology, so that it did not have to utilize its scarce foreign exchange to import telecommunications equipment, hence, C-DOT. Finally, in 1984, this R&D center, funded by the Indian government, was mandated to design indigenous telecommunications switching systems.

Pitroda hired 400 youthful engineers, mainly recent graduates of IITs and regional engineering colleges, and set them to work for long hours per day in a former luxury hotel in Delhi. Under the leadership of Pitroda, who carried the title of "advisor," C-DOT met its goals. He was paid the token rate of 1 rupee (2 U.S. cents) per year. Rural telephone exchanges were developed that could function under tough conditions, and then licensed to private manufacturers. Some 72 private manufacturers of C-DOT telecommunications technologies existed in India in 1999; 450 additional private vendors supply them with components. In this sense, C-DOT has become the "mother hen" of various spin-off telecommunications businesses, contributing to wealth and job creation. In 1999, seven million C-DOT exchange lines, about 30 percent of India's total installed lines, were operational. Consistent with Pitroda's vision, C-DOT products were also exported to various other developing countries including Bangladesh, Nepal, Vietnam, Ethiopia, Russia, Uganda, Ghana, Angola, Namibia, Nigeria, and Yemen.

In 1987, Prime Minister Rajiv Gandhi appointed Pitroda as principal advisor for National Technology Missions, which included telecommunications, immunization, drinking water, literacy, dairy, oilseeds, and wastelands development. Pitroda became in essence the czar of India's development programs. He was also appointed head of the Department of Telecommunications (DoT) and chairman of the newly founded Telecommunications Commission.

Pitroda (1993) cited an example of the importance of telecommunications in every type of development. The goal of his drinking water mission was to make 40 liters of clean water available per person per day in 100,000 problem villages. Officials in the Ministry of Rural Development proposed to purchase 40 imported drilling rigs at a cost of several million dollars. But no one knew how many drilling rigs were already in India, or how many wells per year each rig could drill. Pitroda found a UNICEF official who reported that India already had 1,200 drilling rigs. Analysis showed that a well could be drilled in 10 hours, but then 10 days were required to move the rig to the next site. These 10 days were spent in bureaucratic wrangling in selecting the site, negotiating political priorities, and moving the rig (which only took a day or two). An adequate telecommunications network would allow Ministry officials to cut the 10 days down to five days; thus India would have the equivalent of 1,200 new well-drilling rigs without importing a single one! Here the informatization strategy saved India millions of dollars in foreign exchange.

By 2000, India had about 30 million telephones, or one telephone for every 34 persons. In comparison, Americans have one telephone for every 1.5 persons. In order to provide greater accessibility to telephone service, Pitroda equipped ordinary telephones with small meters. This equipment was sold to local entrepreneurs who set up manned public call offices (PCOs) on makeshift tables in bazaars, at street corners, or in shops whose owners use them to attract customers. The telephone entrepreneurs are billed only six times per year, and get a 25 percent discount as their commission. The metered telephones are in such constant use that the income from one telephone is enough to support an entire family. By 2000, some 650,000 of these public call offices (PCOs), each identified by a bright yellow sign, had been installed across India.

After the fall of the Rajiv Gandhi government in 1989 and Rajiv's assassination in 1991, Pitroda lost his powerful influence in government circles, and eventually moved back to Chicago. However, his interest in improving telecommunications in developing countries continues. In 1995, he founded WorldTel, a multilateral funding organization dedicated to developing telecommunications in Latin America, Africa, and Asia. WorldTel is headquartered in London, and has an office in Geneva to facilitate its sponsorship by the International Telecommunications Union (ITU). Pitroda and his colleagues at WorldTel identify potentially profitable telecommunications projects in developing countries, and then bring together telecommunications operators, governments, and private investors. In order to catalyze the process, WorldTel has its own seed capital of $10 million, provided by a Kuwaiti investment group, by GE Capital, and other private companies to help developing countries harness the power of telephony, the Internet, and other telecommunications technologies.

In 1999, the state governments of Andhra Pradesh, Tamil Nadu, Kerala, Karnataka, West Bengal, and Gujarat contracted with WorldTel to help upgrade PCOs to Internet community centers (ICCs), each equipped with a multimedia capability to send and receive text/voice-mail, provide Internet services, videoconferencing, and photocopying. Some 1,000 of these ICCs are being established across Tamil Nadu; they are similar to the cyber cafes found in urban areas, but charge about half the latter's user fees. Over 90 percent of all Web pages are written only in the English language. So the WorldTel ICC projects in India involve providing relevant, needs-oriented, demand-driven application software and databases in the local language, for example, in Telugu in Andhra Pradesh. The ICCs will allow both urban and rural people to apply for school or college admission, check farm prices, locate the nearest hospital, and so forth, on-line. WorldTel has similar projects under way in Mexico, Azerbaijan, and Peru, and has projects planned in four African nations.

Through WorldTel, Sam Pitroda is expanding the informatization strategy that he developed in India, on a worldwide basis.

■ The New Economic Policy

When the Rajiv Gandhi government fell in 1989, Pitroda's influence with the DoT bureaucrats waned, and the pace of telecommunications reforms slowed down until the Narasimha Rao government came to power in 1991. Led by Finance Minister Manmohan Singh, the Rao government, responding to a national economic crisis, announced a series of path-breaking policy changes. These came to be referred to as the New Economic Policy (NEP). At the time, NEP looked like bitter medicine for India.

The five main components of NEP include: (*a*) *devaluation* of the Indian rupee in order to increase exports,[9] (*b*) *deregulation* or dismantling of government controls over domestic industry, (*c*) *privatization*, including formation of jointly owned public–private enterprises and the sale of public sector enterprises, (*d*) *liberalization* or opening up of monopoly markets to increase foreign and domestic competition, and (*e*) *globalization* by opening the Indian economy to foreign investment (Sinha, 1996). Essentially, the NEP was a massive and radical change in India's political economy toward free-market forces, an about-face that occurred across the continuum of political economy from left to right. Adam Smith's "invisible hand" of business competition would determine prices, the volumes of sales, and other economic factors in the Indian economy.

Under the NEP, infrastructural sectors such as power, telecommunications, roads, ports, harbors, and civil aviation were especially targeted for liberalization, de-monopolization, direct foreign investment, and privatization. The winds of macroeconomic change, spurred by the NEP, were blowing hard enough to force the monolithic DoT to respond, albeit slowly and with great reluctance (Athreya, 1996; Chowdary, 1998). The pace of telecommunications reform picked up in 1993 when N. Vittal, previously Secretary in the Department of Electronics and a visionary technocrat, was appointed head of DoT. Championing the cause of private industry and of telephone users,[10] Vittal was instrumental in the formulation of the National Telecommunication Policy of 1994 (NTP-94), which (a) aimed to provide telephone service on demand to consumers (before NTP-94, customers had waited[11] for one or several years before getting a telephone connection; (b) promoted rapid expansion of the telecommunications network, (c) sought to achieve international standards of service quality, and (d) invited direct foreign and private investments for telecommunications expansion (ibid.).

❑ Keeping Up with State-of-the-Art Technology: WLL

One advantage of deregulation, privatization, and liberalization in India's telecommunications sector was the rapid deployment and assimilation of state-of-the-art technology. In this sense, the 1990s are a far cry from the 1960s and 1970s, when India consciously adopted the obsolescent analog Strowger telephone exchanges while the emerging tigers of the Asian economy were going digital. One state-of-the-art telecommunications technology of the late 1990s, which India quickly adopted and indigenized with foreign collaborators, was the Wireless Local Loop (WLL) system. This system makes possible a high-quality, two-way radio connection between a telephone set and a local exchange, providing an expeditious and cost-effective way of bringing basic telephony services to previously unconnected areas, bypassing traditional wireline solutions.

Deployment of WLL began in India in 1997, when MTNL began offering mobile telephony services in Delhi. By the year 2000, WLL was expected to reach 60 million subscribers worldwide, of which an estimated eight million would be in India (Chowdhary, 1999a). Telecommunications giants Ericsson, Qualcomm, Nokia, Lucent Technologies, and others are aggressively pushing WLL systems in India. Tata Lucent Technologies has already received a $340 million contract from Tata Teleservices in Andhra Pradesh to supply 50,000 fixed wireless terminals. Systems based on WLL are ideally suited for expansion of telephony services in rural areas, where the costs of laying telephone lines from a digital exchange to end-users may not make economic sense. WorldTel's telecommunications and Internet initiatives in India, Peru, Mexico, and Azerbaijan (see the case on Sam Pitroda earlier in the chapter) employ WLL technology.

Also in the final phases of trial in India is CorDECT, an indigenous version of WLL developed by the Indian Institute of Technology, Chennai, in collaboration with Midas Communications Technologies of Chennai and U.S.–based Analog Devices. This technology offers wireline voice quality and integrates seamlessly with the existing public-switched telephone network (PSTN) in India. It also offers high-speed data transmission facilities, Internet access, and ISDN services. Establishing a CorDECT telephone line costs from $275 (U.S.) to $375 (U.S.), less than half of the cost of a wired telephone line, $750 (U.S.).

India's present experiments with CorDECT, and its past experience with C-DOT's technologies, demonstrate that, given a facilitative policy environment, the nation can forge state-of-the-art indigenous solutions to meet telecommunication needs.

■ Problems in Implementing Policy

The Indian experience with NTP-94 showed that "while policy formulation is difficult, policy implementation is even more beset with problems," especially in "a hitherto state-run telecommunication service, with 425,000 unionized employees" (Athreya, 1996, p. 20). While private investments, from both domestic and overseas sources, poured into India for basic fixed services and cellular services, DoT's complex rules and procedures, self-serving tariff structures, and painfully slow procedures for bidding and granting licenses led to unnecessary delays, snags, and low returns on investment for most private operators (S. Rekhi, 1998; Chowdhary, 1999b). Several foreign telecommunications companies like Bell Canada, US West, Swisscom, and AT&T,[12] which entered India in 1995–96 when the government opened up the telecommunications sector, were disillusioned by the unfriendly tariffs and fees, and either froze their investments or pulled out of India. They realized that the license fees they had committed to DoT were unreasonably high and far beyond the returns envisaged.[13] However, DoT, the state-run telephone operator and licensor, demanded that private operators maintain their payment schedules or else face termination of their licenses.

Consequently, the Telecommunications Regulatory Authority of India (TRAI) was established through an Act of Parliament in 1997 to regulate telecommunications services.[14] Its role was envisaged as an autonomous regulator, responsible for formulating new telecommunications policies, settling disputes, managing competition by ensuring a level playing field, and, foremost, preserving the long-term interests of the customer. However, DoT and TRAI have been locked in a bitter turf battle from the day that TRAI was founded (Ahluwalia, 1999). In most cases, DoT continues to believe, often mistakenly, that it is the prerogative of the government to formulate policies, even if they are monopolistic.[15] So several matters of contention between DoT, the private operators, and TRAI were being litigated in India's courts in 2000.

Although the story of private investment in the telecommunications sector spurred by NTP-94 was beset with many problems, the growth of telecommunications infrastructure in India continued at a rapid rate in the late 1990s. Some 1.7 million new telephone connections were provided in 1994–95, 2.2 million in 1995–96, 2.6 million in 1996–97, 3.3 million in 1997–98, and 3.8 million in 1998–99. Also, several private operators such as Bharati Telecom (in Madhya Pradesh), Hughes Ispat (in Maharashtra), Essar Commvision (in Punjab), and others began offering fixed and cellular services in several regions of India, further expanding India's telecommunications network, offering value-added services (like voice-mail), and establishing higher standards of customer service. Consequently, DoT also introduced several customer-friendly initiatives.[16] For instance, as part of its "Phone on Demand" scheme, DoT officials personally visit the residence of the individual requesting a telephone connection, to install a telephone within two to three days. Such customer responsiveness was unthinkable a few years ago. Competition from private operators is also compelling DoT officials in various states to come up with different service–price packages for different customer needs.[17]

To strengthen the resolve reflected in NTP-94 to boost India's telecommunications sector, Prime Minister Atal Behari Vajpayee constituted a Group on Telecommunications (GOT) as part of the National Task Force on Information Technology and Software (NTFIT&SW). The GOT, headed by leading industrialist Ratan Tata, submitted its recommendations for a National Telecommunications Policy (NTP-99). The New Telecom Policy '99 marked a significant juncture as it opened the telecommunications market to increased competition in both cellular and basic telephone services, which may result in lower telephony prices and improved customer service. As a follow-up to NTP-99, the government opened up the domestic long-distance market to private competition in mid-2000. Also, TRAI was vested with greater jurisdiction to ensure a level playing field, especially between DoT and other private operators (Chowdary, 1999c). The New Telecom Policy '99 holds several advantages for private operators who can enter all areas of telecommunications services with a one-time entry fee. Also, instead of paying a fixed license fee for every customer (previously set by DoT at $12 per month per customer) irrespective of their earnings, private operators pay a predetermined percentage of their revenues to DoT. Industry analysts feel that NTP-99 could usher in new investments in the telecommunications sector, as regulatory laws have become more investor-friendly and equipment prices have been lowered substantially (Roy, 1999).

In summary, the Indian telecommunications sector has come a long way since the 1980s. The sector's efforts at reform, restructuring, and growth, especially in the 1990s, were a function of the economic transformation experienced by India, spurred by the

New Economic Policy (Athreya, 1996; Sinha, 1996). The telecommunications reforms represent a compromise among the various political, economic, and bureaucratic interests in the telecommunications arena, including multinational and domestic companies, local equipment manufacturers, DoT's 425,000 unionized workers, and millions of telephone users (Petrazzini, 1996; Sinha, 1996). The telecommunications scenario of the early 1980s, characterized by limited access, monopolistic control, customer neglect, and the perception of "telephones as luxury," was transformed in the new millennium into one of increased access, private investment, increased competition, customer responsiveness, regulation of services, and the perception of "telephones as a necessity." These changes indeed represent a telecommunications revolution in India.

While slow to formulate policy and implement reforms, India's telecommunications sector is guided by a growing understanding of the important role of telecommunications in national development, and the importance of adopting state-of-the-art telecommunications technologies; it is guided, that is, by the informatization strategy of development.

❑ Get a Mobile Phone, Pay Income Tax

Many observers view India's telecommunications reforms as "one step forward, two steps backward." Compromises are made at each step between various political, economic, and bureaucratic interests, as the following illustration demonstrates.

New subscriptions to mobile telephony services dropped by about 50 percent in 1998 when the Indian Income Tax Department (India's IRS) decreed that anyone owning a mobile telephone must submit their income tax.[18] This decree was premised on the notion that if an individual could afford a "luxury" item such as a mobile telephone, the individual earned enough income to file a tax return. As less than one-fifth of all Indian households file income tax returns (the agricultural sector is exempt from taxation), this decree was highly unpopular with both private telephone operators and their consumers.

In 1988, the Indian Home Ministry banned the open sale of pre-paid cash cards for mobile telephones, arguing that a number of criminals were using these pre-paid cash cards so as to leave investigators with no way of tracing them. While the use of telephone cards by criminals is a miniscule part of overall numbers, telephone operators have been mandated to verify the name and address of a customer before retailing a cash card. Private operators believe that they are losing almost 50 percent of their business because of this needless verification. Customers are also unhappy about the added burden imposed by this heavy-handed government policy.

The Indian government demonstrates a strong reluctance to give up its control over telecommunications services. Government control is not always benign; in most instances, in India, it has been neither customer- nor industry-friendly.

Telephony for Rural Development

While 75 percent of India's population lives in rural areas, almost 90 percent of telephones in India are in urban areas (Westerveld and Prasad, 1994). The expansion of the telecommunications infrastructure in the 1990s, while paying attention to rural needs, was driven primarily by the needs of businesses, corporations, and upper-middle-class residential users. The telecommunications initiatives in rural areas were geared mostly to improving telephone connectivity and access. By 2000, nearly half of India's villages were connected by telephone, an amazing feat given that in 1988, only 4 percent of Indian villages had telephone access. Increasing access in rural areas is especially critical given that most poor people cannot afford their own telephone service. They may only need to use a telephone a few times a month, which is not enough to justify having their own telephones.

■ Grameen Bank in Bangladesh and Telecommunications Access

One answer is for rural people to use fixed public telephones such as in public call offices, but this telecommunications service is difficult to provide in remote areas where there is no dedicated electrical power, and where the cost of installing and maintaining such services is cumbersome. A solution to this problem is provided by the Grameen (rural) Bank in Bangladesh. Founded in 1983 by Professor Muhammad Yunus, the Grameen Bank is a system of lending small amounts of money to poor women so that they can earn a living through self-employment. No collateral is needed, as the poor do not have anything to offer as collateral. Instead, the women borrowers are organized in groups of five friends each. Each group member must repay her loan on time, while ensuring that other group members do the same, or else their opportunity for a future loan is jeopardized. This delicate dynamic between "peer-pressure" and "peer-support" among Grameen borrowers is at the heart of its widespread success (Papa, Auwal, et al., 1995; Yunus, 1999). In 1999, the Grameen Bank loaned money to 2.5 million poor women borrowers, and had an enviable loan recovery rate of 98 percent (Yunus, 1999). The idea of microlending, based on the Grameen Bank experience, has spread throughout the world, and has everywhere proven effective in gaining a high rate of repayment of the loans. In short, interpersonal networks are effective collateral for poor women.

In 1997, Professor Yunus established Grameen Telecommunications, which provided a nationwide cellular network throughout Bangladesh. One Grameen borrower in each of the nation's 68,000 villages[19] becomes the "telephone lady" for her village. She operates a mobile pay-phone business with the cheapest cellular rate in the world: 9 cents per minute during peak hours and 6.7 cents in the off-peak (Yunus, 1999, p. 226). Her "mobile" presence means that all village residents can receive and make telephone calls, obviating the need to install expensive, large-scale telephone exchanges and digital switching systems. In 2000, a Grameen village-based mobile telephone earned three times more revenue than an urban cellular phone (http://www.telecommons.com/villagephone, 2000). By 2003, Grameen Telecommunications anticipates one million Grameen telephone subscribers in Bangladesh, over 50,000 mobile "human pay-phones" owned and operated by Grameen Bank members, and a net annual profit in excess of $25 million (Yunus, 1998).

Another telecommunications technology venture is the Village Internet Program (VIP), a pilot project in which borrowers obtain loans to purchase and operate "cyber kiosks" for profit. The purpose of "cyber kiosks" is to provide Grameen borrowers with increased access to agricultural and market information for business use, to provide distance and virtual education through remote classroom facilities, and to provide computer-based employment (such as data-entry and transcription services) in rural areas as an alternative to massive migration to the cities (Yunus, 1998).

The VIP is supported by established infrastructures and technologies within the Grameen family of companies. For instance, Grameen Shakti ("energy") is now experimenting with photovoltaic solar systems to provide electricity to villages that lie beyond the national grid of central station electricity. Eventually, the plan is to have cyber kiosks that run on solar power and connect to the Internet by wireless, microwave, and laser connections. Each cyber kiosk will be run as an independently owned and operated franchise of Grameen Communications, in which the borrower will earn money by selling Internet, telephony, and other computer-related services (Yunus, 1998).

In response to the criticism that the poor do not need the luxury of a telephone or of Internet services, Yunus pointed to contributions made by the "telephone ladies" of Grameen Telecom in spurring village-level businesses and in increasing their efficiency. Further, the "telephone ladies" of Bangladesh generate enough revenues to repay their loans, earning almost three to four times the average per capita income in Bangladesh (Yunus, 1998).

The key lesson of the Grameen Bank approach to the use of mobile telephony and Internet services is that poor people should not just be the passive consumers of communication technology, but rather its owners. This philosophy also explains the tremendous success of India's public call offices (PCOs) which are owned and operated by local entrepreneurs. Here is "penny capitalism," operating at the grassroots level to provide telecommunications access to the socio-economically disadvantaged sections of society.

❏ **The Kittur Rural Telephony Project[20]**

Kittur is a village in Karnataka state in South India with a population of 12,500. This village served as the site of a pilot project in which a 128-line rural automatic exchange (RAX), developed by C-DOT, was installed in mid-1986. The 74 subscribers consisted of local farmers and small businessmen. They averaged an amazing 2,400 calls per telephone per year. An evaluation of the impacts of telephones in Kittur found an 80 percent increase in cash deposits at local banks, an increase of 20 to 30 percent in local business incomes, and more rapid access to doctors for local residents in case of emergencies. The Kittur villagers reported the following benefits accruing from rural telephone service:

1. Savings in time and money
2. Higher prices for agricultural products
3. Increased sales of farm products
4. Quicker medical attention
5. Increased social interaction with friends and relatives
6. Better law and order
7. Faster information and news flows

The Kittur Project represented a watershed, demonstrating that, even in village India, telephones were a business and a social necessity rather than a luxury. Fourteen years later, in 2000, some 25,000 C-DOT rural automatic exchanges operate in villages like Kittur in India.

Conclusions

India represents a spectacular case study of the role that telecommunications can play in a nation's socio-economic development. Despite a monolithic telecommunications bureaucracy (DoT), and continued political wrangling over telecommunications policies, the past two decades have seen vast improvements in telephone services. Aided by the vision of Prime Minister Rajiv Gandhi and returned expatriate Sam Pitroda, Indian policy-makers have realized the importance of telecommunications as a tool for socio-economic development.

Although telephone ownership in India is relatively low, the 650,000 public call offices (PCOs) which dot the Indian landscape bring the benefits of telephony to non-owners. By 2000, over half of India's 600,000 villages had access to reliable telephone service, with some 50,000 new villages being connected each year.

The telecommunications revolution intensified in India with the rise of wireless telephony and the increased participation of the private sector. The higher quality of its telephone service has enabled India to compete more effectively in the global marketplace, especially in high-technology industry. Remember that the Bangalore technopolis went global in the mid-1980s owing to the satellite connection linking the Texas Instruments semiconductor design center with company headquarters in Dallas. As the world increasingly moves toward global competition, telecommunications services become even more important. Telecommunications services can also aid business activity and enhance the quality of life in India's rural areas, as exemplified by the "telephone ladies" in Bangladesh and by the Kittur Rural Telephony Project.

Notes

1. The Social Audit Panel of the Ministry of Communication from 1992 to 1996, convened under the leadership of Justice P.N. Bhagwati and Dr N. Bhaskara Rao, was influential in speeding up telecommunications expansion in India.
2. The overall worldwide telephone density in 1999 was approximately 13 per 100, and was increasingly rapidly thanks to fast expanding telecommunications infrastructures in such countries as China and India.
3. In 2000, the Nokia Company sold about 40 million mobile phones worldwide, accounting for nearly 30 percent of market share.
4. Costs of cellular airtime have dropped 20 to 25 percent in India in the past five years, which has, in part, encouraged the adoption of mobile phones.
5. Despite various attempts to reduce its staff, the Department of Telecommunications in 1999 had 425,000 employees. However, from 1989 to 1999, the number of DoT employees per 1,000 telephone lines was reduced dramatically from 87 to 24 (Bahadur, 1999). In Western, industrialized countries, in comparison, the staffing level is between 7 and 12 per 1,000 telephone lines (Mody, 1997).

6. The word "telecommunications" did not come into wide use until the mid-1980s (Athreya, 1996).

7. A reform-minded, market-driven DoT employee, T. Hanuman Chowdary, headed VSNL. Even after retirement, he continues to work tirelessly for breaking DoT's stranglehold on this area.

8. These missions were principally in core sectors like literacy, immunization, drinking water, dairy, telecommunications, and wasteland development.

9. The devaluation of the rupee, which happened overnight, hit many middle-class families very hard. However, no mass revolt against this government policy occurred.

10. Once again, the Social Audit Panel (see note 1) helped to bring customer concern and service orientation to the DoT.

11. In certain parts of India, it is still not uncommon for subscribers to wait for a telephone connection for many years, although the situation has improved dramatically with DoT's "phone-on-demand" and other customer-friendly programs.

12. Among the multinationals, AT&T has invested over $500 million in two cellular networks in the southern and western parts of India.

13. The operators owed the government over $870 million.

14. The U.S. Department of Commerce lobbied the Indian government to establish TRAI in order that U.S.–based telecommunications businesses in India, notably AT&T which had invested over $500 million in India, could compete on a level playing field in certain telecommunications markets.

15. Consider the following example of an uneven playing field between telephone service providers: Mahanagar Telephone Nigam Limited (MTNL), a subsidiary of DoT, was offering mobile telephony services to its WLL system subscribers in 1997 at about 3 cents (U.S.) per outgoing call, and at no cost for incoming calls. Private operators, on the other hand, had to charge at least 38 cents (U.S.) per outgoing call, and half that amount per incoming call during peak hours. Is this fair competition?

16. While DoT's customer service has improved, it still has a long way to go. A 1998 national consumer survey found that about 70 percent of telephone owners in India want private firms to enter the telecommunications market, thus providing competition to the government monopoly. More than 64 percent said that they had to register a complaint more than once before their telephones were repaired. Some 30 percent said they had to call at least six times before repairs were carried out. More than half the surveyed consumers said that they

had to bribe the DoT or MTNL personnel before repairs were carried out (*Cable Waves*, 1999).

17. Similarly, in the Indian civil aviation sector, competition from private airlines helped improve the customer responsiveness of the state-run domestic carrier, Indian Airlines.

18. The Income Tax Department established various other criteria which bound an individual to submit income-tax returns, including, for instance, for undertaking overseas travel.

19. Grameen Telecom hopes to cover all Bangladeshi villages with mobile telephone service by about 2005.

20. This case illustration is based on Singhal and Rogers (1989).

6 The computer and internet revolution[1]

"We are convinced that the information technology industry would make India one of the fastest growing economies of the next decade."

> Dawang Mehta, Secretary, NASSCOM, India (quoted in http://www.nasscom.org/).

"The Internet will become like furniture, just like running water and the telephone."

> Sterling (cited in Richtel, 1999, p. 92).

"The Internet is the single most important event in the U.S. economy since the Industrial Revolution."

> Jack Welch, CEO of General Electric (quoted in Lewis, 2000, p. 251).

The present chapter analyzes the computer revolution in India, focussing on the expansion of both computer hardware and software services, and the rise of the Internet. India holds a particularly advantageous position in the global computer software industry, in part due to a supportive government policy. Centuries ago, India introduced the world to the decimal system of "Arabic" numbers, and to the numeral zero. So there is a long history of Indian technical excellence in mathematics. But in the field of computer technologies, India has not been a world leader, although this situation is rapidly changing.

The key technology in an information society is the computer because of the immense information-handling ability of these machines. The United States has led the way in the computer era, and the English language has dominated computer hardware and software development. India, with its millions of educated, English-speaking people, is in an advantageous position for future global competition in the information era.

The Growth of Computers in India

The world's first computer, ENIAC, was developed in 1945, funded by the U.S. Department of Defense, and used for military purposes (for calculating the trajectory of artillery shells). ENIAC cost millions of dollars to build, took up most of the space in a large room in the Moore School of Engineering at the University of Pennsylvania, and was used for massive number-crunching tasks (Rogers, 1986). When ENIAC was turned on, it so drained the power supply that the lights of Philadelphia dimmed. The world's first mainframe computer used vacuum tubes for its millions of off/on switches. These tubes frequently blew out, causing ENIAC to shut down.

In the early days of computers, only large corporations and businesses could afford a mainframe computer, and these machines were used for tasks like issuing payrolls and for analyzing huge data-sets (like a population census). The Indian Statistical Institute in Calcutta acquired the first computer in India in 1955. Additional computers were purchased in India, mainly from IBM. By 1972, there were 172 computers in India, and three-fourths of these were made by IBM.

In 1977, the Indian government refused to allow more than 50 percent ownership by foreigners of any company operating in the nation. IBM refused to sell majority ownership of its Indian operations, and was thus forced to leave India. Later, after 1984, Prime Minister Rajiv Gandhi changed government policies to encourage an indigenous microcomputer industry. Imports were liberalized, and international standards were followed by Indian computer manufacturers so that their products could compete more effectively in the global marketplace.

Eventually, with the miniaturization of computer components, the minicomputer was developed. It was about the size of a refrigerator, cost about $50,000, and was also used mainly for number-crunching tasks. The microcomputer was created in the early 1970s using semiconductors as components. It was small enough to sit on a desktop, and the cost dropped to a few thousand dollars. The microcomputer was designed to be owned and used by a single person (hence it was called a "personal computer" or PC). The first personal computer was developed at Xerox PARC (Palo Alto Research Park) in Silicon Valley by a dozen or so long-haired, jeans-and-T-shirt clad young men. Xerox PARC researchers also invented or developed the bit-mapped computer display, pull-down menus, icons, the mouse, and laser printing. Gradually, personal computers began to be used not for number-crunching but for communication messaging purposes, especially as millions of people throughout the world began to use the Internet during the 1990s.

A boom in microcomputers began to take place in India during the 1980s, and expanded rapidly in the 1990s. The computerization of the railway passenger reservation system in 1986, followed by computerization of banks in urban areas, helped spread awareness about computer technology. In the 1990s, growth in the demand for personal computers, along with the rising popularity of the Internet, were two major forces driving the growth of the domestic information technology industry (Figure 6.1). Sales of personal computers in India crossed the one million mark in 1999. The installed base of PCs in the country was about five million in 2000, translating into about five computers for every 1,000 people. Figure 6.2 shows the growth of computers in India.

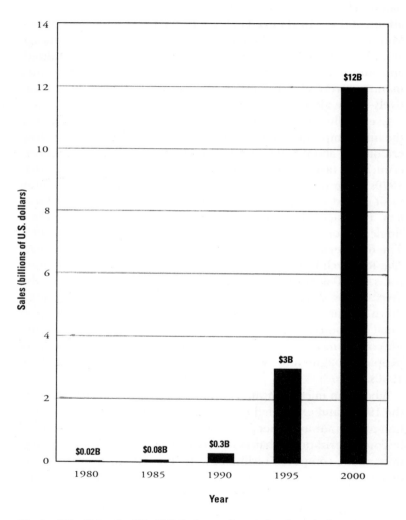

Figure 6.1: Growth of India's information technology industry

The information technology industry, which includes computer hardware, software, peripherals, networking, and training sectors, expanded at a rapid rate in the 1990s.

Source: Based upon Singhal and Rogers (1989) and http://www.nasscom.org/.

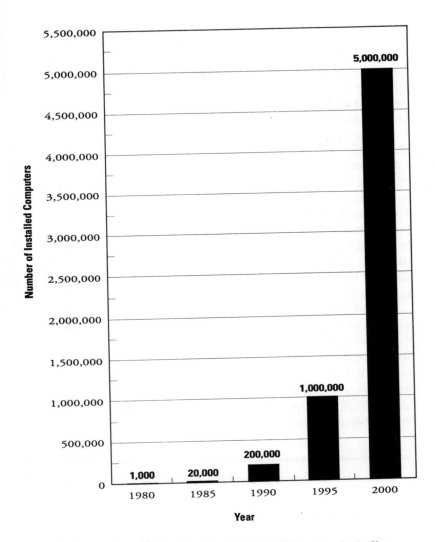

Figure 6.2: Growth in the number of installed computers in India

The cumulative number of computers used in India has skyrocketed, but in 2000 there are still only five computers per 1,000 population.

Source: Based upon Singhal and Rogers (1989) and http://www.nasscom.org/.

- Computer Adoption in India

One important factor promoting the diffusion of personal computers in India in the late 1990s was the rise of various financing schemes. More and more middle-class families were able to buy computers with the help of these purchasing plans. In 2000 the typical cost of a Pentium II desktop computer with printer, modem, and multimedia kit was about 50,000 rupees. For most Indian families, this high price represented a major consumer decision.

An alternative way of acquiring a new computer was by purchasing an "assembled" piece, often from the operator of a cyber cafe. In this scenario, the consumer built his/her own computer by choosing the speed, amount of random access memory (RAM), speakers, modem speed, and the size and make of the monitor. For example, in 1999, one of our colleagues, Sheena Malhotra, helped her mother in Bangalore buy a computer package of a Samsung monitor, a 400 Mhz Celeron chip (made by IBM), disk drives by Sony, Samsung keyboard and speakers, and a Hewlett-Packard laser printer. Total price: Rs 40,000 (Rs 10,000 less than buying a brand-name computer), or about $1,000.

The other incentive in purchasing a computer in the late 1990s was that one could get financing from a bank or from some other finance company for consumer durables. The down payment on a Rs 40,000 computer is typically Rs 10,000, with monthly payments of Rs 4,000 at an interest rate of from 3 to 20 percent. Many families who could not afford to pay cash for a home computer could afford the down payment plus monthly charges. So home computers are becoming more ubiquitous in India.

❏ Arjun Malhotra: From HCL to Techspan

Hindustan Computers Limited is one of the early computer companies that started in India. Its "Busybee" PC was ubiquitous in Indian government offices and corporate businesses in the 1980s. The evolution of HCL as a spin-off from the Delhi Cloth Mills (DCM) is an unusual story of high-tech entrepreneurship by its six co-founders, one of whom was Arjun Malhotra.

Malhotra earned an electronics degree from IIT Kharagpur in 1970 (Plate 6.1). He then joined Delhi Cloth Mills as a management trainee in New Delhi. After several years with the company, Malhotra, like many other DCM employees, left for another job. It happened in this way: Malhotra and his colleague Shiv Nadar were assigned to establish a marketing division for DCM Data Products in 1972. This unit was earning big profits for the parent company through its sale of pocket calculators. But the main textiles division of DCM was suffering heavy losses, and the corporation's top officials curtailed all salary raises and employee promotions throughout the corporation. The employees at DCM Data Products were very unhappy with this company policy.

Plate 6.1: Arjun Malhotra, co-founder of HCL and now CEO of Techspan, a global Internet-based software solutions company

A graduate of IIT Kharagpur, Malhotra is a consummate computer entrepreneur who launched HCL in India in 1975, and Techspan in 1999 in Silicon Valley.

Source: Arjun Malhotra (used with permission).

In mid-1975, Malhotra, Nadar, and several of their co-workers re-signed, and pooled their resources to found their own company, Micro-comp Limited. The spin-off had a starting capital of only $4,250,[2] raised mainly from personal savings and loans from friends and family members of the six co-founders. Malhotra's grandmother provided a two-room *barsati* (terrace) apartment at her home in Golf Links, New Delhi. This *barsati* was the equivalent of the Hewlett-Packard garage in Palo Alto, or Steve Jobs's parents' garage in which Apple Computer was founded.

The new company's primary goal was to get into the computer business, but first they needed more capital. So Microcomp marketed pocket calculators for another company, a task in which they had prior experience. Then Microcomp started manufacturing and marketing its own calculators. Within a year, Microcomp had overtaken DCM Data Products in the sale of pocket calculators, an accomplishment that gave the young entrepreneurs considerable satisfaction. Microcomp had the advantages of low overheads, lower prices, and flexibility in its decision-making. As is often the case in a high-technology industry, a smaller firm can fill a market niche more efficiently than a giant corporation.

In 1976, Microcomp recruited a particularly capable cadre of MBAs from the IIMs and promising engineers from the IITs in order to develop its own microcomputer. Microcomp did not have much to offer them except hard work and a company vision. The company's offices were decrepit and they had to scrimp on daily operations. Microcomp told the new recruits: "It's not a job. It's an adventure." Microcomp secured a license to manufacture its microcomputer in collaboration with the Uttar Pradesh Electronics Corporation, a state corporation. The new company, called Hindustan Computers Limited (HCL), was founded in 1976. Start-up capital totaled $47,000, of which three-fourths was Microcomp's. Later, HCL bought out the state corporation's ownership for several million dollars.

The main strength of HCL was aggressive marketing and pricing, coupled with high-profile advertising. In 1977, a month before IBM wound up its operations in India, HCL shrewdly introduced commercial data-processing for corporations in India. In 1986, HCL stunned the Indian computer market by cutting its microcomputer price to half the prevailing price. In 1988, HCL began to manufacture and sell computer work stations, the first in India. Over the next decade, HCL was India's number one company in sales in information technology products, including computers, photocopiers, electronic typewriters, fax machines, and telecommunications equipment. However, the company began to lose the high ground it had gained because of its primary focus on the hardware business, and in the late 1990s turned to the more lucrative computer software business.

Hindustan Computers Limited has spun off several dozen high-tech companies, including NIIT (the computer education and training powerhouse), pioneering the concept of the "fractal" organization in Indian business. The parent company grew from its original six employees to 1,600 by 1987, and to about 10,000 in 1999. A majority of the workers are engineers or MBAs. Malhotra believes that paying high salaries is needed to retain brainpower, an essential in a high-tech industry. The gross sales of the HCL group of companies increased from $72,000 in 1976, to $4 million in 1981, to $23 million in 1987, to over $800 million in 2000. The company expects to increase sales to $5 billion by 2005 by aggressively focussing on the booming software exports market.

In 1989, Arjun Malhotra moved to Silicon Valley to head operations for HCL-America. In 1998, after building a highly lucrative business for HCL in the U.S., he was bitten again by the entrepreneurial bug. Convinced that the future of information technology lay in Internet and Web-based applications, Malhotra launched a global company called Techspan, headquartered in Sunyvale in Silicon Valley, with a presence in several countries including a wholly owned Indian subsidiary. Techspan seeks to deliver solutions in the high-growth areas of e-commerce services, Web-enabled enterprises, and telecom network management systems. The Internet represents a "new frontier" for high-tech business. Malhotra says: "I am betting on it" (personal correspondence, 4 November 1999). Techspan was financed by Goldman Sachs, the New York investment company, the Walden International Investment Group, and some of Malhotra's previous business partners. Techspan provides technical assistance and business management expertise to "e-babies," Internet-related start-ups, mainly in Silicon Valley, about half of whom are headed by Indians.

What happened to the six founders of HCL? All are now multimillionaires. Malhotra strongly believes in responsible entrepreneurship and supports various development initiatives. He endowed a professorial chair and contributed $1 million to launch the G.S. Sanyal School of Telecommunications in the Department of Electronics at IIT Kharagpur, his alma mater. In 2000, Malhotra and four other IIT Kharagpur alumni in the U.S. (including Suhas Patil of Cirrus Logic and Vinod Gupta of American Business Information) pledged an additional gift of

> $5 million each (a total of $25 million) to IIT Kharagpur to make their alma mater a world-class teaching and research institution, much like MIT, Caltech, and Stanford. Malhotra maintains homes in Golf Links, New Delhi, and in Saratoga, California, while engaging in cross-continental entrepreneurship.

Impacts of Computers in India

In the United States in 2000, almost 50 percent of households owned at least one personal computer. Almost every office-worker had a computer sitting on his/her desk. Access to the Internet and other computer-based information resources is thus facile for most individuals.

But in India, where the rate of adoption of personal computers by households in 2000 was about 1 percent, and where only a small percentage of all office-workers have computers, access is a much more difficult matter. How can this barrier to access be overcome? By providing *public* access to computers in cyber cafes, telecenters, and Internet community centers, akin to what the Grameen Bank's "telephone ladies" do for telephone access in Bangladesh.

■ Inequalities and Growing Information Gaps

Do computers and other new communication technologies (like the Internet) widen or narrow the existing gaps between individuals who are socio-economic elites and those who are less advantaged? At the turn of the century, computers are diffusing in India mainly among the information-rich, making them even more advantaged in an information sense.

Compared to the mass media of radio, television, and film, the new communication media have a higher ratio of information to entertainment. Many individuals adopt computers because these tools allow them to obtain information about financial data, world news, government actions, travel schedules, etc. These users tend to be highly educated and of higher socio-economic status. This close relationship between socio-economic status and computer adoption widens the information gap between the information-rich and the information-poor, at least in the initial stages of computer diffusion in a nation like India. Once public access to computers becomes more widespread through cyber cafes, Internet community centers, and public schools, the digital divide will eventually be crossed.

When applied in the workplace, computers have the potential to replace labor, such as in manufacturing plants like textile factories, thus increasing unemployment rates. In a country like India, where labor is in abundance, this labor-replacement capacity of computerization is a mixed blessing. For this reason, trade unions in India initially opposed computerization, particularly resisting the introduction of computers in banks and insurance companies. In 2000, computers are becoming ubiquitous in Indian banks, offices, and corporations.

Deskilling is the process through which new communication technologies downgrade an occupation to a lower socio-economic status by replacing human skills with information-handling equipment. An illustration of deskilling in the United States is the checkout stands in supermarket stores. Until the early 1980s, checkout clerks were mainly adults who were proficient in memorizing hundreds of prices, and who could quickly add and subtract the items in a grocery bill. They used a cash register that simply recorded the results of their mental calculations.

Today, the checkout clerk is more likely to be a young person, like a high school student. Each grocery product is identified with a bar code consisting of 20 vertical lines (some short and others long), which is read by a computer-based optical scanning machine. It automatically tabulates the grocery bill, so that all the checkout clerk needs to do is to make the correct change for the customer. The benefits of this deskilling at the supermarket checkout stand were passed along, in part, to the consumer as cheaper food prices and fewer errors in grocery bills. But what happened to the adults who were formerly checkout clerks? Perhaps a few of them are working for the computer company that makes the optical scanning machines. Many former checkout clerks sought other work, or are unemployed.

In contrast to such undesirable effects of computerization as unemployment and deskilling, computers can have desirable impacts such as making certain jobs more enriching, enjoyable, and productive. Robots increasingly perform the most repetitive and dangerous tasks on an automobile assembly line, for example. So computer-based technologies can improve our lives, if we have access to them. The vast majority of the Indian population does not yet have such access, but the situation is beginning to change with the establishment of cyber cafes and Internet community centers. Also, the rise of e-governance initiatives in several Indian states (as noted in Chapter 1) will help in bringing the benefits of computer technology to ordinary Indian citizens.

Computer Software in India

The early years of the Indian software industry in the mid-1980s were mainly characterized by bureaucratic hurdles and government bottlenecks. Import duty on software was 160 percent, and the Reserve Bank of India's approvals were needed for overseas travel to negotiate software contracts. Setting up overseas offices or subsidiaries meant excruciatingly slow and painful government approval processes (Srivastava, 1999). Further, high-speed communication links and the infrastructure of software technology parks were unavailable. There was little understanding in government or in banking circles about software, and little venture capital was available in India. Therefore, the software industry embarked on the most viable option for software export, that is, on-site consulting (also called "body shopping"), in which Indian software engineers traveled overseas to work at their customers' sites. The high quality of Indian software engineers gradually provided credibility and increased sales for Indian software companies overseas.

Once this tenuous foothold was acquired, Indian software companies diligently leveraged their growing resources, aided by now-favorable government policies (many instituted by Prime Minister Rajiv Gandhi) and an improving infrastructure, to move up the value chain (Srivastava, 1999). Leading Indian software companies now have their own overseas offices, subsidiaries, and joint ventures. A world-class software industry emerged in India, giving the nation a long-term sustainable competitive advantage in the world market in much the same way that Singapore, Taiwan, Japan, and Korea have dominated the computer hardware industry.

Indian software companies are no longer just Indian exporting companies, but rather have become international companies doing the bulk of their software development in India. To realize this goal, Indian software companies increased their local presence on a worldwide basis, ushering in the era of the India-headquartered multinational corporation. This business strategy entailed staffing overseas offices with local teams of professionals. In 2000, some 212 Indian software companies have either subsidiaries or branch offices overseas, mostly in the U.S. Indian software companies have an increased presence in European countries, where Euro-currency conversion represents a highly lucrative market opportunity.

Over 1,000 software companies operated in India in 2000. From 1994 to 1999, the compound annual growth rate (CAGR) of the Indian software industry, including both domestic and export sales, was 57 percent. This figure represents very rapid growth, almost twice the growth rate of the U.S. software industry. The CAGR for software exports was 61 percent, while the domestic software industry's annual growth was about 50 percent. By 2010, the combined revenues of Indian domestic software sales and software exports are expected to reach U.S.$150 billion, of which $50 billion will come from domestic sales and $100 billion from software exports (Figure 6.3). Maximum growth in the domestic software market is expected in the banking and insurance sectors, e-governance, defense services, and the boom in Small Office Home Office (SOHO) business.

❏ Narayana Murthy: Software Tycoon[3]

In addition to Azim Premji of Wipro (see Chapter I), India's other well-known software tycoon is N.R. Narayana Murthy, 53, who owns 7.7 percent of the shares of his software company, Infosys Technologies

Ltd (Plate 6.2). The headquarters of this 4,100-employee corporation (16 percent of whom work on-site for Infosys's overseas customers) are located 20 kilometers outside Bangalore city on Hosur Road. The Infosys headquarters sprawl over a garden-like setting, complete with a gymnasium, basketball courts, and an amphitheater. Murthy's salary is only $36,000 per year, but his main reward is the stock-market value

Plate 6.2: Indian software tycoon Narayana Murthy, President of Infosys

A graduate of IIT Kanpur, Murthy grew up with leftist leanings, but later realized the importance of creating wealth before it could be shared. His software powerhouse Infosys Technologies, headquartered in Bangalore, has created over 250 dollar millionaires and 4,000 rupee millionaires, including Kannan, Murthy's chauffeur.

Source: Infosys Technologies (used with permission).

of his company's shares, which shot up during the late 1990s making him a multibillionaire. Infosys is traded on the NASDAQ stock exchange in the United States, the first Indian company to be so recognized. Infosys's shares made their debut on the NASDAQ in March 1999 at $34 and had climbed to $500 a year later, representing a market capitalization for the company of $30 billion.[4] Infosys followed Wipro as the second largest company in India in 2000. Not bad for a 19-year-old company.

Murthy earned his Master's degree in electrical engineering at IIT Kanpur, and then founded the computing center at IIM, Ahmedabad. In 1981, with six other software writers, and drawing on $250 of their wives' household finances, Murthy launched Infosys. At that time, the import duty on computer hardware was 335 percent, and government regulations hamstrung the rise of high-tech companies. But Infosys persevered and in 1983 moved to Bangalore. The "air-conditioned" city was troubled by brownouts and overburdened telephone exchanges. Under these conditions, it was difficult for companies like Infosys to compete in the global marketplace. They lost overseas customer orders through lack of adequate telephone connections. Their founders and their employees had to travel to America and other overseas sites in order to write software code for their customers. Electronic working-at-a-distance from Bangalore was not yet feasible for an Indian company.

A turning point was reached in 1988 when John F. Welch, Jr, Chairman of General Electric, visited India. He met with Prime Minister Rajiv Gandhi, who told Welch of India's potential in computer software. Welch shortly dispatched a scouting team to Bangalore. Then GE contracted with Infosys and Wipro and two other Indian companies for software services. This business deal put Indian software companies on the global scene. Infosys began to grow, and grow, and grow. Its stock-market price took off, creating 250 Infosys dollar millionaires and 4,000 rupee millionaires, including the waiters in Infosys's cafeteria, along with several vehicle drivers. Murthy's chauffeur, Kannan, has stock options valued at $500,000 (Padmanabhan, 2000c). The average employee is 26 years old, so these are young millionaires. How did this wealth creation occur? The company's employees are given generous stock options; 20 percent of Infosys's shares are owned by employees. As the company's stock-market value rises, almost instant wealth is created. A rising tide lifts all boats, including those of Chairman Murthy, the waiters, and his chauffeur, Kannan. Here is capitalism, squared.

Murthy absorbed the socialistic ideals of Nehru's India when he was growing up. Then he spent three years designing the cargo-handling system at Charles de Gaulle Airport in Paris. This experience cured the young Murthy of what he now calls his "leftist stupidity." He realized that wealth had to be created before it could be distributed. So capitalism could be a path to greater equality if it is managed in an equalitarian manner. He eats lunch with his employees in the canteen, and lives in a modest three-bedroom house in a middle-class section of Bangalore. This frugality is reflected in his remarkably low salary. The chief executive of an American firm the size of Murthy's Infosys would be paid 10 or 20 times as much.

The success of Narayana Murthy (and others such as Azim Premji) shows that substantial wealth can be created within one generation by means of hard work, technological ability, and good timing in seizing a business opportunity. Young Indians thus have an alternative to migrating to the United States. They can stay home and become software tycoons.

■ Offshore Software Development

In the late 1990s, India made rapid strides in offshore software development, meaning that Indian engineers now develop software for overseas clients *from* India, as opposed to being on-site at the customer's location. High-speed data-communication links allow Indian software programmers to network with computers anywhere in the world on a real-time, on-line basis. A client sitting at a desk in the U.S. can monitor software being developed in India on a minute-by-minute basis, ensuring quality checks. The 12-hour time difference between opposite sides of the world can provide a U.S. client with a virtual 24-hour work day, cutting the software development life cycle by half, ensuring speedy deliveries, higher quality, and substantially reduced costs. With the establishment of dozens of software technology parks in India (for instance, in Bangalore, Pune, Hyderabad, Mumbai, Thiruvananthapuram, and other places), the high-speed data-communication services provided by Videsh Sanchar Nigam Limited, India's liberalized economic policy, and eased visa restrictions between India and the U.S. and other Western European countries, India-based

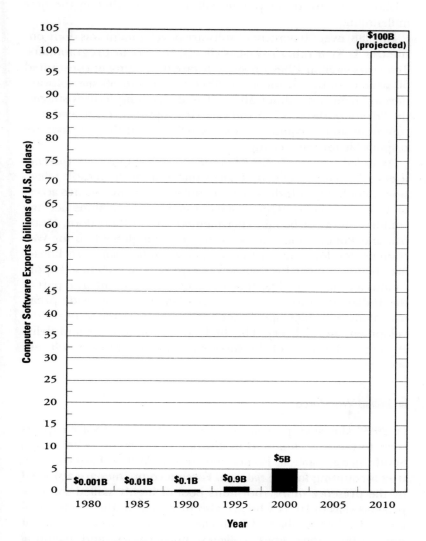

Figure 6.3: The rise of Indian computer software exports

The Indian computer software industry has exploded in the 1990s, in part due to the Internet and other means of high-speed data communication, which allow software engineers to work from India for overseas customers.

Source: Based upon Singhal and Rogers (1989) and http://www.nasscom.org/.

offshore software development will increase further in the new millennium.

In 1988, over 90 percent of software development was done on-site (for U.S. or other overseas clients) by Indian programmers. Ten years later, in 1998, on-site software development constituted 60 percent of the business. By 2000, on-site and off-site software development were about 50:50. These changing figures suggest the "death of distance" in software development. Improved tele-communications, communication satellites, and the Internet are responsible for these changes.

As noted previously (in Chapter 3), an explosion of Internet users will occur in India in the new millennium when cable television households in India—over 35 million of them—secure access to Internet services. Once cabled Internet connections become common (they are being experimented with in Bangalore, Mumbai, and Pune), India will be positioned as a global hub for Web content development and e-commerce. Indian software houses are creating a niche for themselves in providing Web-based applications and services. The Internet is becoming an integral part of the Indian software business, as is evident from its widespread use, along with high-speed satellite connectivity for software development and delivery. This high-speed connectivity and delivery are at the heart of the success of India's computer software industry.

■ Skilled Workforce

In 2000, almost 60 percent of Indian computer software exports were to the U.S., followed by Europe (23 percent), with Japan, South Africa, Canada, France, and several Middle Eastern countries accounting for the balance. Foreign companies are attracted by the presence of an enormous pool of highly skilled software professionals in India who are also proficient in the English language. By 2000, India had 4.5 million technical workers trained at some 1,900 universities, colleges, polytechnics, and technical training institutes. In 2000, these institutions were training about 70,000 computer software professionals *per year*!

The Indian software industry employed about 400,000 people in the year 2000, some 70 percent of whom were directly involved in software development. The overall median age of Indian software professionals in 2000 was 26. Some 80 percent of software professionals in software companies were men; 20 percent were women. However, this ratio is predicted to change to 65 percent men and 35 percent women by the year 2003, as women are increasingly attracted to this profession. Salaries in the software sector rise by an average of about 20 percent every year. Increasingly, compensation includes stock options for employees. In 1998 alone, 41 software companies announced employee stock option plans. The turnover rate of jobs in the Indian software industry hovers between 15 and 20 percent, higher than in other sectors.

■ Competitive Advantage

India has a special competitive advantage in computer software because of its relatively lower salaries and widespread fluency in the English language. The salaries of software engineers in India are one-sixth, or less, of comparable pay in the United States.

Indian software companies have earned a global brand equity for providing efficient software solutions of high quality, at low cost, and by using state-of-the-art technologies. Indian software powerhouses like Tata Consultancy Services (TCS),[5] Infosys, Satyam, Wipro, Pentafour, Mastek, and others have demonstrated that they can handle very large and complex software development projects, and deliver solutions on time. The virtual 12-hour time zone difference between India and the U.S., as noted previously, can cut down software development time by one-half. Also, Indian software companies offer cost-effective, innovative, and extensive e-commerce and e-business applications, a market that is growing by leaps and bounds.

India's software industry has also achieved a remarkable distinction for providing excellent quality. By 2000, some 200 Indian software companies acquired the ISO 9000 quality certification, and another 100 were in the process of being certified. In fact, the Indian software industry has more ISO 9000–certified companies than any other country in the world. By 1999, 32 Indian software companies had acquired the coveted Software Engineering

230 INDIA'S COMMUNICATION REVOLUTION

Institute–Capability Maturity Model (SEI–CMM) certification, with six of them, including Wipro, certified at Level 5 (only 12 software companies worldwide are certified at this level; half are Indian). It is not surprising that Microsoft chairman Bill Gates picked the Indian city of Hyderabad in which to establish his company's first-ever software development center outside of the U.S.

■ Supportive Government Policy

The boom in Indian software would not have occurred without a supportive government policy. Since 1986, when the first computer software policy was announced during Prime Minister Rajiv Gandhi's administration, computer software has been singled out as a high-priority thrust area for expansion. Over the years, the Indian government has provided special fiscal benefits to software developers, built high-speed data-communications networks, established free trade zones and software technology parks (STPs), eliminated the import duty on software, and provided a 100 percent tax exemption on profits from software exports.

In 1998, the Prime Minister's Task Force on Information Technology further initiated bold measures to boost software development by simplifying clearance procedures, deploying additional resources for technical manpower development, enhancing India's global brand equity in software, and providing state-of-the-art infrastructure for software development. As a result, by 1999, some 32 Indian state governments and union territories had announced IT policies and/or formed IT Task Forces. A computer software revolution is under way throughout India. The Indian software industry zoomed from a mere $150 million (U.S.) in 1990 to $5 billion in 2000 (see Figure 6.3). No other industry has created as many millionaires in India in such a short period of time. In fact, the Indian computer software industry has created more millionaires in the past five years than all the other industries/sectors put together in the past 50 years. Informatization, in this sense, acts like a gigantic money-making machine for corporations, entrepreneurs, and the government (in the form of taxable profits and wealth).

Computer Software versus Hardware

While the Indian software industry has matured into a global powerhouse with Indian software developers targeting well-defined, lucrative market segments through differentiated applications, the computer hardware industry, relatively speaking, has done poorly. Despite the 30 percent annual growth of the hardware sector, and the presence of over 135 major computer hardware manufacturers (supported by over 800 ancillary companies), hardware manufacturing is not as profitable in India because so many of the components are imported.[6] Many analysts feel that computer hardware has been treated as a stepchild by the Indian government. Indian hardware firms (like HCL and Wipro) are increasingly shifting into software exports, or reorganizing themselves in other ways. For instance, Godrej Pacific Technology, which sells Compaq, Hewlett-Packard, and IBM PCs in India, is reorganizing itself to become a supermarket distributor of computers.

While the economies of Southeast Asian countries like Taiwan, Korea, Singapore, Thailand, Indonesia, Malaysia, and the Philippines, and of China have been fueled by IT and computer hardware manufacturing, India has missed the boat in these industries. In 1999, Singapore exported almost $100 billion worth of IT hardware products, China about $25 billion worth, and the Philippines over $2 billion (Parpia, 1999). These hardware manufacturing activities created several million jobs in these countries, led to industrial agglomeration and spin-offs, fueled foreign investments, and helped train local manpower in information jobs. So leadership in computer hardware manufacturing led to phenomenal growth rates in GDP, and thus to an increase in levels of living in Taiwan, Korea, and other Southeast Asian nations.

Unlike the software industry, the IT hardware sector in India was an unfortunate victim of government rules, regulations, lack of foresight, and rampant dogma. In a world that demanded just-in-time delivery, India insisted on a 24-hour "cooling period" for all air exports (Parpia, 1999). In a world that demanded lower transaction costs, India insisted that all imports be accompanied by a certificate of origin. Such dogmatic government practices raised costs, fueled delays, bred corruption, and drove IT manufacturing to India's more amenable Southeast Asian neighbors.

The prospects of IT hardware manufacturing are bright world-wide, and it may not be too late for India to get into this industry. The global PC market sells more than 100 million PCs per year, plus new devices such as personal organizers, interactive Web TV, smart Internet appliances, and telecommunications equipment. Most of these new products are outsourced for manufacturing. Government policies can be modified to make India a more attractive location for such hardware manufacturing.

The Internet Revolution

The most important impact of the computer on society has been generated by the Internet. The origins of the Internet, as described earlier, trace to the Cold War era. Because the U.S. Pentagon feared a nuclear attack from the Soviet Union, computer scientists designed and implemented ARPANET, the predecessor of the Internet, without a central headquarters. Each networked computer passes along a message to another computer in the direction of the message's destination (indicated by its address) by means of an open terrestrial or satellite telephone line, with no predetermined or prescribed route. Thus, an email message on an Internet server from Bangalore to Silicon Valley may travel through any one of millions of possible routes.

The ARPANET computer network, designed for national defense purposes, evolved into the Internet in the late 1980s when the number of users in the U.S., and then in other countries, began to explode (Figure 6.4). Compared to other communication channels like postal mail or long-distance telephone calls, communication via the Internet is quicker, cheaper, and more reliable. A very rapid rate of adoption of the Internet, including the World Wide Web, occurred during the 1990s. One reason that the Internet was adopted so rapidly was the prior adoption of personal computers through which the Internet was accessed.

Many observers consider the Internet one of the great transformational technologies (ranking with the steam engine, railroads, electricity, etc.) that at first challenged, and then fundamentally changed, the way that people learn, play, create, communicate,

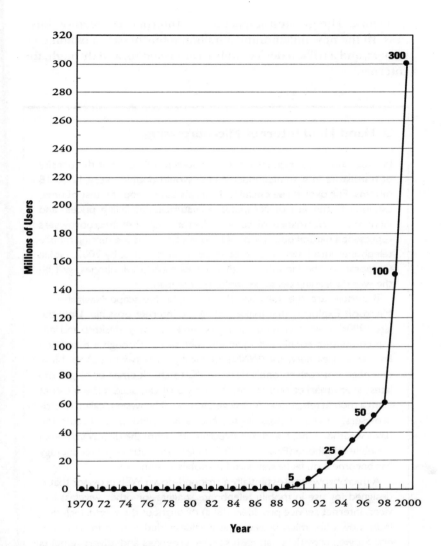

Figure 6.4: The rate of adoption of the Internet on a worldwide basis increased sharply in the 1990s

After a long, 20-year tail to the left, the rate of adoption of the Internet took off in about 1989, and began increasing at an increasing rate. Much of the diffusion of the Internet occurred in the United States and other Western nations in the 1990s, but in recent years adopters are increasingly located in developing countries, including India.

and work. The greatest impact of the Internet has been on business. In the new millennium, a million e-businesses, a billion consumers, and a trillion devices will be connected to, and through, the Internet.

❏ Hand-Held Internet Microbrowsing

In 1965, Intel's co-founder Gordon Moore predicted that the density of transistors in a semiconductor chip would double every 12 to 18 months. For over three decades, Moore's Law stood the test of time, ushering in the era of computer miniaturization, falling prices, and increased performance of semiconductors. Internet microbrowsers represent a natural outgrowth of Moore's Law, and are turning mobile telephones into hand-held personal computers. Thus, by 2002, Nokia Corporation, the Finnish firm that makes mobile telephones, will be the world's leading personal computer company.

Browsers are the software (for example, Netscape Navigator or Microsoft Explorer) that make surfing the Internet possible. Until the late 1990s, most Internet browsing occurred through desktop and laptop computers connected to an Internet server through a telephone line, wide area network (WAN), or local area network (LAN). Now one need not rush to one's desktop PC to check email or to get the latest stock market quotations. An individual can access the Internet from a mobile telephone. A new generation of browsers, called microbrowsers,[7] makes it possible to receive and send email, access the day's weather report, and surf selected sites from the display screen of a mobile telephone (Prakash, 1999). In fact, microbrowser technology has become a de facto standard for mobile telephones.

A microbrowser is essentially a stripped-down Web browser that is designed for use in mobile telephones, pagers, or other wireless devices. Internet service providers (ISPs) throughout the world, including India, now offer microbrowsing as a value-added service for consumers. Service providers can flash specific greetings and advertisements to users in an unobtrusive manner. Also, location-specific networks can display special invitations and sales for neighborhood businesses. What mobile phones did to fixed telephones, microbrowsers will do to desktop browsers.

Growth of the Internet in India

In 1998, the Internet had 70 million users worldwide. The United States and Canada accounted for 62 percent of all users, while Asia accounted for only 12 percent. Global Internet users were expected to rise to more than 325 million by 2000. By early 2000, India had an estimated three million Internet subscribers and about 15 million users.[8] With the favorable Internet service provision policies of the government, these numbers are projected to explode to about eight million subscribers or roughly 40 million users by 2001. Further, in 2000, India had 35 million cable households; once cable Internet services begin to take off in India (as they have on an experimental basis in Bangalore and Mumbai), the rate of Internet adoption will skyrocket. A survey conducted by the International Data Corporation (IDC) showed a high latent demand for Internet connections in India. While only 9 percent of households owning personal computers could access the Internet in 1999, some 37 percent were eager to sign up for the Internet. This survey also showed that more than 50 percent of Indian households planning to buy a computer would like to have an Internet connection; about half planned to get it along with their PC purchase (*India Abroad*, 1999b). However, having a PC is not essential to access the Internet, which is why cyber cafes and telecenters are rapidly mushrooming in India and in many other nations.

■ Cyber Cafes

A profitable new venture sprang up as part of the communication revolution in India: cyber cafes.[9] Prior to 1995, Internet connections in India were only available to non-commercial organizations through a Department of Electronics Education and Research Network (ERNET) scheme. However, in 1995, when Internet connectivity became available to individuals and organizations on a commercial basis, Indian entrepreneurs were quick to enter this business.

The first commercial cyber cafe began in 1995 on Brigade Road in Bangalore; it was called the "Coffee Day Cyber Cafe."[10] The concept of this cyber cafe was to combine coffee drinking, a popular local habit, with surfing the Net. At first, this cyber cafe served only South Indian coffees and a limited menu of snack foods. Late in the 1990s, the Coffee Day chain expanded to a dozen outlets, and the menu expanded to sandwiches, burgers, chips, ice cream, etc., while the coffee choices included Western variations such as cappuccinos, espressos, and lattes. The snacks and electronic services are reasonably priced, and the Coffee Day Cyber Cafes are especially popular with the college crowd. Cyber cafes soon became hangout headquarters for the youth of Bangalore.

The main attraction of the cyber cafes is the computer-related services that are offered: a customer can log onto the Internet, surf the Net, check his or her email, and so forth, for about Rs 60 ($1.30) per hour. Many cyber cafes have only one or two computers, but larger establishments may have a dozen or more. A customer can scan in pictures (Rs 20 per page), or laser print from the Internet (at Rs 7 per page). Small businessmen who cannot afford their own computer use the services of cyber cafes to produce more professional-looking documents, or to contact other businesses by email. Teenagers use the cyber cafes to play games on the Internet, to access pornographic material (when the computer screen is not visible to adults), and for email, especially through the free Web-based email accounts offered by companies such as Hotmail, Yahoo!, or Excite.

Cyber cafes have become very popular in Indian cities: Bangalore, Mumbai, Chennai, Delhi, Calcutta, and Hyderabad, for example, have shops offering Internet services on almost every street, at least in middle-class areas. In Hyderabad alone, 600 new Internet cafes were established in the first six months of 1999 (Chowdary, 1999b). One software entrepreneur equipped 200 of these cyber cafes with a Web server. Several PCs are connected in a local area network (LAN) so that multiple users can simultaneously access one dial-up line, carrying out multiple Internet activities. Many of the customers are youths, but one also observes traditional-looking women in *saris*, older men, and individuals from all walks of life in these cyber cafes.

India is likely to experience, perhaps as no other country has, an explosion of cyber cafes in the new millennium. In 1999, the information technology unit of the S. Kumars Group, a large textile manufacturing and retail company, announced that its 30,000 distribution outlets, spread over 1,008 Indian cities and towns, would establish cyber kiosks. Hundreds of India's 650,000 public call offices (PCOs) that provide local and long-distance telephone services are already upgrading to become telecenters or Internet community centers (ICCs).[11] Such telecenters offer telephony, multimedia, Internet, videoconferencing, and photocopying services. Much as the *cablewallah* facilitated the cable television revolution in the early 1990s, the cyber cafes are bringing the telecommunications, Internet, and computer revolution to many lower-middle-class Indians who cannot afford to own a personal computer or a telephone. They can afford Rs 30 to check their email for half an hour every few days.

■ Internet Policy in India

Internet services were introduced in India in 1991 by the Department of Electronics (DoE) through the Educational and Research Network (ERNET) for use by public departments, universities, public and private research bodies, and by non-profit organizations (McDowell & Pashupati, 1999). In 1995 VSNL, the state-owned international telephone service provider, began offering commercial Internet services to individuals and organizations, charging about 80 cents (U.S.) per hour of connection time. Deliberations on a comprehensive Internet service provision (ISP) policy in India began in 1996, and, consistent with the reformist agenda of the telecommunications policy, there was a push toward inviting private companies into this sector (Balakrishnan, 1999). The ISP policy faced similar difficulties in formulating and implementing as the National Telecommunications Policy, and was delayed and officially announced only in 1998.

The ISP Policy-98 represented a bold, liberal policy for Internet service provision by private telecommunication companies in India. Internet service providers (ISPs) in India were allowed to establish their own customer access networks and gateways to the global Internet network without depending on the infrastructure of the Department of Telecommunications' VSNL. Private ISPs can also provide infrastructure services for e-commerce, tele-medicine, distance learning, and other IT-enabled services without paying license fees (Chowdary, 1999a). Further, under the ISP policy, the Indian Railways, the Power Grid Corporation, the State Electricity Boards, and Indian oil and gas companies can now build communication infrastructure for resale or lease to any Internet service provider. These competing infrastructures, ana-lysts feel, will lead to the lowest prices and to better services for customers, speeding the informatization of Indian society.

The new ISP policy caused frenetic market activity. Several pri-vate service providers like Satyam Infoway and Dishnet began to offer Internet services in India,[12] shaking the monopoly of VSNL's Internet gateway, and creating more customized Internet pack-ages for various customer needs (Natarajan, 2000).[13] In late 1999, Satyam Infoway's $125 million buyout of the Web portal India-world.com, whose 1998–99 revenues and profits were $300,000 and $60,000 respectively, reflected Satyam's confidence in the future growth and earnings potential of Internet services in India. Dishnet, a Chennai-based Sterling Infotech company, began offer-ing Internet access at 5 cents an hour in 1999, provided subscrib-ers signed up for one hour of daily browsing for a period of five years.

The ISP Policy-98 is fueling the market for Internet service pro-vision equipment and leading to new business alliances, both national and global. For instance, Intel Corporation, Lucent Tech-nologies, and other global players geared up quickly to offer tai-lored Internet servers and technology solutions to Indian Internet service providers. Wipro and KPN (Royal Dutch Telecommunica-tions) joined hands to provide Internet services in India through Wipro Net, a subsidiary company of the Wipro Corporation. Wipro Net currently manages a nationwide fault-tolerant network, 24 hours a day, seven days a week, through communication hubs in eight major Indian cities. Since the mid-1990s, it has been the leading intranet/extranet services provider in India. With its established leadership in the business segment, Wipro Net, in syn-ergistic cooperation with a global telecommunications company, is expected to emerge as a key Internet service provider in India.

❑ U.S. Hegemony on the Net

Between 1993 and 1997, Internet users in Asian countries grew at a rate of 120 percent annually (Vijay, 1999). While Internet users increase in number outside the U.S., most data flows out of the U.S., rather than flowing in. Often the quickest Internet route between two points, even if they are in the same country, is through the U.S. In fact, most Indian content sites accessed by Indians are housed on servers in the U.S. So a user in Kanpur downloads data from a site in Bangalore, courtesy of the U.S. (ibid.). In 2000, some 60 percent of the world's Internet hosts were based in the U.S., and 90 of the 100 most-visited Web-sites were in the U.S. Some 40 percent of these were in California.

The U.S. hegemony of the Internet is complete, as it owns most of the networking and bandwidth infrastructure, controls most of the Internet's R&D initiatives, and directs site content. Will this dominance be challenged at some time in the future?

Internet: The Highway for a Global Economy

The Internet spawned the era of e-business (electronic business), which consists mainly of e-marketing and e-commerce. *E-marketing* is the use of the Internet to market one's products or services; *e-commerce* is commercial transactions between two parties on the Internet. An estimated one trillion dollars of commercial transactions will occur on the Internet by 2002. Some observers feel that the rise of e-business in the 1990s is establishing a New Economy (Arthur, 1996) that operates under different economic assumptions (increasing returns rather than diminishing returns, as we discussed in a previous chapter) from those of the Industrial Society.

The Internet is the highway of the global economy. In 1998, companies such as Compaq, Dell Computer, IBM, Intel, and Gateway, among many others, revamped their marketing strategies to become Internet-centric. In 1999, IBM earned about $20 billion, a quarter of its total revenues, through its electronic business (Kaur, 1999b). During the late 1990s, Dell opened an on-line superstore offering computer peripherals and software, grossing sales of over $10 million per day globally. Dell allows customers to select the particular computer configuration they want. Then, when a buyer has decided on the monitor, keyboard design, modem speed, amount of memory, and other specifications, the individual can pay by credit card. Then the product is assembled and shipped. The entire transaction is handled through the Internet. Dell's use of the Internet represents a radically new business strategy (Dell, 1999).

In 1999, over 150 million home-based shoppers made purchases in the cyber marketspace (Kaur, 1999b). In 2000, some three million items were up for bidding at eBay auctions; over 20 million people shopped for discounted books and music at Amazon.com; and on-line brokers managed $600 billion in assets. These numbers will rise exponentially in the new millennium.

The mother of all Internet retail companies is Seattle-based Amazon.com, which can ship almost any book (that is currently in print) to a customer. These books are stored in several gigantic warehouses which serve all parts of the globe. When a customer contacts Amazon.com through its Web-site to order a particular book, the buyer is asked for a credit card number, and the book is then mailed by overnight/priority mail service. The cost, including postal charges, is comparable to a local bookstore's price. In 2000, Amazon.com expected to cross the line into the black for its book sales. However, it will still be some time before the other products that Amazon has added to its repertoire—CDs, videos, toys, prescription drugs, etc.—begin to yield company profits. With 20 million customers, Amazon.com's stock market value soared in the late 1990s, on the basis of expected future sales and profits.

As stated earlier, Amazon.com is noteworthy in its use of computer records to promote customer reminders. For instance, if you buy a book on some topic, say a South Indian cookbook, Amazon.com will send you an email notice two months later to let you know that another book on this topic has just appeared.

❏ Goodbye Silicon, Hello Internet

The U.S.–based semiconductor giant, Intel, with sales of over $30 billion in 2000, views the Internet as just as important to its future as silicon was to its past success. Intel focussed on the development of

Internet technologies, and used the Internet to streamline its internal and external business processes. Among global manufacturing organizations, Intel is the world's largest e-commerce company.

Of Intel's 65,000 employees in 2000, some 40,000 were involved in manufacturing operations (Vijaykar, 1999). Until January 1998, Intel took customer orders by telephone or fax. A few months later, with a user-friendly Web-based e-commerce system in place, Intel had completely automated its order-handling and delivery, reducing costs and increasing efficiency. Intel transacted business over the Internet with 550 partners, distributors, and customers in 46 countries worldwide through thousands of personalized Web-sites. By the end of 1998, Intel was transacting over $1 billion (U.S.) worth of business per month over the Internet, making it larger than Dell Computer or Cisco Systems in terms of the value of its e-commerce transactions.

Several Indian companies, realizing that the Internet renders distance irrelevant while allowing for interactivity, are becoming Net-centric. For instance, in 1999, the National Institute of Information Technology (NIIT) Ltd, a major Indian player in computer-related educational services, invested $15 million to implement on-line computer classrooms and Web-centric curricula in eight metro-cities in India. The Internet is helping NIIT design, maintain, and facilitate global learning standards.

India's Knowledge-Based Virtual Age

The Internet has brought in a new era where wealth creation is not only based on the production and transportation of physical goods, but occurs through information networks, using sound knowledge management practices, the reduction of interaction costs, and remote processing (Sagar, 1999). Business activities that previously required face-to-face communication between a service provider and a consumer now flow through electronic channels in computer networks.

The global trend is increasingly to outsource such remote services as transcription, translation, data-entry, project design, and accounting (Sagar, 1999). Other value-added remote-processing services include network management, data search and analysis,

Web-site services, remote education, monitoring services, secretarial services, and customer help desks. Numerous new occupations have been spawned by the Internet: email management, Internet patrol and security, Web-page designing and updating, and the management of Internet commerce. In this respect, the Internet can be a great equalizer of global talent, as these new services can be provided from any place in the world. Physical distance is simply no longer a limitation to human communication.

■ Remote Processing: A Gargantuan Opportunity for India[14]

Remote processing, or, simply, "teleworking" (working from a distance), is undermining geographical barriers. India is uniquely positioned to capitalize on the global market of remote processing, with its large pool of English-speaking university graduates. By mid-1999, 25,000 Indians based in Hyderabad, Bangalore, New Delhi, Mumbai, and Chennai were employed in remote-processing work for U.S., European, and East Asian companies, generating $250 million in sales revenues (David et al., 1999). The National Association of Software and Service Companies (NASSCOM) estimates that by the year 2008, remote processing will employ 1.1 million Indians, earning revenues of over $13 billion, a 52-fold increase in 10 years (Mukerjea & Dhawan, 1999). Former finance minister Manmohan Singh's New Economic Policy of the early 1990s has positioned India to capitalize on this remote-processing business opportunity. The presence of a solid telecommunications infrastructure, favorable policies for free global trade, and the availability of low-cost, English-language talent, provide India with a tremendous competitive advantage. Many analysts view the potential of remote processing in India as even greater than that of its software exports, an industry in which Indian expertise is considered world-class.

Consider GE Capital, which in 1998 employed 600 teleworkers in its $6 million facility in Gurgaon, Haryana, south of Delhi. A swank, multistoried building, with glass walls and tasteful interiors, this is General Electric's only remote-processing center in the world (Mukerjea and Dhawan, 1999). The GE center manages payroll accounting for several GE units across the world, houses an around-the-clock customer service call center where Indian teleworkers answer questions from GE's card holders in Europe and the U.S., and processes mortgage loans and insurance claims for a GE subsidiary company. General Electric plans to increase its remote-processing operations in India by hiring 1,500 new employees in the year 2000, and another 3,000 workers by 2005.

Another flourishing remote-processing center in India is Healthscribe India, a medical transcription firm in Bangalore which provides services to 18 U.S.–based hospitals. In the U.S., doctors maintain careful records of patient diagnoses and medical advice, in the event that a malpractice suit is filed against them. These notes are usually recorded by doctors on dictaphones and then transcribed by retired nurses and pensioners who are paid $25,000 (U.S.) a year. Healthscribe, which employs 440 people, processes about 80,000 lines of transcription every day, paying its Indian workers $1,500 per annum, about one-twentieth of what a U.S.–based transcriber would charge, but four times the per capita income in India (Mukerjea and Dhawan, 1999). Healthscribe planned to triple its number of employees in India by 2000.[15]

Michael Dertouzos, Director of MIT's Computer Sciences Lab, believes that India, more than any other country, is uniquely positioned to take a worldwide leadership position in the global market for remote on-line services (Arora, 2000). Critics of remote processing contend that India is heading toward becoming a low-tech "sweatshop" for multinational corporations. Supporters argue that remote processing offers opportunities for creating hundreds of thousands of white-collar jobs in India, especially for educated but unemployed youth. Further, remote-processing jobs need not be low-tech. The remote-processing center of U.S. construction giant Bechtel, located in Gurgaon (a neighbor to GE's India center), employs 400 engineers who provide on-line technical and modeling support to Bechtel's 1,000-odd construction projects, located in 63 countries.

❑ A 24-Hour Cyber Office

A few years ago, a Web-site address on an Indian visiting card would have certainly raised eyebrows; these days *not* having a Web-site would be surprising. Many Indian companies are discovering that having a Web-site is almost like having a 24-hour working office without personnel. People can visit a company in cyberspace, look over the company profile, and make specific queries and suggestions.

Scores of Internet solution companies providing Web design services have emerged in India. For instance, Delhi-based Combit Advertising, which started operations in 1996, had about 400 clients in 1999. Chennai-based EasyLink, which began operations in 1994, had, by 1999, established offices in 12 Indian cities including Madurai, Coimbatore, Erode, Tiruppur, Vizag, Kakinada, Thiruvananthapuram, Cochin, Bareilly, and Delhi.

How much does it cost to establish a cyber office? In the mid-1990s, setting up a Web-site in India, complete with graphics and animation, cost from $1,200 to $1,600 (*Computers Today*, 1999b). Setting up the same Web-site in 2000 cost about half that amount. And this cost will continue to drop.

■ E-Commerce in India

India is in the infant stages of e-commerce. In 1998, only $3 million worth of e-commerce (both business-to-business [B2B] and business-to-consumer [B2C]) was transacted; this figure will rise 750 times to an estimated $2.32 billion by 2002 (Sodhi, 2000). McKinsey's, the global consulting company, projects the e-commerce market in India at $10 billion by 2010. An industry survey in 1998 showed that 77 percent of Internet users in India were either small, medium, or large business houses (Figure 6.5). Some 86 percent of the top 100 Indian corporations view e-commerce and the Internet as integral to their corporate strategy.

However, at the present time in India, a great deal of hype exists about the business-to-consumer advantage of e-commerce. For instance, in glorified versions of e-commerce, even the neighborhood *paanwallah* has a Web-site to sell his products. Barring notable exceptions, the focus is mostly on "brochure-ware," that is, hawking products by establishing a Web-site. By 2000, few Indian vendors had linked their Web-sites to their application systems, although this activity will greatly increase once cyber laws are

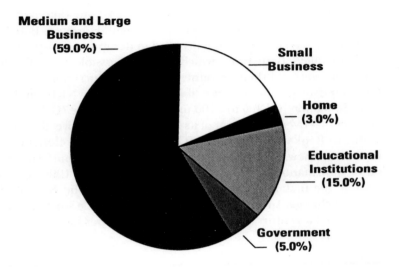

Figure 6.5: Internet users by segment in India

At present, use of the Internet is dominated by larger companies, but this situation will probably change in the future with the expansion of Internet community centers in Indian cities, towns, and villages.

Source: Cable Waves (1998).

passed, back-office services like accounting, order processing, and transportation scheduling are computerized, and transactions over the Internet secured. Leased line charges (which drive corporate Internet access) are at present very high in India (about six times what they are in the U.S.), stymieing the corporate sector in its adoption of the Internet for the lucrative business-to-business segment.

Some Indian companies are already demonstrating that Internet Web-sites can be used as strategic business tools to enlarge markets and enhance customer service. The ICICI Bank, established in India in the early 1990s, created a user-friendly Web-site targeted to non-resident Indians (NRIs) in the Middle East, U.K., and the U.S. in an effort to increase deposits (Kohli, 1999). Non-resident Indians can easily download the account-opening form, print it at home or at work, and mail it to ICICI with a check. Customer queries can be answered by email within a 24-hour time period, not the usual two to three weeks by postal mail. However, ICICI's big leap forward came when it invested in designing a customized software called Bankaway, which made it possible for NRIs to check the status of their accounts on-line, conduct money transfers, and issue payment advice (ibid.).[16] Deposits by NRIs climbed from $8 million in 1995 to $100 million in 1998. The ICICI Bank believes that over 60 percent of its NRI deposits are directly attributable to Bankaway. Today, ICICI's Bankaway site offers up-to-the-minute news from India, a selection of Hindi film CDs, and other information services to overseas Indians. In 1999, ICICI became the first Indian company to be listed on the New York Stock Exchange. In 2000, ICICI introduced on-line stock trading and floated a venture capital fund to fuel Internet start-ups.

❑ **Love Goel: Direct Selling through the Internet**[17]

Not all of the successful young Indian technologists/entrepreneurs are in Silicon Valley, and not all are starting up cutting-edge high-technology companies. Love Goel works for the very staid Federated Department Stores Inc. in Minneapolis. Goel is the 28-year-old multimillionaire chief operating officer of the fast-expanding e-commerce business unit of this $18 billion parent company (Plate 6.3). He has 125 employees, up from 15 one year ago. His revenues double every 10 to 12 weeks. During 1999, 50 million individuals visited the Federated Web-site, and 3.5 million made purchases. Goel's e-commerce division harnesses the power of computer databases and the Internet to gain competitive advantage in the cutthroat retail market.

Goel migrated from Delhi to the United States in 1992, and earned a Bachelor's degree in computer science and finance at the University of Minnesota. While still a student, he worked part-time for Apple Computer Inc., helping the company with its sales strategy for college students. As he neared graduation, Goel wrote to 200 mutual fund managers and investment bankers on Wall Street. He had not attended an Ivy League school, nor lived in New York, and he was not from a wealthy American family. He did not receive a single response to his applications. So Goel smashed up against the glass ceiling.

Plate 6.3: Love Goel, the hard-driving chief operating officer of Federated's e-commerce business unit

Goel migrated from India in order to attend the University of Minnesota. Then he rose rapidly in a mail order company as head of its e-commerce division. He was rewarded with stock options, and when his company was acquired by Federated Department Stores, Goel became a multimillionaire. A decade younger than the managers under him in Federated's e-commerce unit, Goel is on a super-fast career track.

Source: Love Goel (used with permission).

Undiscouraged, he joined a prestigious management consulting company in Minneapolis, where he spearheaded several key client projects for Prudential Insurance, Sears, Deloitte and Touche, Cargill, and the U.S. Navy. He was then hired by one of his customers, Fingerhut, a large mail order company specializing in lower-income consumers, to help run its information services unit. A few days after arriving at Fingerhut, Goel was asked to salvage a contract with a big company for order-processing work; he mobilized a task force of 50 people for a few days, drove hard, and landed the contract, worth hundreds of millions of dollars to Fingerhut. He thus became a company hero.

When Fingerhut started an e-commerce unit in 1998, company officials selected Goel as the chief operating officer. This choice rocked the company, as Goel was a decade younger than the managers who worked under him. He drove them hard. He was single. He was global. And his rapid rise on the organizational chart created widespread hostility.

But his work unit grew rapidly in size. Fingerhut's stock value tripled in less than a year. In March 1999, Federated bought Fingerhut for $1.7 billion, making Goel, who had received generous stock options from Fingerhut for his accomplishments, a multimillionaire. He now works for Federated, launching Internet sites that sell electronics, flowers, food, and other products. Federated is America's largest department store, operating such brands as Bloomingdale's, Macy's, Bon Marche, Sterns, Burdines, and Fingerhut.

High-fliers like Love Goel combine technological expertise with marketing know-how. He works long hours, arising at 4:00 A.M. to work at home until he goes to the office (he has learned that it is best not to come to work until after 8:00). He parks in an unreserved lot at Federated. As he walks by a message board outside his office, he notices that an employee has scrawled: "The word for today is… scream!" Many people at Federated think Goel is a hard-driving taskmaster. A boss says, "He breaks a lot of glass." Goel knows that he is pushy: "We have people here who think growth is 3 percent a year. But we're growing 500 percent this year. People… know how to do [things] in six months. I want them to do it in six days."

Goel leaves his office at 6:00 P.M. As he climbs into his car, he says that he may some day become a venture capitalist, or return to India to enter politics. "People like me don't have the patience to do this for 20 years," Goel says. He will work at home until 10 P.M.

Hard-working hard-drivers like Goel symbolize the cutthroat nature of Internet-based e-commerce, in which brainpower is the basis of competition. More importantly, Goel symbolizes the new generation of Indians who are making a dent in corporate America—outside of Silicon Valley.

■ The Internet and Privacy

Millions of Internet users worldwide, including Web-surfers in India, perceive the Net as a bundle of Christmas presents with free email accounts, free home pages, free disk space, and free memberships in cyber clubs. However, the price of these seemingly "free" services is personal information about the user's age, location, profession, interests, hobbies, etc. (Ranganathan, 1999). Web-sites use such information to choose and display specific ads that match the interests of the individual. Other Web-sites gather the email addresses of customers and send them periodic emails with marketing and promotional material. Even if Internet users do not voluntarily disclose personal information, their preferences are derived by noting their link-movements and the Web pages visited, providing intelligence for audience segmentation for on-line advertising. Hotmail's "free" service, as discussed earlier, is not really free to the user. It is more correctly described as the exchange of personal information for the use of a Hotmail address.

There is no free lunch on the Internet. As the Internet becomes more integrated with the lives of its Netizens, the issue of privacy will assume greater importance, as will the ethical aspects of trading personal information about the individuals in a database.

Conclusions

Here we have traced the history of computers over the last half of the past century, as they evolved from clumsy, expensive mainframe computers to cheap, small-sized personal computers. Although most of the initial development of computers happened in the United States, by the turn of the century the computer industry was well established in India. The main function of computers has changed from number-crunching to communication, for instance via the Internet. As computers diffuse more widely in India, their impacts are being even more widely felt.

The Indian information technology sector, including both computer hardware and computer software services, is growing six to eight times faster than the Indian economy. In the 1990s, the speed of computer penetration in India in banks, schools, government offices, and urban homes was breathtaking. The software boom continued in India at the turn of the century at an even more rapid rate, nearly 10 times the growth rate of the Indian economy, despite a laggardly business cycle, a roller-coaster stock market, and reduced dependence on Y2K projects (Bakshi, 1999).

The rise of Indian computer software exports is backed by a highly literate, English-speaking, technically skilled workforce. Indian software engineers provide state-of-the-art software solutions to global companies (located in over 100 countries), carving out a global brand equity in this highly lucrative information technology sector. Government policies toward software development have been extremely supportive, reflective of the informatization strategy of development. The time zone advantage of joint Indo-American work teams, collaborating from opposite sides of the world in a daily dance linked by high-speed data links and the Internet, illustrates the unique nature of India's rise as a computer software powerhouse. The Internet removes the cost of physical distance from person-to-person business relationships.

Computer hardware, software, and Internet-based e-governance and e-commerce are now vital ingredients in the New India, fueling its progress along the route of informatization.

Notes

1. This chapter draws on the NASSCOM Web-site http://www.nasscom.org/ for facts and figures about the Indian information technology industry, including the status of the computer hardware and software industry in India.

2. As explained in the Preface, for the sake of consistency, we report all monetary values in U.S. dollars, with each dollar equaling 43 Indian rupees (the exchange rate at the time of writing in 2000). It is important to note, however, that in 1975, one U.S. dollar equaled about 8 Indian rupees. So Microcomp's starting capital in 1975 was close to $21,000.

3. The present case illustration is based mainly on Karp (1999).

4. Infosys is seen as a "world leader" in software programming, delivering top-quality, on-time, on-budget software results to demanding clients such as Northern Telecom, Apple, and Goldman Sachs. Profits at

Infosys grew eightfold in the five years from 1994 to 1999 (Bellman, 1999).

5. During 1998–99, Tata Consultancy Services (TCS) was the top Indian software exporter ($362 million), followed by Wipro Infotec ($151 million), Pentafour Software ($121 million), Infosys ($119 million), and NIIT ($95 million). The TCS group's IT sales turnover in 1998–99 was $1 billion. With projects in over 50 countries, TCS has built multiple high-speed dedicated links connecting its India offices with 40 locations worldwide (Jain, 1999). In 2000, TCS established three new software development centers in Calcutta, Noida, and Hyderabad, investing a total of $40 million.

6. The computer software industry does not need as much electricity, energy, water, or other logistic facilities as does the hardware manufacturing industry.

7. Like the Microsoft Internet Explorer (IE) and Netscape Navigator on the desktop computer, the browser war on hand-held devices in 1999 was mainly between two firms: Phone.com and Geoworks.

8. Each Internet subscription in India is used, on an average, by five people.

9. Internet cafes have emerged all over the world: from a dilapidated trailer on the island of Bali with an ancient PC in one corner, to a full-service bistro overlooking the river in Singapore with dozens of state-of-the-art computers. Most cyber cafes charge an average of about $5 for an hour of browsing, much more than in India.

10. Prior to 1995, several cyberclubs existed in India, for instance, at Hotel Leela in Mumbai, Hotel Maurya Sheraton in Delhi, and the Green Chillies Cafe in Hyderabad. However, these cyberclubs were not commercial ventures (Sen and Koppikar, 1995).

11. Several Indian banks now offer loans for upgrading PCOs to "cyber kiosks" or Internet community centers. The costs of upgrading range from $7,000 to $10,000.

12. Satyam Infoway became the second Indian company after Infosys Technologies to be listed on the U.S. NASDAQ stock market in October 1999. Two months later, by December 1999, the share price of Satyam Infoway on the NASDAQ had increased five times.

13. Some 18 of the 176 private ISPs in India are planning to establish Internet gateways, overcoming the monopoly of VSNL.

14. This section draws upon Mukerjea and Dhawan (1999) and Sagar (1999).

15. By 2000, several dozen Indian companies in Hyderabad, Chennai, Mumbai, and Delhi were offering medical transcription services through the Internet.

16. Bankaway was developed by software engineers at Infosys Technologies, who had personally realized the need to conduct on-line banking in India when working overseas on a company project.
17. This case illustration is adapted from Kaufman (1999), and is supplemented by our personal email correspondence (of 13 December 1999) with Love Goel.

7 Lessons learned about informatization

"As a great social leveler, information technology ranks second only to death. It can raze cultural barriers, overwhelm economic inequalities, even compensate for intellectual disparities. In short, high technology can put unequal human beings on an equal footing, and that makes it the most potent democratizing tool ever devised."

> SAM PITRODA (1993, p. 67), the visionary technologist who spearheaded India's telecommunications revolution.

"Once you have enough, you want to begin to help. The question is how much is enough? After all, how much can one eat and spend? There is no mechanism to give and we are trying to create it with The Indus Entrepreneurs."

> GURURAJ "DESH" DESHPANDE, a veteran of several successful start-ups, who mentors young Indian high-tech entrepreneurs (quoted in http://www.india-today.com/ctoday/19991216/master4.html).

"Whether it is wealth of knowledge or business wealth, it brings enough 'trusteeship' along with it. To discharge this trusteeship is a tremendous responsibility. It is a bigger job in terms of challenge than creating wealth in the first place."

> AZIM PREMJI, Chairman of Wipro and the richest Indian, in a convocation address to graduates of IIT Mumbai on 6 August 1999.

T he purpose of this chapter is to summarize the main points of the present book. We regard India as a fascinating case study of the informatization strategy of development. Here we ask: to what extent can lessons learned in India be generalized to other nations? We also turn toward the nature of the future information society in India, proposing the increased application of information technology in government and public service, and in improving the quality of life of ordinary citizens. We also see a greater role for responsible entrepreneurship, and emphasis on "growth with equity."

A Summary of Main Concepts

The purpose of this book has been to describe and analyze the recent socio-economic changes taking place in Indian society resulting from applications of communication technologies. We showed that India is moving rapidly from a nation of bullock carts to one of cyber cafes.

Informatization is the process through which new communication technologies are used as a means of furthering socio-economic development. While India as a nation lags far behind many other countries in its degree of informatization, the information strategy is applied enthusiastically in technopolises like Bangalore and Hyderabad. A *technopolis* is a geographically concentrated high-tech complex characterized by a large number of entrepreneurial spin-off companies. A *spin-off* is a new company that is created (*a*) by individuals who leave a parent organization, and (*b*) around a technology that these entrepreneurs bring with them from the parent organization. A *high-technology industry* is one that is at the cutting edge of technology, an industry whose core technology changes rapidly. Worldwide, microelectronics and biotechnology are the leading high-tech industries. India has a special advantage in computer software development due to its large number of computer scientists and its English-language proficiency. Further, Indians are well endowed with entrepreneurial skills, and they are increasingly starting up computer and Internet-related businesses both in India, in Silicon Valley, and in other technopolises. A number of Indian entrepreneurs have become enormously wealthy.

The *global village* is a world that is increasingly interconnected by communication technologies and that is heading toward a more common culture. At least at a superficial level, large cities across the world today resemble major cities in the West in the products sold, movies shown, air conditioning, traffic problems, and fast food, Cokes, McDonalds, Reeboks, and Japanese automobiles. The Canadian media guru Marshall McLuhan coined the term "global village" in the 1960s. Since then, his vision has started to come true. Today, the entire world is interconnected by the Internet, the English language dominates, and Americanization and Westernization grow stronger everywhere, including in India.

Information societies are countries in which information workers are more numerous than such occupational categories as farmers, industrial workers, or service workers. *Information workers* are individuals whose main job responsibilities are to gather, process, or distribute information, or to produce information technologies like computers or telecommunications equipment that are used by other information workers. About two-thirds of the workforce in countries like the United States, Japan, and Germany are information workers. In India, information workers may constitute only about 25 percent of the workforce, but these millions of urban elites may outnumber the information workers of other nations, including perhaps even the United States. Thus, India has an information society within itself.

Information is patterned matter-energy that affects the choices available to an individual making a decision. The computer is the crucial technology in the Information Age, as the steam engine was in the Industrial Age. Computers have become tools for human communication, particularly via the Internet. Business opportunities are emerging, such as the Internet-related companies of the late 1990s, in which information is converted to wealth. Opportunities also abound to create networked information systems that can make governance procedures more accountable, responsive, and transparent to citizens.

Communication technology is the hardware equipment, organizational structures, and social values by which individuals collect, process, and exchange information. The new communication technologies are unlike either interpersonal communication or mass media communication because they are *interactive*, defined as the degree to which the participants in a communication process have control over, and can exchange roles in, their mutual discourse. The exchange of email messages by two individuals on the Internet illustrates interactive communication.

Technological determinism is an approach that considers technology as the main cause of social change. We believe that the social changes represented by India's communication revolution are caused by advances in the new communication technologies, along with such social factors as government policies, international politics, and public opinion. The *social construction of technology* is the process through which people give meaning to a new technology by talking about it with each other. Gradually, such discussion helps individuals understand what a new technology is, and whether they should adopt it. Talking about a new technology such as the Internet helps shape its meaning for us.

Development is a widely participatory process of directed social change in a society, intended to bring about both material and social advancement (including greater equality, freedom, and other valued qualities) for the majority of people through their gaining greater control over their environment. *Development communication* consists of the uses to which communication is put to further development. Much mass media content in nations like India consists mainly of entertainment, intended to attract a large audience in order to be sold for a profit to advertisers. The entertainment function of the mass media in India was facilitated (*a*) by the privatization of television broadcasting in the 1990s; and (*b*) by the 1991 New Economic Policy (NEP) which opened Indian markets to foreign companies.

The privatization of television meant a shift away from the previous rhetoric of development communication toward more entertainment content, in the competition to achieve higher audience ratings. But the entertainment and the educational functions of mass communication can be combined in *entertainment–education*, the strategy of intentionally incorporating educational issues in entertainment programs. India has been a pioneer in entertainment–education television soap operas and radio soap operas. Such programs attract large audiences and commercial advertising, while promoting educational development messages about family planning, gender equality, and HIV/AIDS prevention. Entertainment–education, in this sense, provides a unique opportunity to balance the mass media's commercial interests with its public service mission.

Lessons Learned

What general lessons have been learned from our analysis of the important social changes under way in India as it moves along the informatization road?

Lesson #1   *The Indian experience,[1] especially in the 1990s, shows that private business initiatives, driven by a sense of ownership and the potential for economic gain, can represent an important force for innovation and social change in a developing society.* Examples include the private vendors who own and operate India's 650,000 public call offices, the 6,000 stock-holding employees of Infosys Technologies in Bangalore (including cafeteria waiters and vehicle drivers), and the 2,000 Indian computer education and training institutions like the National Institute of Information Technology (NIIT), Aptech, and Zee-Education (ZED), which train several hundreds of thousands of computer professionals each year.

Free-market forces can reward creative solutions to development problems. The Indian government should continue its pace of economic reforms, implement e-governance procedures, and streamline bureaucracy. The role of government should be to facilitate innovation, entrepreneurship, and creativity; *not* to stifle it.[2] Will the political leadership in New Delhi be bold enough to re-engineer India's government? Can lessons learned from Chandrababu Naidu's progressive government in Andhra Pradesh be implemented on a national basis? Can opportunities be created to use information technology as a business as well as a socially ameliorative tool (as with the telephone ladies in Bangladesh)?

Lesson #2   *The informatization of Indian society during the 1990s resulted in part from globalization, which allows Indian brainpower to* *freely and "virtually" flow in and out of India.* The main forces bringing about the informatization of Indian society are based on free-market capitalism, building on the basis of a planned, socialistic-style society established earlier. The year 1991 was a turning point, when the New Economic Policy was adopted by the Indian government. This policy marked a radical shift, opening the national borders to international products, services, and capital flows, and allowing Indian companies to join in international competition.[3] The opening of India's economic frontiers, coupled with the domestic expansion of telecommunications and the ubiquity of the Internet (which acts to remove the cost of distance from information exchanges), allowed the rapid rise of India's software industry, which rocketed to world-class status in the late 1990s. In this case, India has a considerable set of market advantages: lower salaries, English-language ability, expertise in computer science and engineering, and a long tradition of numeracy, plus the 12-hour time zone advantage.

The special lead of Indians in Silicon Valley, and in other technopolises abroad and at home, also stems from globalization, capitalism, and the natural fit of Indian culture with high-technology "culture." The technological competence of Indian engineers and scientists, coupled with their business ability, allows them to excel in the game of high-tech entrepreneurship, transforming technological innovations, often in microelectronics or Internet-related fields, into wealth. While the number of Indian citizens in the diaspora and in metropolitan centers like Bangalore, Hyderabad, Mumbai, and Chennai is a small portion of India's one billion population, perhaps about 100 million, the contribution of these information workers to the informatization strategy is far out of proportion to their numbers. The wealth they are creating represents a new gold rush.

Globalization means that Indian brainpower can flow out of India, both in real and virtual terms, and can also move back in. Many Indian technologists migrated to America for graduate education, attracted by the high quality of U.S. universities. Others migrated to pursue high-tech careers. Thousands of overseas Indians return to their motherland each year, bringing with them wealth and expertise. Migration has been good for many

Indians, and, probably, for India. In a globalized world, the importance of national boundaries decreases. New communication technologies of telecommunications, computers, and the Internet allow individuals to live anywhere in the world, and to conduct business on the other side of the world. Globalization means that Indian software houses, remote-processing firms, and Indian meritocracy can now compete on a level playing field with overseas competitors, turning English-language competency, numeracy, and low labor costs into competitive advantage. Globalization also means that poultry farmers in Tamil Nadu and garlic growers in Rajasthan will lose their livelihoods as a result of imported American chicken legs and Chinese garlic.

Lesson #3 *The potential for rapid economic development in India has long been present on the part of its people, and once the bureaucratic and other governmental barriers to innovation, creativity, entrepreneurship, and growth were removed (or at least reduced), rapid social changes occurred.* However, India ranks well below on the listing of the nations of the world in terms of economic indicators (like per capita income, exports, and imports) and informatization (such as the percentage of the total population which has telephones, computers, or Internet access). But if one looks at these indicators for the information workers in India, rather than for its total population of over one billion, the information society within India can compete with the Singapores, Japans, Taiwans, and Koreas of the world. India's rate of growth along the route to informatization in the 1990s was impressive, especially in terms of creating new wealth and jobs, implementing electronic governance, and expanding access of disadvantaged citizens to telecommunications and Internet services. Within a few generations, India could become a world powerhouse in information technology businesses, ranking in the elite grouping of the United States, Japan, and Germany today. Also, developing countries could learn lessons from India about using information technology for governance and public service.

Whether or not this leap occurs depends in part on such unknowns as the political strength and stability of India's central government, its future informatization policies, how the troubled relationships with neighboring Pakistan and China are managed, and the degree to which traditional Indian culture adjusts to rapid technological and material progress. Another fundamental problematic of the future is whether the nation's informatization can be judiciously managed to benefit the huge mass of India's population. The electronic governance policies of Chief Minister Chandrababu Naidu in Andhra Pradesh, a state with a population of 80 million people, and the establishment of Internet community centers by Sam Pitroda's WorldTel in six Indian states, are thus being carefully watched in India, and worldwide.

Lesson #4 *India, especially in its urban areas during the 1990s, underwent a high degree of Westernization and Americanization, which facilitated informatization, but which also contributed to conflicts with India's traditional culture, and caused various social problems.* The rise of private television broadcasting in India during the past decades, made possible by satellite transmission and by cable distribution and by a hands-off government (non)policy, brought a flood of American television programs to India (*Dynasty, Baywatch,* and *The Bold and the Beautiful*). The audience and advertising success of the private cable and satellite-based television networks in India led to the commercialization of the state-run Doordarshan. Its programs now promote consumerist and material values, as Doordarshan seeks to hold on to its dominant audience position.

Along with the entry of Western companies selling consumer products like McDonalds, Coke, Reebok, and Benetton, facilitated by the NEP, and by the widespread television advertising of these foreign companies, Indian values are changing in fundamental ways, especially on the part of urban, educated younger people. Consumerism, individualism, and values of gender equality are surging, while frugality, collectivism, and patriarchy are diminishing. Many material benefits thus accrue to Indian society. The other half of India's human resources, women, are increasingly coming into the workforce, for example. But new social problems can emerge with such progress: parental conflict with adolescents, alcoholism, drug abuse, and the reported incidence of anorexia and bulimia among urban Indian girls who increasingly seek to starve their bodies into the pencil shape of model Cindy Crawford (Ghosh & Merchant, 1999). Along with the economic advantages of individualism, like a mobile workforce, come rising divorce rates and weaker family bonds. Would Mahatma Gandhi approve of present-day Indian television programming? Certainly not.

Lesson #5 *India's tremendous progress in telecommunications services during the 1990s fostered business progress and economic development, illustrating the informatization strategy.* Telecommunications policymaking in India in recent decades has been extremely contentious, contradictory, and multi-directional. Nevertheless, the provision of telephone and other telecommunications services has expanded impressively. Millions and millions of Indian households, which did not even have access to a public telephone a decade earlier, now have high-quality telephone services. India's landscape is dotted with thousands and thousands of privately operated public call offices (PCOs) that are now increasingly adding Internet services. Likewise, the ubiquitous cyber cafes and the Internet community centers (being established in six Indian states through Sam Pitroda's WorldTel) provide telecommunications and Internet services for a modest fee, low enough for millions of Indians who can not afford to own their own telephones, personal computers, or fax machines. Some hundreds of millions of Indian citizens, however, cannot even afford these public access telecommunications services now available at cyber cafes. These lower-income individuals represent a priority segment for further extending these public access services in the immediate future.

Where telecommunications services have been provided, and where their cost has decreased and quality improved, economic development has followed (as exemplified by the introduction of telephones in Kittur—discussed in Chapter 5). Telecommunications are a key factor in the informatization strategy, related to, and ranking along with, high-tech entrepreneurial spin-off companies.

Lesson #6 *Visionaries and champions play a key role in moving a nation forward on the informatization path.* For instance, how did

India's telecommunications revolution get under way in the mid-1980s? Two key individuals, the late Rajiv Gandhi, India's first high-tech prime minister, and Sam Pitroda, the expatriate visionary for informatization, collaborated in the late 1980s to bring about India's leap forward in telecommunications.[4] This revolution was caused in part by technological innovations created by Sam Pitroda's C-DOT, a government-sponsored R&D center, harnessed with the force of private capitalism through (*a*) the indigenous manufacturers of innovative telephone switching equipment, and (*b*) local operators of public access telephone booths. Once these forces were set in motion, the telecommunications revolution continued through the 1990s. And beyond.

Rajiv Gandhi's government instituted favorable policies in electronics, computer software, and telecommunications, and pushed for the application of information technology in computerizing the Indian Railway's reservation system, banks, and land records. During Rajiv Gandhi's tenure, the Center for Development of Telematics (C-DOT), the Center for the Development of Advanced Computing (C-DAC), and the National Informatics Center (NIC) were established. Also, Rajiv Gandhi's government invited Texas Instruments, General Electric, and Hewlett-Packard to do business in India, fueling the rise of the Bangalore technopolis.

So visionaries and technology champions such as Rajiv Gandhi and Sam Pitroda, aided by many other forward thinkers, promoted government policies that shook up the somnolent Indian bureaucracy previously responsible for providing telecommunications services to the Indian people, injecting the dynamics of competition and privatization. Ultimately, the combination of the 1991 New Economic Policy, and new policies for telecommunications, software, and Internet services, along with technological innovations, led to the communication revolution in India. Since the mid-1990s, Andhra Pradesh Chief Minister Chandrababu Naidu has championed the cause of informatization in his state, and nationally.

These six lessons learned about the informatization of India's information society center on the new communication technologies of computers, the Internet, and other microelectronics applications such as in satellites and telecommunications. Without these technological innovations, the Public Broadcasting Revolution, the Cable Revolution, the Technopolis, the Telecommunications Revolution, and the Computer/Internet Revolution would not have occurred. But these disruptions and discontinuities could also not have occurred (*a*) without public policies (for example, the New Economic Policy) that removed prior constraints to social change; and (*b*) without the individual actions of visionaries, champions, entrepreneurs, and innovators. Revolutions, after all, do not happen without revolutionaries to lead them. These leaders exist at all levels, from the postmaster (Bapu) and tailor in village Lutsaan, to national figures like Azim Premji and Chandrababu Naidu, and to international personalities like Sam Pitroda and Sabeer Bhatia.

Looking Backward

As explained in our Preface to the present volume, we originally set out to update our 1989 book, *India's Information Revolution*. What are the most important social changes that have occurred over the past 10 years?

#1 The brain drain of young Indian technologists, many of whom were products of the IITs and IIMs, perceived as a major social problem in 1989, is today balanced by a return flow of people, funds, and expertise from the worldwide Indian diaspora, notably from the United States. India's globalization leads its citizens in foreign lands to become outposts and liaisons for Indian business and technology (Khadria, 1999). An example is the software engineer in Bangalore, perhaps an employee of Infosys Technologies, Wipro, or Texas Instruments, who writes code that is transmitted by satellite and the Internet to America, where it is purchased by a U.S. company for use 12 hours later. Or consider the many Indian high-tech entrepreneurs in Silicon Valley who become wealthy, send funds back home, and perhaps return to India with cutting-edge technological innovations.

#2   Indian technologists continue to convert their considerable brainpower into technological innovations that are sold in the marketplace as new products and services. Both at home and abroad, Indian-created technologies are managed by Indian business mavens in order to create high-tech start-up companies, and thus to amass vast wealth. These spin-off ventures fuel the growth of Bangalore, Hyderabad, and other technology cities in India, and vault Indians in Silicon Valley and on Boston's Route 128 into wealth and fame. The rise of Indian entrepreneurs in Silicon Valley is illustrated by their launching four in every 10 new start-ups in the late 1990s. Silicon Valley is home to 80,000 skilled Indian professionals, a majority of whom work as scientists, engineers, and managers (*Computers Today*, 1999a). As before, they are noted for their technical expertise; now they are also respected for their entrepreneurial business skills as they launch high-tech companies. A new set of Indian billionaires who pioneered computer software or Internet-related ventures in 1999 serve as role models for others to follow.

#3   The informatization strategy through which an information society emerges centers (*a*) on new communication technologies like computers, telecommunications, and the Internet, (*b*) on research universities like the IITs, where technical brainpower is trained and R&D is conducted; and (*c*) on favorable government policies. India's New Economic Policy of 1991 was a fundamental shift to free-market capitalism and to open-border globalization. This radical policy change was totally unexpected when we wrote our earlier book in 1989, which reflected the intense frustrations of "wanna-be" Indian entrepreneurs whose progress was blocked by the necessity for dozens of government licenses and approvals. This dismal bureaucratic situation has now been ameliorated, so that indigenous entrepreneurship has been unshackled and allowed to compete in the global marketplace. The incredible business success of Indians and of Indian companies is likely to continue, and grow, in the future.

   The IITs and IIMs were identified as crucial institutions in our 1989 book; today they are even more so. And, to complement them, a horde of private computer training centers—some 2,000 in number—have arisen throughout India. The newly established Indian Institutes of Information Technology in Hyderabad and in Bangalore are also at the core of India's informatization future.

#4 The important role of private cable and satellite television networks in the Westernization of Indian values through television programs and advertising could not have been anticipated in 1989, although the commercialization of public television (Doordarshan) was already under way, accompanied by concerns about rising consumerism. The private television revolution of the 1990s was a product of technology (satellite transmission and cable distribution) plus the appeal that imported television programs and indigenous entertainment programs such as television serials and talk shows produced in local languages held for Indian audiences.

Mass media the world over are driven by market forces gauged by audience ratings. However, broadcasters and advertisers feel, often mistakenly, that in order to achieve high audience ratings, the entertainment content of a media message needs to be degraded to include depictions of overt sex and violence. Recent experience from all over the world, including the findings of media research in village Lutsaan and Kheda and Jhabua districts in India (discussed in Chapter 2), suggests that entertainment–education programs can strike a balance between market demands and social imperatives.

#5 India's computer software industry was already booming in 1989, but we did not foresee the creation of such impressive wealth by India's cyber czars Azim Premji and Narayana Murthy through software export sales, nor did we appreciate the role of the Internet and telecommunications in allowing India-based software programmers to gain a dominant market share worldwide. Texas Instruments, India, had demonstrated the market advantage of their Bangalore–Dallas across-the-time-zones connection, but we did not foresee the coming software explosion. Nor did we visualize the competitive advantage that India has gained in the booming global marketplace of remote-processing services like medical transcription, Web design, database management, and so forth.

In short, many of the forces leading to India's information society were already under way in the 1980s. But during the 1990s, several of these trickles became a flood, pushing the subcontinent into position among the world leaders in computer software and other high-technology industries. The overall result is the need to suggest a different strategy for development, and informatization, than was anticipated previously. What will happen next?

Looking Forward[5]

India's informatization challenge is not only to create the conditions for a vibrant information technology industry that is globally competitive and creates software millionaires by the thousand, but to use information technology to improve the quality of life of the mass of its citizens, to solve their pressing problems, and to empower them through readily accessible information in a language that they can understand (Pitroda, 1998). What can be done to achieve these industry-friendly and people-centered informatization goals?

1. Creation of IT Mindsets in India   A tremendous need exists to enhance awareness and understanding among *all* Indian citizens (not only its many millions of information workers) about what information technology *can* do. India, in 2000, had information technology, but lacked the IT culture of sharing information, organizing, codifying, and streamlining processes (Pitroda, 1998). Information is still mostly the domain of a privileged few, although with expanding public access to television, cable, telephony, and the Internet, this scenario is changing.

How can IT mindsets be created in India? The mass media can play an important role in setting an IT agenda by covering the Chandrababu Naidus, Sam Pitrodas, and Azim Premjis, among others. More importantly, the mass media should cover the creative applications of IT to solve local problems, for instance, the rural telephone exchange in Kittur, the Jhabua Development Communication Project in Madhya Pradesh, the Internet community centers in Andhra Pradesh, and others. Every Monday evening, Chandrababu Naidu, connects with his state's citizenry through a highly rated interactive television program on Doordarshan, Hyderabad, called "Dial Your Chief Minister." A pressing social issue is identified every week (for instance, unemployment, prohibition, or health care), and citizens can dial in and directly communicate with their political leader. Naidu has used this television program to communicate his IT vision to the citizens of AP, and the citizens, in turn, experience firsthand how television, telecommunications, and governance can go hand in hand. Naidu, as discussed previously, regularly holds videoconferences with district-level administrators, creating an IT-led governance culture and mindset in Andhra Pradesh.

An IT culture cannot be created overnight in India; it will take time, decades perhaps. But as concerted efforts are made to take IT to the Indian people through railway reservation systems, banks, PCOs, Internet community centers, distance education, e-commerce, and electronic cash, IT mindsets will emerge (as they have in the U.S. and other Western industrialized countries). Here it is important that IT implementation relate to the felt needs of the common Indian citizen. They need to know the latest market prices for their agricultural produce, how to grow better potatoes, and repair water pumps (Pitroda, 1998). People in India's cities, towns, and villages should be able to access such need-based information from a local facility (a cyber cafe or an Internet community center), in their local language, and at an affordable cost.

2. Applying IT to Governance and Administration   Information technology offers an unprecedented opportunity to take government to the people, as is occurring in Andhra Pradesh and several other Indian states (Pitroda, 1998). It is estimated that most Indian states have about 20,000 forms, for instance to apply for a ration card, make a housing application, obtain a birth certificate, and so on. These forms need to be reduced in number, simplified, standardized, and made available through public access Internet kiosks (Gates with Hemingway, 1999). Citizens should no longer need to travel to the district headquarters, or stand in line for hours, to obtain simple forms, check examination results, or pay their water, electricity, and telephone bills. With adequate training, operators of Internet community centers can offer these public services to citizens at affordable rates.

The potential of IT in streamlining government is monumental, as the experience of Andhra Pradesh in India suggests. Paperless processes can be created, for instance, to streamline bureaucracy. Putting government departments on email can reduce paper filing; also, governments can publish everything on the Internet, saving tremendous publication costs. In addition to convenience, speed, and efficiency, information technology can help create a responsive, accountable, and transparent system of governance. By reducing the need for interpersonal contact between government officials and citizens, a key cause of widespread corruption in India, information technology can potentially transform governance processes. As Pitroda (1999) remarked: "The Internet represents a golden opportunity for India to revolutionize its antiquated, slow, corrupt, inefficient and failing bureaucratic processes with state-of-the-art, instantaneous, user-friendly, convenient, accessible, open, transparent, and productive electronic methods."

Naidu's electronic governance initiatives in Andhra Pradesh have inspired the states of Tamil Nadu, Karnataka, Kerala, Gujarat, and various others to follow suit, creating a healthy competitive environment between Indian states to implement e-governance.

3. Development of IT Infrastructure, Policies, and Business Potential   As noted previously, the Indian government, in the past decade, has done a commendable job to create an infrastructure (of software technology parks, high-speed data-links, export promotion zones) and implement policies to make India a global computer software powerhouse. However, a great deal more needs to be done (Pitroda, 1998). High-speed, high-bandwidth digital backbones are needed that provide universal access to all parts of the country. An integrated communication policy is needed that will integrate Internet and cable services with basic and wireless telephony, as well as data services. With the emergence of digital technologies, the distinction between broadcasting and telecommunications is becoming blurred. It makes sense to have an overarching regulator of these communication services, so that the informatization strategy can be carried forward in India on a more coordinated basis. The challenge for the newly created Ministry of Information Technology in India is to speedily establish and implement such a forward-looking agenda, and not be mired in turf battles with other ministries.

More broadly, clear-cut policies, procedures, and programs need to be instituted with respect to promoting intellectual property rights, patent filing, R&D facilitation, academic–industry collaboration, venture capital, public market access, small business promotion, and entrepreneurship (Pitroda, 1998; D. Sharma, 1999).

4. Developing Human Resources for Informatization The key resource for informatization to occur centers around human resources. In India, the IITs, IIMs, hundreds of regional engineering colleges, and over 2,000 private IT training institutes (run by NIIT, Aptech, ZED, and others) do a good job of training the personnel needed for India's emerging information society. However, for India to emerge as a global industry player, and for it to take IT to its remote corners, a far greater number of people need to be trained, and in different kinds of skills. If informatization is to make a dent in the problems of village India, the education and training challenge includes: how to prepare the teachers in Indian cities, towns, and villages in Internet-based distance education methods; how to train government employees to use email and the Internet; how to train operators of Internet community centers so they can adequately serve the public's (including those who are illiterate) information needs; and how to train village leaders at the local level to access market information, manage accounts, prepare balance sheets, collect taxes, and provide local services.

□ **New Opportunities for Communication Research**[6]

While India has several well-known engineering and business schools that drive its communication revolution, training in communication theory and research hardly exists in India's universities, with few exceptions. This situation seems a strange paradox, given that communication technologies are at the heart of contemporary social changes.

Communication research is the application of social science, humanistic, and critical theories and their accompanying research methods to the study of human communication behavior.[7] Technologies such as email, fax, Internet, and high-speed data-links fundamentally change the way nations, communities, organizations, and individuals communicate. As India moves forward on its informatization road, the study of social science, humanistic, and policy aspects of communication technologies becomes even more crucial.

Communication study as an academic discipline grew to intellectual strength mainly in the U.S. during the several decades following World War II, although its European and American foundations go back another 30 years (Rogers, 1994). Communication teaching and research flourishes in North America, Europe, and Latin America, and is expanding rapidly in several countries of Asia (China, Singapore, Korea, and Hong Kong, for instance) and Africa. This appealing field, attractive to students, often leads to well-paid, glamorous occupations that are growing in numbers, especially in countries that are becoming information societies.

In 2000, approximately 120 communication programs existed in Indian universities, however, most focussed on imparting print journalism skills (as most are founded or headed by former/retired newspaper journalists).[8] The booming job market in television, cable, and other media services have created a need for trained personnel, and universities and private training institutes have hurried to establish communication programs, some of which are of dubious quality. Most of the 120 communication programs in India offer diplomas or Bachelor's degrees, with a handful (for example, the Universities of Pune, Manipal, Bangalore, Osmania, Jamia Milia, and a few others) also offering Master's degrees. Relatively few of these programs are theoretically driven or display a concern for the role of communication media in social mobilization and development.[9] The curricula in most programs are often outdated and lack relevance to pressing national or regional needs. Seldom do courses deal with the social impacts of new communication technologies, a topic that is of much relevance in India at this time. In recent decades, hundreds of Indians have earned Ph.D. degrees in communication theory and research at various U.S. universities (and some in the U.K.). However, only a handful of them conduct studies of the unfolding process of informatization in India, either individually or in collaboration with local scholars.

> At the turn of the century, India is positioned, perhaps as no other developing country is, to provide answers to what role new communication technologies can play in the task of nation-building, governance, and in improving the quality of life of its ordinary citizens. Will communication researchers, in India and overseas, seek such answers through systematic study?

Responsible Entrepreneurship: Sharing the Pie?[10]

Our book shows how India's informatization strategy has created an enormous amount of wealth, in a relatively short period of time, for such individuals as Azim Premji of Wipro, Narayana Murthy of Infosys, Subhash Chandra of Zee-TV, Sabeer Bhatia of Hotmail, Vinod Khosla of Sun Microsystems, Gururaj Deshpande of Sycamore Networks, Arjun Malhotra of HCL, and many others. This wealth was amassed through free-market capitalism, aided by favorable government policies, individual leaders' vision, entrepreneurial spirit, and hard work. Greater socio-economic inequality often accompanies free-market capitalism, creating a wider gulf between the haves and the have-nots. Hence, a tremendous need exists, especially in the contemporary informatization era, to balance corporate profit-taking with a sense of social responsibility. Such "balancing" does not ordinarily happen through market forces; however, it can be consciously, creatively, and thoughtfully forged.

India needs entrepreneurs who believe in making money and doing good at the same time. Several useful lessons in this regard can be learned from the Grameen Bank in Bangladesh, where capitalistic principles serve to empower the poor. Its micro-lending program, its "telephone ladies" program (discussed in Chapter 5), its village Internet program, and numerous other initiatives demonstrate how entrepreneurship and social responsibility can be creatively forged. Further, India needs entrepreneurs who practice "compassionate capitalism" or "creative altruism" for their society (Murthy, 2000). These individuals create wealth through highly competitive ventures, but then give some of it back to society for laudable social initiatives (Yunus, 1999).

Narayana Murthy, Chairman of Infosys Technologies, is a proto-typical socially responsible entrepreneur. As discussed previously, he draws a salary of only $36,000 (U.S.), lives in a modest house in a middle-class Bangalore neighborhood, and takes pride in having created over 250 dollar-millionaires and 4,000 rupee-millionaires in India. In recent years, Infosys has instituted 26 scholarships for Ph.D. students at 13 prestigious national institutions including the Indian Institute of Science in Bangalore and the IITs. Its Catch-Them-Young program identifies bright school students for short-duration courses in computer software programming. As part of its Computers@Classrooms program, Infosys donates used computer equipment to local schools.[11] Its Rural Reach Program conducts computer awareness and demonstration sessions in small towns and villages. Furthermore, the Infosys Foundation promotes literacy among the underprivileged; it has helped establish over 1,000 libraries in underserved areas.

Murthy made a personal gift of $1 million to his alma mater, IIT Kanpur, in the mid-1990s, inspiring his colleague Nandan Nile-kani, Managing Director of Infosys and a 1978 graduate in electrical engineering from IIT Mumbai, to gift $1.75 million to his alma mater. Narayana Murthy and his brand of socially conscious entrepreneurs believe that wealth must first be created before it can be given away. And they do give it away.

The IITs in India have especially benefitted from alumni gift-giving. As noted previously, Kanwal Rekhi, a successful Silicon Valley entrepreneur, gifted $2 million to IIT Mumbai to establish the Kanwal Rekhi School of Information Technology.[12] Arjun Malhotra, co-founder of HCL, donated $1 million to establish the G.S. Sanyal School of Telecommunications at IIT Kharagpur. Other notable benefactors to their IIT alma maters include Rakesh Mathur, the brains behind Internet browser Junglee.com, Vinod Gupta of the U.S. database firm American Business Information, and Suhas Patil, co-founder of Cirrus Logic. Endowed academic programs and professorships, while common in the U.S., were extremely rare in India until the mid-1990s. However, thanks to the Narayana Murthys and the Arjun Malhotras, this is no longer the case. The Indian Institute of Technology Delhi acquired 17 endowed professorships from 1996 to 2000!

The giving away of tens of millions of dollars by Indian entrepreneurs to their IIT alma maters is laudable. Giving back to one's
alma mater, parish, and community is a highly cherished value in
the U.S., and, no doubt, inspirational to successful U.S.–based
Indians (Rekhi, 2000). In 2000, a billion-dollar corpus fund was
being raised by successful Indians in the U.S. to establish a world-
class Global Institute of Science and Technology in India in cooperation with top-notch U.S. universities. Indian prime minister
Atal Behari Vajpayee appropriately labeled this gigantic fund-
raising effort as one that established a "new standard of philanthropy in India."

However, what keeps these successful Indian entrepreneurs
from raising many more billion dollars to equip the hundreds of
thousands of disadvantaged Indian villages with primary health
care centers, *pukka* (solid) school buildings, telephones, or village
Internet connections? Why is it that these successful entrepreneurs, who are veterans at creating and assessing business plans,
do not also forge socially responsible yet commercially viable business plans for implementing village development activities? What
prevents these corpus funds from being used to hire the best talent in the country (whether from the IIMs, or the IITs, or local
institutions) at market rates to solve such national problems? Why
should the best Indian minds not be applied also to boost health,
nutrition, and literacy among people in rural India, as opposed to
just focussing on selling them toothpaste, shampoos, and soft
drinks? What prevents suitable national and local partnerships
from being established between corporations, donors, NGOs, and
the village communities to implement such programs? What keeps
more Khedas and Jhabuas (see Chapter 2) and radio farm forums
from being funded initially through "do-good capital" (as opposed to venture capital), with clear-cut plans to move toward
financial sustainability (like the various Grameen Bank ventures)?
Why should one depend on the government alone to take care of
these most pressing national and local needs? Also, why does the
government not facilitate such privately funded, demand-driven,
socially responsible development initiatives? Why are single-
window clearances and other financial and tax incentives not provided for these activities?

As compared to the U.S., the voluntary sector in India is at a nascent stage. In the U.S. in recent years, the Bill and Melinda Gates Foundation, fueled by Microsoft dollars and managed by Bill Gates's father, made monster contributions for polio eradication, minority scholarships, and the worldwide promotion of reproductive health. Media baron Ted Turner, founder of Cable News Network (CNN), made a billion-dollar gift over a period of 10 years to the United Nations to support its high-priority development programs. Silicon Valley's first two billionaires, Bill Hewlett and Dave Packard (founders of the Hewlett-Packard Company), established well-endowed foundations to support a variety of social initiatives. Corporate philanthropy and the establishment of private foundations in India are just beginning. Corporate giving in India must necessarily be driven to tackle India's most pressing needs.

Another form of socially responsible entrepreneurship is reflected in the work of the Grameen Bank in Bangladesh (see Chapter 5), where small micro-credit loans enable poor women to engage in income-generating activities, including the vending of mobile telephony services in rural areas (Yunus, 1999). The "telephone ladies" of Bangladesh, while in a different league from the Bill Gateses and the Ted Turners, bring the benefits of informatization to remote, rural areas, while making a tidy profit from the services they provide. Muhammad Yunus, through his social invention of micro-lending, may have done as much to help the world, if not more, as the Bill Gateses and the Ted Turners.

Social entrepreneurship can take non-material forms,[13] such as when individuals, after making their fortunes, contribute their time and expertise to develop state-of-the-art technology to solve national and local problems. The role of Sam Pitroda in the 1980s in establishing the Centre for the Development of Telematics (C-DOT), where he served as an advisor at a token salary of 1 rupee (2 cents) a year, is illustrative. After selling his U.S.–based telecommunications company, Wescom, and netting 3.5 million dollars, Pitroda said: "Enough is enough. Now it is time to give back" (personal interview, 16 June 1987). He spent the decade of the 1980s contributing his personal time and money to revolutionize telecommunications services in India. Then, in the 1990s, Pitroda focussed on applying his informatization vision and skills to other poor countries of the world.

As the informatization process moves forward in India, the debate about "Informatization for whom, and with what purpose?" will intensify. It should. A large percentage of India's population of one billion, about 350 to 400 million people, are illiterate and live poverty-ridden lives under harsh conditions. How will the Internet-related technologies that create Indian billionaires also help them? Socially responsible entrepreneurship can balance economic and social interests, much as the entertainment–education strategy can earn high audience ratings and hence advertising dollars, while educating the public for social change (see Chapter 2). As Muhammad Yunus (2000, p. 6), Managing Director of the Grameen Bank, said: "Doing good and doing well are not mutually exclusive. In fact, doing good may be the best way to do well."

The mantra for India's informatization strategy must necessarily be "growth with equity." Will that ever happen? How soon?

Notes

1. The Chinese experience is revealing: China's private sector contributed 60 percent of the nation's GDP in 1999, up from 0 percent in 1979.

2. This often means that the government should simply get out of the way. For instance, despite the NEP, why is the Indian government wasting its time and resources running five-star hotels and airlines? In late 1999, several IIT alumni (including U.S.–based Kanwal Rekhi, President of The Indus Entrepreneurs, and India-based Narayana Murthy of Infosys) offered to raise $1 billion to privatize the five IITs (which presently depend on Indian government subsidies), running them through a council of distinguished alumni, Indian business leaders, and noted academics and policy-makers. The purpose is to make the IITs world-class teaching and research institutions like Stanford, MIT, and Caltech.

3. The advent of Westernized, privatized satellite television opened India's cultural borders as well, making the Western lifestyle appear desirable.

4. In the 1990s, Prime Minister P.V. Narasimha Rao and Finance Minister Manmohan Singh championed the New Economic Policy, which helped speed up the informatization process in India.
5. This section draws upon the IT vision of Sam Pitroda (1998), Chandrababu Naidu (see http://www.andhrapradesh.com/), Dr N. Bhaskara Rao (personal communication, 16 November 1999), and Gates with Hemingway (1999).
6. This section draws on personal conversations with Dr N. Bhaskara Rao, Chairman of the Center for Media Studies, New Delhi, on 5 January 1999.
7. Communication issues are central to academic disciplines such as social psychology, computer science, electrical engineering, linguistics, anthropology, sociology, and political science. The study of communication must necessarily be rather multidisciplinary, drawing on these several fields and contributing to them.
8. Print journalism programs are the preferred route to cash in on this boom, as little capital investment is needed to establish them relative to programs in television production, which need expensive studios, cameras, editing machines, and a highly trained faculty.
9. In recent decades, audience research in India has become increasingly market- and ratings-driven.
10. This case draws upon Lakshman (1999).
11. Infosys also donated $250,000 to the Indian Institute of Information Technology in Bangalore, which has established a technology incubation park modeled after Stanford University's park.
12. Also see note 2 above.
13. Or when seasoned and successful entrepreneurs mentor first-time entrepreneurs, as is done by Kanwal Rekhi and Gururaj Deshpande in the U.S.

Glossary of concepts

Agglomeration is the degree to which some quality is concentrated spatially in one area.

Collaboration is the process through which each unit in a system voluntarily agrees to unite with other units to pursue common goals.

Commercialization of the mass media is the production and transmission of media products intended to attract large audiences and thus to generate large profits from advertising sales.

Communication research is the application of social science, humanistic, and critical theories and their accompanying research methods to the study of human communication behavior.

Communication technology is the hardware equipment, organizational structures, and social values by which individuals collect, process, and exchange information.

Consumerism is the degree to which an individual is oriented toward purchasing products and services.

Deskilling is the process through which new communication technologies downgrade an occupation to a lower socio-economic status by replacing human skills with information-handling equipment.

Development communication is the process of using communication to further development.

Development is a widely participatory process of directed social change in a society, intended to bring about both social and material advancement (including greater equality, freedom, and other valued qualities) for the majority of people through their gaining greater control over their environment.

E-commerce is commercial transactions between two parties on the Internet.

Efficacy is the degree to which an individual feels he/she can control his/her future.

E-marketing is the use of the Internet to market products or services.

Entertainment–education is the process of purposely designing and implementing a media message to both entertain and educate, in order to increase audience members' knowledge about an educational issue, create favorable attitudes, and change overt behavior.

Global village is a world that is increasingly interconnected by communication technologies and that is tending toward a global culture.

High-technology industry is an industry at the cutting edge of technology, whose core technology changes rapidly.

Information societies are countries in which information workers are more numerous than such occupational categories as farmers, industrial workers, or service workers.

Information workers are individuals whose main job responsibilities are to gather, process, or distribute information, or to produce information technologies like computers or telecommunications equipment that are used by other information workers.

Information is patterned matter-energy that affects the choices available to an individual making a decision.

Informatization is the process through which communication technologies are used as strategies for furthering socio-economic development.

Innovation is an idea perceived as new.

Interactivity is the degree to which the participants in a communication process have control over, and can exchange roles in, their mutual discourse.

Interpersonal communication is a face-to-face exchange between two or more individuals.

Mass media communication includes all those means of transmitting messages such as radio, television, newspapers, and film, which enable a source of one or a few individuals to reach a large audience.

Mega-cities are metropolitan areas that have grown to such large size that they are virtually unmanageable by city officials.

Parasocial interaction is the perceived face-to-face interpersonal relationship that develops between a television viewer and a media role model.

Research university is defined as an institution of higher education whose main functions are to conduct research and to train graduate students in doing research.

Soap opera is a dramatic serial that is broadcast mainly in order to entertain audience members.

Social construction of technology is the process through which people give meaning to a new technology by discussing it with each other.

Spin-off is a new company that is created (*a*) by individuals who leave a parent organization, (*b*) around a technology that these entrepreneurs bring with them from the parent organization.

Technological determinism is an approach that considers technology as the main cause of social change.

Technology is defined as information that is put to use in order to accomplish some task.

Technopolis is a geographically concentrated high-technology complex characterized by a large number of entrepreneurial spin-off companies.

Transcreation involves adapting an existing serial's plot, characters, and context to suit the needs of another audience.

Venture capital is money invested in new high-tech companies with a high potential for growth.

References

Agrawal, B.C. (1981). *SITE social evaluation: Results, experiences, and implications*. Ahmedabad: Space Application Center.

Ahluwalia, B. (1999). Wrong number, Trai again. *Outlook*, 5 April 1999, pp. 48–49.

Aiyar, S.S. (2000). Labor, governance, and the information age. *Development Outreach*, Winter, pp. 23–27.

Akash Bharati (1978). *Report of the Working Group on Autonomy for Akashvani and Doordarshan*. New Delhi: Ministry of Information and Broadcasting.

All India Radio (AIR) (1996). *All India Radio 1996: Facts and figures*. New Delhi: All India Radio.

An Indian personality for television (1985). *Report of the Working Group on Software for Doordarshan*. New Delhi: Ministry of Information and Broadcasting.

Arora, S. (2000). A guru's mantra. *India Today*, North American Supplement, March 2000, p. 28.

Arthur, B.W. (1996). Increasing returns and the new world of business. *Harvard Business Review*, 74 (4): 100–109.

Athreya, M.B. (1996). India's telecommunications policy. *Telecommunications Policy*, 20 (1): 11–22.

Bahadur, S. (1999). DoT demystified. *Information Communications World*, Special Supplement, August 1999.

Bakshi, M. (1999). Touching Kargil heights. *Computers Today*, 1–15 August 1999, http://www.india-today.com/ctoday/19990801/.

Balakrishnan, A. (1999). India, still Internet-shy. *Computers Today*, 1–15 July 1999, http://www.india-today.com/ctoday/19990701/.
Ballon, M. (1999). Where the dough is. *Inc.*, June 1999, p. 107.
Bansal, S., & Carvalho, B. (1998). India's Murdoch. *Business World*, 9 July 1998, http://www.zeetelevision/com.
Bean, S.S. (1989). Gandhi and *khadi*, the fabric of Indian independence. In A.B. Weaver & J. Schneider (eds), *Cloth of human experience*, pp. 355–76. Washington, D.C.: Smithsonian Institution Press.
Bellman, E. (1999). Software powerhouse Infosys trades on the Nasdaq, a first for India. *Bloomberg Personal Finance*, July–August 1999, p. 48.
Bhagwati, J. (2000). The next Jews. *India Today International*, 27 March 1999, p. 32.
Bhargava, S. (1987). Ramayan: Divine sensation. *India Today*, 30 April 1987, pp. 170–71.
Bhasin, U. (1997). *The role of All India Radio in formal education in India: A case study*. Paper presented at the Global Knowledge Conference, Toronto, Canada, May 1997.
Bhasin, U., & Singhal, A. (1998). Participatory approaches to message design: *'Jeevan Saurabh'*, a pioneering radio serial in India for adolescents. *Media Asia*, 25 (1): 12–18.
Bhatia, S. (1988). An epic goes electronic and India gets hooked. *Far Eastern Economic Review*, 4 February 1988, pp. 70–73.
Bhatt, K. (1998). The power of digitized dreams: The role of Indian-Americans in Silicon Valley. http://www.indiapost.com/bus_news/APR98/.
Bhatt, S.C. (1994). *Satellite invasion of India*. New Delhi: Gyan Publishing House.
Branigin, W. (1998). High-tech's hired hands: Critics say visa program, immigrants exploited. *The Washington Post*, 26 July 1998.
Bumiller, E. (1990). *May you be the mother of a hundred sons: A journey among women of India*. New York: Random House.
Cable Quest (1998). A sign of maturity. 15 December 1998, p. 2.
Cable Waves (1997). Government wants a license or two. 16–31 August 1997, p. 9.
—— (1998). Audience share of key channels in Indian market. 15 March 1998, p. 4.
—— (1999). Consumers want private firms in basic telephony. 16–28 February 1999, p. 11.
Chopra, A., & Baria, F. (1999). The beauty craze. *India Today*, 15 November 1999, pp. 20–29.
Chowdary, T.H. (1998). Politics and economics of telecom liberalization in India. *Telecommunications Policy*, 22 (1): 9–22.

Chowdary, T.H. (1999a). Don't turn around now. *Computers Today*, 1–15 July 1999, http://www.india-today.com/ctoday/19990701/.

—— (1999b). PCs in the PCO booths. *Computers Today*, 15–31 August 1999, http://www.india-today.com/ctoday/19990815/.

—— (1999c). *Telecom de-monopolization in India*. Hyderabad: Center for Telecom Management and Studies.

Chowdhary, S. (1999a). Wireless Local Loop: Where there's W(I)LL. *Computers Today*, 15–31 July 1999, http://www.india-today.com/ctoday/19990715/.

—— (1999b). New telecom policy: Sputter, sputter. *Computers Today*, 15–31 August 1999, http://www.india-today.com/ctoday/19990815/.

Computers Today (1999a). E-millions. 16–31 December 1999, http://www.india-today.com/ctoday/19991216/master4.html.

—— (1999b). Turmoil will churn the IT marketplace. 15–31 August 1999, http://www.india-today.com/ctoday/19990815/.

Contractor, N.S., Singhal, A., & Rogers, E.M. (1988). Meta-theoretical perspectives on satellite television and development in India. *Journal of Broadcasting and Electronic Media*, 32 (2): 129–48.

Crabtree, R., & Malhotra, S. (2000). The genesis and evolution of commercial television in India: Organizational mechanisms of cultural imperialism. *Journal of Broadcasting and Electronic Media*, in press.

David, S., Ghosh, L., & Jagadheeshan, L.R. (1999). On the fast track. *India Today International*, 2 August 1999, pp. 38–45.

Dell, M. (1999). *Dell direct: Strategies that revolutionized an industry*. New York: Harper Business.

DeVol, R.C. (1999). *America's high-tech economy: Growth, development, and risks for metropolitan areas*. Santa Monica, CA: Miliken Institute Report.

Dey, S. (1999). MTV to go regional by year-end, steps up reach in neighboring countries. *Financial Express*, 14 July 1999, p. 3.

Dolan, K.A. (1999). What the doctor ordered. *Forbes*, 25 January 1999, p. 74.

Doordarshan (1998). *Doordarshan 1998*. New Delhi: Prasar Bharati Broadcasting Corporation of India.

Dutt, E. (1999). Trio in venture to create on-line shopping guide. *India Abroad*, 10 September 1999, p. 28.

—— (2000). Epinion's multimillion dollar ad campaign. *India Abroad*, 31 March 2000, p. 40.

Dutta, J. (1999). Delegation from Maharashtra showcases state's attractions. *India Abroad*, 9 July 1999, p. 32.

Easwaran, A. (1999). Web magazine by Texas couple turns into a hit. *India Abroad*, 30 April 1999, p. 43.

Ebiri, B. (1999). How the world uses the Net. *Yahoo! Internet Life*, September 1999, p. 118–19.

Fernandez, M. (1998). Asian Indian Americans in the Bay area and the glass ceiling. *Sociological Perspectives*, 41 (1): 119–49.

Forbes (1999). Thoughts on business of life. 4 October 1999, 164 (8): 160.

Frauenheim, E. (1999). India Inc. *Techweek*, 20 September 1999, http://www.tie.org/TechWeek%20India%20Inc_%20%5B9-20-99%5D.htm.

Gates, W., with Hemingway, C. (1999). *Business@the speed of thought*. New York: Warner Books.

Ghosh, L., & Merchant, R. (1999). New age addiction. *India Today*, 18 October 1999, pp. 46–47.

Gibson, D.V., & Rogers, E.M. (1994). *R&D collaboration on trial: The Microelectronics and Computer Technology Consortia*. Boston, MA: Harvard Business School Press.

Gibson, D.V., Kozmetsky, G., & Smilor, R. (eds) (1992). *The technopolis phenomenon: Smart cities, fast systems, and global networks*. Baltimore, MD: Rowan and Littlefield.

Gladwell, M. (1999). The science of the sleeper: How the information age could blow away the blockbuster. *The New Yorker*, 4 October 1999, pp. 48–50, 52–55.

Gupta, N. (1998). *Switching channels*. New Delhi: Oxford University Press.

Halarnkar, S., & Ramani, P. (1999). Digital dawn. *India Today*, 5 July 1999, pp. 34–39.

Hegel, J., & Singer, M. (1999). *Net worth: Shopping markets when customers make the rules*. Boston, MA: Harvard Business School Press.

Horton, D., & Wohl, R.R. (1956). Mass communication and para-social interaction: Observation on intimacy at a distance. *Psychiatry*, 19 (3): 215–29.

—— http://smartm.com/news/html (1999). SMART Modular Technologies, Inc., outfits Silicon Valley high school with extensive new computer lab.

India Abroad (1999a). Briefs: 39th in competitiveness. 30 April 1999, p. 22.

—— (1999b). Bits & bytes. 2 July 1999, p. 32.

—— (2000). Wipro's Premji is world's fourth richest person. 25 February 2000, p. 38.

Jain, A. (1999). Leading firms. *India Abroad*, 23 April 1999, p. 26.

Johnson, K. (2000). *Television and social change in rural India*. New Delhi: Sage Publications.

Kalwachwala, D., & Joshi, H. (1990). *Nari tu Narayani: A retrospective look*. Ahmedabad: Development and Education Communication Unit, Space Application Center.

284 INDIA'S COMMUNICATION REVOLUTION

Karp, J. (1999). The IT guys: New corporate gurus tap India's brain-power to galvanize economy. *Wall Street Journal*, 27 September 1999, pp. A1, A24.

Kasturirangan, K. (1999). *Communication for development*. Paper presented at the CMS Communication Colloquium, New Delhi, India, Center for Media Studies, June 1999.

Katakam, A. (1999). Towards e-governance. *Frontline*, 10 December 1999, pp. 78–80.

Kaufman, J. (1999). Young love: What happens when a 20-something whiz is suddenly boss. *Wall Street Journal*, 8 October 1999, pp. A1, A10.

Kaur, K. (1999a). Radio on the Net: Listener is King. *Computers Today*, 15–31 August 1999, http://www.india-today.com/ctoday/19990815/.

——— (1999b). State of the mart: World view. *Computers Today*, 1–15 July 1999, http://www.india-today.com/ctoday/19990701/.

Khadria, B. (1999). *The migration of knowledge workers: Second-generation effects of India's brain drain*. New Delhi: Sage Publications.

Khanna, H. (1987). Socio-cultural dynamics of Indian television's search for balance. Paper presented to the Indian Social Science Congress, Mysore, March 1987.

Kivlin, J.E., Roy, P., Fliegel, F.C., & Sen, L.K. (1968). *Communication in India: Experiments in introducing change*. Hyderabad: National Institute of Community Development.

Kohli, V. (1999). How smart companies are casting on the Net. *Business World*, 7–21 January 1999, pp. 76–82.

Kripalani, M. (1997). Read all about it! Newspapers go for a face-lift! *Business Week*, 2 June 1997, p. 27.

Krishna, B.M. (1999a). Research body evaluates Canada's Software Development Worker Project. *India Abroad*, 23 April 1999, p. 26.

——— (1999b). 4 entrepreneurs receive AIA's Kautilya awards. *India Abroad*, 23 April 1999, p. 22.

Krishnan, P., & Dighe, A. (1990). *Affirmation and denial: Construction of femininity on Indian television*. New Delhi: Sage Publications.

Kumar, K.J. (1998). History of television in India: A political economy perspective. In S.R. Melkote, P. Shields, & B.C. Agrawal (eds), *International satellite broadcasting in South Asia: Political, economic, and cultural implications*, pp. 19–46. Lanham, NY: University Press of America.

Lahiri, A. (1998). Media mogul. *Business India*, 7–20 September 1998, pp. 54–59.

Lakshman, N. (1999). Tapping the old boys' net worth. *Weekend Business*, 24–30 July 1999, p. 1.

Lewis, M. (1999). The search engine. *The New York Times Magazine*, 10 October 1999, pp. 77–83, 100, 108, 112–13.

—— (2000). *The new new thing: A Silicon Valley story.* New York: W.W. Norton.

Malhotra, S. (1999). *The privatization of television in India: Implications of new technologies for gender, nation, and culture.* Ph.D. Thesis, Albuquerque: University of New Mexico.

Malhotra, S., & Rogers, E.M. (2000). *Satellite television networks and the new Indian woman.* Paper presented to the Western States Communication Association, Sacramento, February 2000.

Mankekar, P. (1999). *Screening culture, viewing politics: An ethnography of television, womanhood, and nation in post-colonial India.* Durham, NC: Duke University Press.

Mansell, R., & When, U. (eds) (1998). *Knowledge societies: Information technology for sustainable development.* New York: Oxford University Press.

Mathur, J.C., & Neurath, P. (1959). *An Indian experiment in farm radio forums.* Paris: UNESCO.

McDowell, S.D. (1997). *Globalization, liberalization and policy change: A political economy of India's communication sector.* New York: St Martin's Press.

McDowell, S.D., & Pashupati, K. (1999). *India's Internet policies: New media metaphors and communication development.* Paper presented to the International Communication Association, San Francisco, May 1999.

McMichael, P. (2000). *Development and social change: A global perspective.* Thousand Oaks, CA: Pine Forge Press.

Mehta, V. (1977). *Mahatma Gandhi and his apostles.* New York: Viking.

Melkote, S.R. (1991). *Communication for development in the Third World: Theory and practice.* New Delhi: Sage Publications.

Mendoza, M. (1999). Not all Silicon Valley workers are in the chips. *The Columbus Dispatch*, 19 September 1999, pp. 1–2H.

Mishra, N. (1999). Zipping down the info highway. *Outlook*, 5 April 1999, pp. 37–39.

Mitra, Ananda (1993). *Television and popular culture in India: A study of the Mahabharat.* New Delhi: Sage Publications.

Mitra, Anjan. (1999). MTV draws up millennium plan. *Business Standard*, 14 July 1999, p. 9.

Mitra, S. (1999). Cyber czars. *India Today*, 15 March 1999, pp. 10–16.

Mody, B. (1979). Programming for SITE. *Journal of Communication*, 28 (4): 90–98.

—— (1987). Contextual analysis of the adoption of a communication technology: The case of satellites in India. *Telematics and Informatics*, 4 (2): 151–58.

Mody, B. (1991). *Designing messages for development communication*. New Delhi: Sage Publications.

—— (1997). Liberalization of telecommunications in India in the mid-1990s. In E.M. Noam (ed.), *Telecommunications in Western Asia and the Middle East*, pp. 3–37. New York: Oxford University Press.

—— (2000). The Internet in a majority world. *ICA News*, March 2000, p. 11.

Mohan, J. (1997). Discovery channel aims for a slice of market. *India Abroad*, 12 September 1997, p. 30.

Mukerjea, D.N., & Dhawan, R. (1999). Teleworking! The hottest business opportunity for India. *Business World*, 7–21 January 1999, pp. 20–28.

Murthy, N.N.R. (2000). NRI high-tech entrepreneurs are compassionate capitalists. *Siliconindia*, April 2000, pp. 26–28.

Nariman, H. (1993). *Soap operas for social change*. Westport, CT: Praegar.

Natarajan, A. (2000). Start-up fever in India. *Siliconindia*, February 2000, pp. 62–66.

Nayar, K.S. (1999). Minnesota entrepreneur sees nation as IT power. *India Abroad*, 2 July 1999, p. 32.

Neurath, P.M. (1962). Radio rural forum as a tool of change in Indian villages. *Economic Development and Cultural Change*, 10: 275–83.

Niejahr, E. (1997). From boom town to gloom town. *World Press Review*, December 1997, pp. 31–32.

Nieves, E. (2000). Many in Silicon Valley cannot afford housing, even at $50,000 a year. *The New York Times*, 20 February 2000, p. 16.

Padmanabhan, A. (2000a). Contributions of Indian diaspora stretch beyond business. *India Abroad*, 25 February 2000, p. 32.

—— (2000b). Of incubators, angel investors, and venture capitalists. *India Abroad*, 14 April 2000, p. 26.

—— (2000c). ESOPs and the many fables of the Internet age. *India Abroad*, 14 April 2000, p. 26.

Pais, A.J. (1998). Growing presence. *India Today International*, 28 December 1998, p. 24c.

—— (1999). Memorable merger. *India Today International*, 18 October 1999, p. 24k.

Papa, M.J., Auwal, M.A., & Singhal, A. (1995). Dialectic of control and emancipation in organizing for social change: A multitheoretic study of the Grameen Bank in Bangladesh. *Communication Theory*, 5: 189–223.

Papa, M.J., Singhal, A., Law, S., Sood, S., Rogers, E.M., Shefner-Rogers, C.L., & Pant, S. (2000). Entertainment–education and social change: An analysis of parasocial interaction, social learning, collective efficacy, and paradoxical communication. *Journal of Communication*, 50 (4), in press.

Parpia, M. (1999). Hardware manufacturing: Grab the hard opportunity. *Computers Today*, 1–15 July 1999, http://www.india-today.com/ctoday/ 19990715/.

Pathania, G. (1998). Responses to transnational television in a STAR-struck land: Doordarshan and STAR-TV in India. In S.R. Melkote, P. Shields, & B.C. Agrawal (eds), *International satellite broadcasting in South Asia: Political, economic, and cultural implications*, pp. 61–80. Lanham, NY: University Press of America.

Pendakur, M. (1991). A political economy of television: State, class, and corporate influence in India. In G. Sussman & J. Lent (eds), *Transnational communication: Wiring the Third World*, pp. 234–62. Newbury Park, CA: Sage Publications.

Petrazzini, B.A. (1996). Telecommunications policy in India: The political underpinnings of reform. *Telecommunications Policy*, 20 (1): 39–51.

Piotrow, P.T., Kincaid, D.L., Rimon II, J., & Rinehart, W. (1997). *Health communication: Lessons from family planning and reproductive health*. Westport, CT: Praeger.

Pitroda, S. (1993). Development, democracy, and the village telephone. *Harvard Business Review*, 71 (6): 66–77.

—— (1998). Changing IT focus: From industry to people. *Silicon India*, http://www.silicon-india.com/magazine/dec98sam.html.

—— (1999). In light of the Internet. *Silicon India*, http://www.silicon-india.com/magazine/oct99sam.html.

Pitroda, S. (2000). Comfort and strength in chaos. *Siliconindia*, February 2000, pp. 92–93.

Prakash, V. (1999). Microbrowsers: The Net in your pocket. *Computers Today*, 15–31 July 1999, http://www.india-today.com/ctoday/19990715/.

Rajadhyaksha, N. (1999). 1988: A to Z. *Business World*, 7–21 January 1999, p. 18.

Ranganathan, C. (1999). No free lunch on the Net. *Computers Today*, 15–31 July 1999, http://www.india-today.com/ctoday/19990801/.

Rao, J. (1999). SMART Modular Technologies: Staying smart in the high-tech world. *Indzine*, 5 (6), June 1999, http://www.indzine.com/1999/june/tcoverstory.html.

Rao, S. (1998). The new Doordarshan: Facing the challenges of cable and satellite networks in India. In S.R. Melkote, P. Shields, & B.C. Agrawal (eds), *International satellite broadcasting in South Asia: Political, economic, and cultural implications*, pp. 47–60. Lanham, NY: University Press of America.

—— (1999). The rural–urban dichotomy of Doordarshan's programming in India: An empirical analysis. *Gazette*, 61 (1): 23–37.

Rao, S. (2001). From pre-television to a post-cable community: Two decades of media growth and use in Bangalore, India. In S.R. Melkote & S. Rao (eds), *Critical issues in communication: Looking inward for answers.* New Delhi: Sage Publications, in press.

Ratnesar, R. (2000). The faces of India's future. *Time,* 27 March 2000, p. 47.

Rekhi, K. (2000). Taking Silicon Valley culture to India. *Siliconindia,* April 2000, p. 22–24.

Rekhi, S. (1998). Please dial after some time. *India Today,* 18 May 1998, pp. 54–55.

Richtel, M. (1999). Back to the future. *Yahoo! Internet Life,* December 1999, p. 92.

Richter, S. (2000). The immigration safety valve. *Foreign Affairs,* 79 (2): 13–16.

Rogers, E.M. (1976). Communication and development: The passing of the dominant paradigm. In E.M. Rogers (ed.), *Communication and development: Critical perspectives.* Newbury Park, CA: Sage Publications.

—— (1986). *Communication technology.* New York: Free Press.

—— (1994). *A history of communication study: A biographical approach.* New York: Free Press.

—— (1995). *Diffusion of innovations,* fourth edition. New York: Free Press.

Rogers, E.M., & Larsen, J.K. (1984). *Silicon Valley fever: Growth of high-tech culture.* New York: Basic Books.

Roy, S. (1999). Telecom policy to bring in foreign investment. *India Abroad,* 9 July 1999, p. 28.

Sagar, V. (1999). Piggyback on the Web. *Computers Today,* 1–15 July 1999, http://www.india-today.com/ctoday/19990701/.

Saran, P.S. (1997). Golden jubilee year of independence: Progress of telecom services in India and looking ahead. *IETE Technical Review,* 14 (4–5): 263–72.

Saxenian, A. (1999). *Silicon Valley's new immigrant entrepreneurs.* San Francisco: Public Policy Institute of California.

Sen, A. (1999). *Development as freedom.* New York: Alfred A. Knopf.

Sen, S., & Koppikar, S. (1995). Surfing past the rules. *India Today,* 15 December 1995, p. 161.

Sharma, D. (1999). Nation said to be unprepared for patent regime. *India Abroad,* 28 May 1999, p. 2.

Sharma, N. (1998). Yahoo! We are rich. *India Today International,* 24 August 1998, p. 24C.

Shekar, M. (1999). And now, TVs you can talk to. *Business World,* 7–21 January 1999, pp. 60–61.

Shridharani, K. (1946). *The Mahatma and the world*. New York: Duell, Sloan, and Pearce.

Siliconindia (2000a). U.S. index. April 2000, p. 104.

—— (2000b). India index. April 2000, p. 104.

Singhal, A., & Aikat, D. (1993). *Champions of Bangalore*. Unpublished manuscript, Athens, OH: Ohio University, School of Interpersonal Communication.

Singhal, A., & Brown, W.J. (1996). The entertainment–education communication strategy: Past struggles, present status, future agenda. *Jurnal Komunikasi*, 12: 19–36.

Singhal, A., & Rogers, E.M. (1989). *India's information revolution*. New Delhi: Sage Publications.

—— (1999). *Entertainment–education: A communication strategy for social change*. Mahwah, NJ: Lawrence Erlbaum Associates.

Singhal, A., Rogers, E.M., & Mahajan, M. (1999). The gods are drinking milk! Word-of-mouth diffusion of a major news event in India. *Asian Journal of Communication*, 9 (1): 86–107.

Singhal, A., Doshi, J.K., Rogers, E.M., & Rahman, S.A. (1988). The diffusion of television in India. *Media Asia*, 15 (4): 222–29.

Sinha, N. (1996). The political economy of India's telecommunication reforms. *Telecommunications Policy*, 20 (1): 23–38.

Sodhi, A. (2000). Plastic fraud threat hampers e-commerce growth. *India Abroad*, 14 April 2000, p. 28.

Space Application Center (1996). *Jhabua Development Communication Project*. Ahmedabad: Space Application Center, Development and Educational Communication Unit.

Springer, R. (1999a). Global voice messaging service is started. *India Abroad*, 2 July 1999, p. 32.

—— (1999b). Juniper Networks surges after IPO. *India Abroad*, 9 July 1999, p. 31.

—— (1999c). TiE's sixth annual conference is a sellout. *India Abroad*, 4 June 1999, p. 30.

Sreenivas, I.S. (1998). Microsoft acquires Hotmail: CEO Bhatia strikes gold. *India Currents*, February 1998, pp. 1–2.

Srivastava, S. (1999). Software exports: Is vision $100 b achievable? *Computers Today*, 1–15 July 1999, http://www.india-today.com/ctoday/19990701/.

Stremlau, J. (1996). Dateline Bangalore: Third world technopolis. *Foreign Policy*, 102: 152–69.

The Hindu Business Line (1999). IT companies will get red carpet, not red tape. 11 December 1999, p. 7.

Tiwari, S. (1999). Infotainment: The new paradigm. *IT Vision*, 1 (6): 10–11.

Upside (2000). India starts up. 22 February 2000, http://www.upside.com/texts/mvm/ebiz/story.

Venkataram, P. (1999). Getting our act together. *Computers Today*, 1–15 July 1999, http://www.india-today.com/ctoday/19990701/.

Vijay, S. (1999). Internet dominance: Who serves the Net game? *Computers Today*, 15–31 July 1999, http://www.india-today.com/ctoday/19990715/.

Vijaykar, A. (1999). Riding the Internet wave. *Computers Today*, 1–15 July 1999, http://www.india-today.com/ctoday/19990701/.

Vittal, N. (1999). IT strategy: India's new lever of growth. *Computers Today*, 1–15 July 1999, http://www.india-today.com/ctoday/19990701/.

Westerveld, R., & Prasad, R. (1994). Rural communications in India using fixed cellular radio systems. *IEEE Communications Magazine*, October 1994, pp. 70–77.

Yunus, M. (1998). Alleviating poverty through technology. *Science*, 282: 409–10.

—— (1999). *Banker to the poor: Micro-lending and the battle against world poverty*. New York: Public Affairs.

—— (2000). International Center for Information Technology to eliminate global poverty. *Grameen Dialogue*, 41: 1–6.

Name Index

Subject Index

INFORMATION AND COMMUNICATION TECHNOLOGY IN DEVELOPMENT

CASES FROM INDIA

Edited by
Subhash Bhatnagar and Robert Schware

This book documents the successful use of information and communication technology (ICT) in rural development. Written by administrators who have implemented successful projects, the sixteen case studies in this volume spell out the various applications of information technology that have made a difference in the delivery of services or products in rural India or that have increased productivity.

Among the services covered are healthcare, milk collection, disaster management, postal services, telephones, and services for the disabled. Applications in these areas involve the use of simple and inexpensive technologies at one end, and sophisticated satellite-based communication at the other. Their effect is to improve the planning and monitoring of development programmes, empower citizens through access to information and knowledge, generate employment opportunities and encourage entrepreneurship in rural areas. This important and practice-oriented volume will interest those involved in information and communication technology, rural development, public administration, management, development economics and planning. Government and voluntary organizations in the development sector, IT professionals and training institutes will also find it useful.

'The in-depth assessment of rural problems [in this book] is exhaustive and contains both rich information and practical insights.'

Business Standard

220mm × 140mm/2000/Hb/Pb/232pp.

Sage Publications
NEW DELHI/THOUSAND OAKS/LONDON

INFORMATION AND COMMUNICATION TECHNOLOGY IN DEVELOPMENT

CASES FROM INDIA

Edited by
Subhash Bhatnagar and Robert Schware

Sage Publications
New Delhi/Thousand Oaks/London